Contents:

Foreword

That school leaders face increasing challenges is a well-worn truism: operating under austerity budgets in the background of historic underfunding; managing the ongoing recruitment crisis, responding to the latest edict from OfSTED and, at present, the small matter of a world-wide pandemic. Accompanying this, a seemingly insatiable expectation of schools as agents of social change: championing the PREVENT agenda, ensuring students emerge from school financially literate, having avoided teenage pregnancies and the gang culture, free of prejudice and ready to meet the economic needs of the country. *Perhaps we should be flattered by the confidence in our capacity?* Sadly, I suspect most would adopt a rather more sceptical view.

So, is this just a case of, 'teachers moaning about their lot again'? My experience is that this is not the case. School leaders recognise that the challenges facing us are multi-faceted, insistent and visceral; however, we also appreciate that they motivate us in our work to affect social change: the, somewhat tired but nevertheless genuine, desire to 'make a difference.'

But where to start amidst the plethora of competing nestlings demanding to be fed? My contention is that, as school leaders, we cannot and should not resort to becoming operationally blinkered, succumbing to the 'tyranny of the immediate'. We are, after all, employed to lead, to empower, to affect progress. To achieve that, we must strive to be aware and informed. This means engaging fully with emerging issues: informing ourselves and others; devising focused responses and measuring impact. Many of the challenges are chronic, requiring us to draw upon experience; however, when something completely new appears we need to start from scratch: *Never has this been more true than in the case of County Lines.*

On a personal level, I've worked with Phil Priestley for a number of years and have always been struck by the contrast between his easy-going, unassuming demeanour and the relentless, driven determination to affect change. Following discussions with Phil, I was fortunate enough to be able to support his transition from a flourishing career in the Police Force to stepping into fulltime school work. It's fair to say that I've not regretted that decision for a second and neither have our students.

In this book, Phil provides an insightful, lived narrative to all aspects of County Lines. At once comprehensive, compelling and illuminating, it demands a response from the reader. Drawing upon his own experiences, he effortlessly draws us into the shadows, to a world of subtle radicalisation, grooming and abuse. Here the spotlight is shone on the 'key players', the nature of the drugs in circulation, and business model that is now ubiquitous across the country. All of this information is

4

crucial for the school leader: if you don't know the geography or speak the language, how can you negotiate the landscape and engage with the natives?

Moving forward, we are led to consider how children are drawn into County Lines activities. Crucial and, without this recognition, we are powerless to be able to 'go in after them,' to secure their trust and to bring them out again. We also examine the variety of approaches adopted by schools, learning that many of the techniques we've successfully employed over the years for other needs don't and won't work in this context. Instead, we are guided to alternative methods, grounded in experience and practice, that can support our growth and provide the tools to affect change.

And which students are we talking about? Who are the County Lines management seeking to recruit? We are led to see the link between those who have suffered trauma in their early lives, making them susceptible to grooming. We are also faced with the notion that schools are unwittingly funding recruitment centres for County Lines by supporting the use of Alternative Provision centres. Each school knows the students that are being referred to these institution and there is an uncomfortable truth in the portrait painted of the creation of training grounds for County Lines. This is, however, not an attack on these centres or the great people who work in them; just a reflection on some potential unintended consequences.

Helpfully, having set out the challenges of County lines, we are then provided with a model for responding. However, what is immediately clear is the financial challenge at a moment in history when we are seeing major investments in nuclear weapons, the military in general and infrastructure projects such as HS2 in particular. *This at a time when public services are suffering from over a decade of austerity and appear to be entering into a second, coronavirus-inspired, tightening of belts.* If the county lines phenomenon is to be effectively addresses, the full range of public services need to be allowed to step up to the plate. That the people working within these institutions are ready to do just that is not in question; the villain of the piece is lack of capacity through chronic underfunding. Regardless, as long as this is our reality, all duty is to think differently, to do all we can to make the most of the expertise and limited resource available.

A series of recommendations concludes the main body of this work; potentially the most provocative section. Here the reader is left to grapple, not only with the macro level policy decisions, but their translation in the day-to-day functioning of schools. On reflection, it is hard to fight the logic of the conclusions which are reached; at least, any internal objections from the reader necessarily lead to the retort (also internal) of, 'if not this, then what?' We are made to rethink our perspectives, our prejudices and our practices. And once we have taken this time, there is the imperative to adjust to affect change, albeit local.

Some books are of academic interest, you read and you move on. In contrast, with this book, you read and it moves you on.

Chris Tooley has thirty years of professional experience as a secondary school and post GCSE educator. He is the Principal of the Netherhall School and Sixth Form Centre in Cambridge. He holds a Masters degree from the University of Cambridge in Educational Assessment, Testing and Measurement. His bachelors degree (also from the University of Cambridge) is in Natural Science and Education.

About the Author and Inclusive Development

Phil Priestley was educated at the University of York and graduated in 2001. He joined North Yorkshire Police in 2003. In November of 2005 he transferred to Cambridgeshire Constabulary where he spent the rest of his policing career – until September 2019.

The first nine years of the author's career were spent investigating crime as a qualified Detective Constable and Detective Sergeant. This included the specific investigation of violent crime and also controlled drug offences leading to successful prosecutions at both Magistrates and Crown Court levels. The author spent two years in the Public Protection Unit focusing on offences of Domestic Abuse, Serious Sexual Offences, Honour Based Violence and Child Abuse.

Phil Priestley was awarded three commendations in relations to his work during this period.

A transition from investigating crime to the prevention of crime happened in the latter half of his career – and a role in Neighbourhood Policing saw him lead the Constabulary relationship with Schools and Young People across the areas of East Cambs, South Cambs, Cambridge City and the Huntingdonshire districts.

In 2016 Phil founded the Cambs Youth Panel to improve the relationship and levels of rapport and trust that existed between the police and young people in East Cambridgeshire. This group is still active today and Phil continues to lead and organise it. At the time of writing the Cambs Youth Panel is a socially active group that represents the views and opinions of young people to a wide spectrum of statutory and elected partners across the whole of Cambridgeshire South.

Phil is an experienced multiagency practitioner who is used to working inside the world of collective problem solving. He has extensive experience of Child in Need / Child at Risk case conferences, of working with Social Care, Probation, Health, Education, Housing, YOT/YOS (Youth Offending Teams/Services) and local authorities at Parish, District and County levels.

In the course of his time as a police officer Phil has dealt with and interviewed a substantial number of young people directly involved in, and on the fringes of County Lines and Criminal Exploitation. Phil has worked with several young people who have been seduced, exploited and harmed by the County Lines phenomenon.

The author has spoken to parents, teachers, and young people in the writing of this book and in his professional capacity – trying to help young people to avoid being harmed by County Lines, or trying to help them extract themselves or loved ones from the web of coercion that County Lines represents.

Today Phil runs his own business – Inclusive Development. This company grew out of the need for a bridging service to replace the professional skills deficit left by years of harmful (and at times misleading) government led austerity measures.

Phil now works with several schools across Cambridge City, South Cambs and on the borders of the adjacent counties. The work that he undertakes involves an advisory and 'critical friend' role to educators. Schools are now at the very forefront of diagnosing risk around a child, and in the first instance responding to it and mitigating potential harm. Phil works on a daily basis with children in the highest bands of risk, as they are recognised by their respective schools. His mentoring work focuses on rapport building, mutual understanding, trust and positive influence.

2019/2020 saw a success for Phil and Inclusive Development – with several cases of acute vulnerability offering significant improvements in school cooperation, attainment, behaviour and other lasting outcomes.

Phil is passionate about social contribution and helping the vulnerable. During the COVID-19 crisis Phil led the Cambs Youth Panel in supplying more than 700 computers to young people (across Cambridgeshire, Essex, Suffolk, Norfolk, Bedfordshire and Hertfordshire) who otherwise didn't have the means to access online learning during the period of limited school access. Phil has raised more than £50,000 for good causes including the women's domestic abuse charity Refuse, the Great Ormond Street Children's Hospital and towards COVID-

11

19 relief and the provision of computers for disadvantaged children in his region.

Preface

I left policing in September 2019. Despite what I believe were the very best efforts of the most senior officers in the Constabulary to preserve resources in neighbourhood policing and community engagement, it was absolutely clear that this form of preventative policing had, at the very least, been significantly compromised.

I know for a fact that police leaders, and rank and file officers, feel passionately about engagement, problem solving and harm prevention. Relationship building is acknowledged to be a huge part of the spectrum of policing responsibilities. This being said, austerity has been an incredible challenge – and it remains an incredible challenge. Even now Chief Constables across the country are being given impossible choices to make between where very finite and much reduced resources (financial and headcount) should be employed or withdrawn. Not one of the decisions made has been a happy decision to make.

I've been fortunate enough to be in the room where some very experienced and knowledgeable professionals (who I respect massively) have had passionate debates about where we can do with less, and what communities can do without. I know that these conversations have been repeated across all of our public services – and today our School Principals resemble Chief Executives – being required, more than ever, to make very complicated financial decisions and structured plans as best they can around forecasts offered by central government and local authorities.

My move to create my own business to serve schools (predominantly) and to utilise my multiagency knowledge was not an easy one. It was an intimidating choice that has been full of personal risk. There is a clear need for what I do and what I provide – but being a police officer was a huge part of my identity for almost seventeen years. I am passionate about what I do, and the difference that I make working with some very vulnerable young people.

In the course of this book I hope you will gain insight into the huge threat that is posed by criminal gangs who seek to exploit children, and the County Lines model they utilise to achieve their aims. This is a journey that I've been on for a long time. I am acutely aware that the victims of Child Exploitation and County Lines don't possess the tools to sit down and write their own book. They are invisible, they walk past you on the street, you see them for a moment and then they are gone. You rarely recognise them, or what is happening to them. Some of what I write and present is clearly aimed at giving you as much of what they experience through their eyes. I want you to see what they see, and feel how they feel.

I hope that in reading this you will gain a valuable insight. I think that what I am writing here will not be a revelation to many professionals in public services today – but I don't think there are many accounts out there that will go to the same lengths to pull this together from so many perspectives and with the breadth of views that I hope to achieve. This book is ambitious – forgive me if it only gets us partially to where we need to be.

As adults I think that we have a huge responsibility to realise the responsibility that we hold to halt the trend towards drug supply based on the movements and the trafficking of child victims. There is so much more we can do. That is – above all else – what this book is about, and why I have written it.

Phil

Introduction

Kylo is a young man who is struggling with early life trauma, stress and anxiety. He is not what you would call 'a bad lad' – he is not a threatening or intimidating figure. He's not particularly streetwise and he doesn't cause many issues inside school. He was never on anyone's radar as a particular risk. Of all the many agencies that are tasked with keeping children and young people safe in our communities – nobody really knew about Kylo.

It all began when he went to a party. He went along reluctantly – he was invited along by a friend and turned up in an awkward way – there were a lot of older people there and he felt out of his depth very quickly. People he recognised from years above him in school were talking in the kitchen. There were a lot of people that he didn't recognise. There was loud music, there was a fog of herbal smoke in the air, there was booze – the people that he arrived with kept saying "This is lit!" and talked excitedly. Kylo wanted them to shut up – *it made them seem obviously less mature than anyone else*. There were girls there – one of the girls Kylo knew from school and his own year – Macy - but he'd never seen her looking quite like this before. She even looked different in her eyes. She was like a totally new person unconstrained by school uniform. He probably wouldn't look twice at her in school to be honest. At this party he couldn't keep his eyes off her – he would steal a look – then stare down or away to deliberately stop himself from just looking like a weirdo. She brushed past him deliberately on her way to the kitchen. He was blushing and completely on the back foot. He tried to say "Hi" and immediately moderated it into a cooler "Yo". It came out "Yi". He was sure that he was blushing. It was so embarrassing. For some reason he wanted to wave – but he was grateful that his hands didn't seem to be obeying him and his whole body seemed disconnected. She didn't hear his cringeworthy greeting. Or she ignored it. *Or she didn't hear it*. In any regard, he didn't feel in control at all.

The whole situation felt like an enormous pressure – all he could actually think about was what he looked like to everyone else, how bad he probably looked. He felt vulnerable – he thought that the other lads were going to turn on him at any minute, and ridicule him and use him to make each other laugh. He looked round the room. In the dimly lit corner one of the older boys was all over a girl that he didn't know – or maybe he did – he didn't know for sure. Someone had kicked over a bottle of beer and it was seeping into the carpet in gulps. Kylo wanted to make a dive for it and shout to someone to get a tea towel or something – but he stopped himself, he knew *that* would be deeply uncool. Whose house was this anyway? He thought he was going to George's house – but George shook his head. Kylo felt like an imposter. His breathing was getting short. The smoke hanging in the air made him cough. There was an internal dialogue running through his head. *"How do I get out of here without looking stupid?"*. Scanning for the exits he actually thought about going to the bathroom and bailing out of the window. He just wanted to go home and be in his room, on his own. He could just go home and go back to hating himself in the safety of his own bedroom. Why the fuck was he even there? Then Macy passed him the cigarette, she physically put it between his lips – *"I get anxious when it's wearing off too – have a drag on this…"* she leaned over towards him, he stared obviously into her fairly prominent cleavage.

And that was how it happened. Kylo previously had never even smoked – but he had seen people smoke and he was not going to embarrass himself in front of this version of Macy and he went with it. He wasn't about to be the 'just say no' kid. *He didn't think he had the power in him to say no to anything she asked him to do.* He just took the cigarette, held it awkwardly in his mouth and sucked on in. He immediately choked and coughed and spluttered as the cigarette bounced up and down. Macy looked at him in his eyes and said "Slow down!" – she was smiling. "Hold it in your mouth – hold it – breathe it in slowly…" She put her hand on his face when she said it – and that alone felt like an electrical impulse running through his entire body.

It didn't take long for Kylo to feel dizzy – but relaxed – somehow calmer, less inhibited, more confident – *oh my God thank you*. It was like a wave of relief. He was looking for it again "Don't be greedy!" she was flirting now and he was actually able stay cool and flirt back… he was beginning to feel ok there now – the crushing sense of inadequacy that was constantly shadowing him seemed to fade. It was cool. The focus *wasn't* on him, or he didn't care if it was. Another thing he wasn't worried about was his mother's cancer, he wasn't preoccupied with making sure his brother had socks for the morning. He didn't even think about his Dad – who he hated – *it was the first time in an unquantifiable amount of time that he didn't think about his fucking Dad who he hated.*

Instead – he just felt chilled out – got lightheaded. He had a sweet, warm, tingling feeling – he wanted to laugh. He just wanted to laugh. And when he laughed, the others laughed with him. Not at him. With him. They just all felt so connected to this positive vibe.

As they drank someone toasted and said "And fuck the feds man. Fuck the po-leese" – the word was over pronounced in an artificial way "Fuck the po-leese" they all chimed and drank. "Yo man, if you ever get any shit off the feds, and you don't know what to say – just tell them 'no fucking comment'". And the bottle clanked together.

The darkness in the room seemed to envelop him like an arm around his shoulders. It shrouded his horrible spotty skin. It threw a blanket over his worn out clothes and his crappy trainers. He just melted into this evening – it felt like just what he always needed – a holiday from himself.

It ended hours later with him throwing up outside the back door next to the bins. Not in the bins, next to the bins. His throat burned from the acid reflux coming up from his stomach – it was like the problematic personality he had been supressing all evening. He had eaten nothing. He had drunk too much. His head was lost in a fog of weed. Who knows how he got home? He woke up the following morning with a proper headache, like a splitting headache that needed a doctor. In a pretty foul mood, still dressed in the same clothes, late for school – Mum was shouting up the stairs asking him what was wrong. "Just shut the fuck up will you!" he shouted back venomously without even thinking. He couldn't remember most of what happened. He couldn't even remember being sick by the bins.

His phone went off and someone send him a Tik-Tok video of him throwing up at the back the house with a music track running behind it while people cheered him on. He looked completely wasted with a green complexion and the video showed him wiping his mouth on his sleeve. He looked down at his sleeve – which was stained with his dried sick. He smelled his own clothing and it was grim. Musty, sweaty, pungent, stale. His head was still banging. His phone kept going off. Normally he didn't get messages from *anyone*. It was like he was popular or something "Nice one mate – see you next week yeah?" "You ok? lolz".

His incoherent thoughts pieced themselves back together in an illogical pattern. There was no sense of order – what happened when – nothing like that. What he did remember was that warm feeling that he got, that tingle, that chilled out sense of bliss when he hit that cigarette. It was the drink that made him puke – *but the weed* – that was what he needed. He'd like to get some more of that.

So now a week later he had headed out on his bike. He had his hood up and a rucksack on. He'd pulled together a tenner and he hoped that would be enough. One of his new mates gave him a phone number and told him that the guy was decent and would sort him out. After a couple of text messages he had agreed to meet up in a part of town that he didn't usually fancy roaming round in – he didn't really know anybody up there – but he agreed to the meet up and went out there on his BMX.

Down at the park it was dark. Not dark in a nice way like at the party – but properly dark – *murky and damp.* Outside dark. At night. There was perhaps one orange lamp offering a poor attempt at illumination – all it managed to do was highlight the drizzle. It was a bit rainy, it was cold. This was not glamourous or enjoyable. An older lad stood by a moped and nodded at him – he nodded up and not down, like as if to say, "Come over here". He talked to him quietly and took out a little bag of green herbal. It was then that Kylo realised that he didn't have any papers, a lighter, anything at all basically.

For some reason he kind of thought that this guy would hand over a rolled-up cigarette or something. More issues – where was he going to get papers – how do you get them? He asked the guy if he had any papers...

Suddenly from the corner of his right eye he saw a much older male – an adult, a proper adult – come charging towards him "Is this the fucking one is it?!"

"Er, Yeah, yeah that's him" the lad with the moped said with a worried edge in his voice, nodding anxiously.

That was all.

Kylo didn't feel the knife going into his stomach, or being pulled out. He just felt like he'd been punched hard. He was winded. He looked up and instinctively grabbed his stomach where he received the blow and his hands were wet. Time slowed right down. He felt the damp on his stomach. It wasn't that wet outside. It was only drizzle. It didn't make sense. He was properly wet. He was short of breath. His heart was racing. He felt lighted headed. Why was he so wet? "Oh my god have I wet myself?" he thought.

The man shouted at the lad with the moped.

"That's what they fucking get you see?! That's what you fucking have to give them! We let them know! That's what you fucking do! Why do I have to come down here and get this shit done?! You better fucking step it up bro or you're fucking next, you get me?"

Kylo staggered – his knees were weak – he saw blood on his hands, lots of blood and he was panicking. Shock was starting to set in. Why would nobody help him?

"And you, you fucking little pussy – I want every penny for that fucking merchandise – you get me?! You'll see me again and if I don't get every fucking penny you pussy, you're a fucking dead man. It was three-fifty, but now it's five-hundred – you fucking get it sorted!"

The man was shouting at him. As Kylo slumped down to his knees, confused about the numbers, and as his head started to go, his knees were in a puddle – his tracksuit bottoms were wet. He didn't know if it was rainwater or blood or piss. Every second seemed like five minutes. He took every detail – every detail in slow motion. The man talked him down to the ground – with threats and abuse "Five hundred!" he kept saying. "Fuck you!". It was like he was putting a landline phone down on someone he hated "Fuck you! Fuck you! Fu..."

There was blood on a knife. His blood.

This time Kylo woke up in hospital. He jolted like he'd come up from a bad dream. A monitor was bleeping out the rhythm of his heart at the side of his bed. His mum was in the cubicle, his little brother was sat there too. "Don't get up Kylo" said a compassionate female voice. "It's ok. You're ok. You've been attacked. You got hurt – but you're going to be ok." She leaned into him, over him, he looked up at her.

Someone said to his Mum "Will you sign this? He is going to require surgery".

His mother, bald from chemotherapy, looked even more ashen white that she usually did. Her lips were grey anyway. Her eyes were dark baggy circles. Kylo can remember when her eyes used to be lively and she used to prank him and tickle him and they'd play fight. "I'll catch you! I'll catch you!" she used to say.

After his dad took off, his Mum ended up having a baby with another man years later. She had always said it would only be him and her – together – but this other man came along and she lied to him. She ended up knocked up and all she did was spend time on 'Baby' Richie. He's not even a fucking baby anymore, he's fucking nine.

Then she got sick – really fucking sick and dying – so he had to forgive her or she'd fucking die. He didn't forgive her really. He loved her but he was so angry.

"It's going to be alright Kylo".

She was using that voice that she used when she lied. That voice that she used when she got told about the cancer. When Dad fucking left them. When she got fucking pregnant. When there was no fucking presents at Christmas time.

"It's going to be alright Kylo".

Nothing is alright. Nothing is fucking even right. Everything is all fucking wrong. What even happened? At least on one level Kylo didn't really want to live. Fuck all of this.

Kylo slumped back down – what was actually a couple of inches of flex in his back and stomach felt like a full sit-up, like the twentieth sit-up, but now he felt a sharp pain and he winced. His eyes rolled back involuntarily. Even though he wasn't moving the pain didn't stop.

"Abdominal pain. Would you like something for that Kylo?" the nurse didn't wait for the reply, she just nodded at another nurse, and the other nurse started rummaging about in a cupboard over to one side. Kylo noticed that one nurse was kind of fit, the other nurse was a bit of a troll. He liked the fit nurse more, straight away, even like that, laid out on a bed, in a hospital. That's when he realised that he wasn't in his clothes – he was in some flimsy little gown and he was horrified. Who the fuck had undressed him – was it her or was it his Mum? "Fuck didn't I wet myself?" he suddenly thought.

He tried not to think about the fit nurse. He instinctively put his hands over his genitals. There were no blankets, no nothing, he couldn't hide behind anything. Anxiety shot through his head, his stomach, his bowels. It coursed through his forearms, he felt it burning in his chest. A pain like an electric shock went through his stomach.

As the nurse to his right moved towards him out of the corner of his eye he heard a voice "Five hundred! You fucking get my five hundred" he lurched away and he screamed "No!" tears went down his face. In one split second he realised it wasn't real – it was a nurse – it was ok but he was going crazy. He was mental.

A young police officer came into the cubicle "Can I talk to him quickly?" he whispered.

"We have to get him to theatre – he's going to be under a general, he needs surgery for that wound pretty immediately".

"I just want two minutes before he goes up?"

"I don't know if he's up to it".

"Do you know who did this to you?" the police officer spoke to him, regardless of the nurse.

"No, no I don't" he said honestly.

"Do you have any idea why this happened?"

"I just got jumped by the park, that's all I know" now he was lying.

"Would you recognise the person who did this?"

"I don't think so" (another lie).

"Could you try – we think we might know – do you think you could?"

"No… no comment".

The words just fell out of his mouth, and as they did someone coincidentally dropped a metal tray in the next cubicle.

The police officer, the nurse, his Mum all stopped for a heartbeat – it was like an X-ray - they looked into him, right inside him – and they were horrified by what he said.

"What did you say?" His Mum said – half shock and half anger *"What did you say young man?!"*

"Where did you get that from? Where did that come from?!"

The police officer's brow furrowed, he looked to the side and made eye contact with the nurse. He clicked his pen and slid it back into a flap in his uniform. His pocket notebook folded away neatly into his body armour with a sense of resignation. His body language betrayed everything – just such a slight shake his head.

"Come on, he's got to go" the nurse – the ugly nurse, not the pretty one – briskly threw a light blanket over him from the waist down. She kicked the wheels to release a brake on the trolley bed. She threw up a side rail that clanked into place. The bed lurched forward into the corridor as the doors swung open Kylo felt like he was on a ghost train. He'd gone through a boundary. No way back. He was about to be rendered unconscious *again*.

Kylo's injury was serious. It required a surgical intervention to deal with the wound, the loss of blood, the infection that he received and to reconstruct the damage to his bowel. His rehabilitation was a slow and painful process – while his physical injury healed successful and he avoided having to have a bowel transplant – his psychological injuries were deep and would never really find complete resolution.

Post-traumatic stress disorder set in very quickly – and aside from jumping away from anything that approached out of the corner of his right eye – particularly behind and to the right – Kylo suffered night terrors, panic attacks, bed wetting, unpredictable and severe mood swings, incidents of rage and fear.

Kylo became reclusive, he developed agoraphobia, and he couldn't cope with school. Classroom environments became impossible. Shopping centres became impossible. Anything that involved a crowd was intolerable. Driven to increasing levels of introspection Kylo developed problems with his diet and with the routines by which he lived his life.

The wound itself was long healed while the mental health problems persisted and got worse. A long scar across his stomach reminded him of the incident every time he showered. For a long time he couldn't even touch the scar tissue – and it was only after a process of talking therapy that he could bring himself to run his fingers along the length of its line.

You wouldn't describe this young man as being 'caught up in' County Lines. He wasn't a dealer, he wasn't a runner, he wasn't even really a user. Driven by a combination of different early life traumas he tried to self-medicate through a new experience – through cannabis – to release a bit of the stress and anxiety that he felt as a young carer for his mother and his younger brother.

An absence of healthy self-esteem, a fear about social acceptance, a constant nagging doubt about his appearance – all of these things crippled his ability to lead a day to day life. His relationship with his Dad was like an amputation. He was never rehabilitated from losing his Dad. It was a bereavement of sorts – but he knew that his Dad was still out there. He tracked him on social media. He knew that his Dad had a new family now – a start over. Kylo saw himself as the 'do-over' – something that went so wrong that his Dad had to abort him *after* he was born. It was incredibly painful.

The stress of having a mother diagnosed with a potentially terminal illness – in and out of hospital all the time – he couldn't think of himself as anything less than other people. He didn't know anyone else who had to live life like this...

We know that early life trauma – and a lack of support around early life trauma – massively increases the likelihood of negative later life outcomes[1]. This ranges from health to social achievement. For every rags to riches story of a kid that drags themselves out of a gutter to become a millionaire or billionaire there are thousands that go by the wayside into the more likely outcome of drug dependency, crime, custodial prison sentences and premature death.

Kylo – smothered by a complicated but overwhelming web of traumatic circumstances turned to weed – and inexplicably within days of doing so was stabbed in a case of mistaken identity.

The young man sat on his moped – there to sell cannabis to Kylo that evening – had been running for a County Lines handler. He ignored the oldest adage in the drug dealing business:

"Never get high on your own supply".

In a spiralling use of the drug, that young runner ran up a £350 debt quickly and easily. His vicious handler – himself from some extraordinary circumstances of

---

[1] https://www.health.harvard.edu/diseases-and-conditions/past-trauma-may-haunt-your-future-health#:~:text=Early%20childhood%20trauma%20is%20a,stroke%2C%20cancer%2C%20and%20obesity.

depravation, neglect and abuse – lived only by the law of the jungle. Kill or be killed. Our moped runner knew that he was in deep trouble – so he simply told his boss that he'd been mugged off by someone who owed him money and that he couldn't get it back. He was meeting him tonight. *It was all going to be ok.*

The handler knew that Kylo wasn't his guy. He could tell in a split second that Kylo didn't owe anything and wouldn't steal drugs or run up a debt. The handler simply didn't care – he wanted to make a statement to his runner – he wanted to scare the shit out of him. He wanted everyone to see that he was a cold-blooded killer – and that he got his money or there would be consequences. In the most Machiavellian terms – he lived by the rule that it is always better to be feared than loved.

Kylo was little more than collateral damage, bleeding in a puddle outside of a children's park. The offender had come up from London – wasn't a local guy – and made frequent runs back and forward, usually driving a hire car, staying over in motels. He supervised a network of boys – like a latter day Fagin – but very cruel and unpredictable in his moods. One day your best mate – nothing is too good for you – but most days following you like a vulture.

He wasn't arrested for stabbing Kylo – he got away with it. He got away with other horrendously cruel and sadistic acts against young people too. His methodology was very clear – no half measures, show no remorse – go way over the top and inspire the kind of fear that stops anyone from talking. "I might turn up at your mother's house and burn it down in the middle of the night". He joked "I'm the devil. I burned down Grenfell. You mean nothing to me." He wanted the lads to genuinely believe it.

'County Lines' is a training environment for hostility that turns into brutality. It is a process of radicalisation all of its own. Someone on your patch? *Fuck you, stab them*. A member of your family? *Fuck you, stab them*. You have a pretty girlfriend? *She's mine now* – I can make some money out of her at parties. She's only 14? *Fuck you, she'll love it. Don't worry you can have her back when we're done...*

The County Lines machine only gets darker and more vicious the closer you get to the centre of it. You brush up against the outer circles and you're already gambling with your personal safety. It might begin with a good time – gifts, clothes, electronics, cash, computer games, parties and of course drugs... but it only ends up in violence, coercion, and trauma. For some it ends in addiction or death – through suicide, murder or misadventure. "Kill yourself" has become an internet insult that is handed round in chat forums casually now – and the viral nature of such things, and the traction it has, is a thing to behold.

Inspector John Hallworth of Essex Police wrote a lengthy academic paper[2] (20,0000 + words) as part of his Masters Degree in Applied Criminology at Swelwyn College Cambridge, in 2016. This paper has been published online and offers interesting statistical insights into County Lines offenders operating in Essex. While accepting that precise definition of the County Lines model remains flawed, Hallworth clearly stipulates an evidential base to believe:

> *"...offenders to be more demographically consistent, more violent and more dangerous. They travel great distances for the more lucrative criminal markets. They commit less total, yet significantly more harmful offences... and pay a higher price for their criminal enterprise being more likely to die than non-County Lines offenders."*

For young people trapped – *and bullied doesn't begin to adequately cover a County Lines relationship* – suicide can seem like the only way out. This is particularly true if they are a teenager 'in care' who has been trafficked from one part of the UK to another, and find themselves in a strange and hostile environment where they can trust absolutely nobody. While County Lines is about

---

[2] 'County Lines': An exploratory analysis of migrating drug gang offenders in North Essex (Selwyn College Cambridge, 2016);

criminal coercion and exploitation – we believe that it absolutely goes hand in hand with Child Sexual Exploitation (CSE) and every other form of organised illicit profit making. Where drugs are sold at parties, so is sex.

This is the oppressive, smothering world of organised crime that is 'County Lines'. It is about criminals who will violently destroy the fragility of a child – *boy or girl* – from the age of 11 or 12 – over a period of years, just to make money. Money is the bottom line – and the industry is worth billions – based on the drugs aspect of the activity alone.

The National Crime Agency, writing a national briefing in 2018[3] wrote:

> *"The true scale of county lines activity is difficult to determine with accuracy as its nature is fluid and the intelligence surrounding the threat is not always clear, nor is it recorded consistently. Elements of county lines drug supply are likely to exist in all forces across England and Wales. It is also likely that the number of forces with exporting lines will increase as more criminal groups adopt the county lines methodology."*

---

[3] https://www.nationalcrimeagency.gov.uk/who-we-are/publications/234-county-lines-violen-ce-exploitation-drug-supply-2017/file

What this means in a nutshell is that County Lines – as a business model – is so successful that it has taken control of the vast market for cannabis and other illegal controlled drugs being supplied in the UK. The Institute of Economic Affairs (IEA) suggested in 2018[4] that the illegal market for cannabis alone was worth £2.6 billion. This does not take into consideration other controlled substances such as heroin and cocaine – which are also commonly made available with severe addictive properties.

"Teenagers find it easier to buy cannabis than alcohol" they write in an article that is clearly supporting the argument for legalisation. This is an assertion I can corroborate from disclosures made to me repeatedly by young people in schools who are using cannabis *and* drink alcohol.

You will be initially relieved to know that Kylo is a fictional character – *but very sadly his personal circumstances and the details of 'his' experiences are not*. You might think that focusing on one such character is too idiosyncratic to be useful – my message is that all of the circumstances where young people are seduced into contact with County Lines, and particularly those who really become entrenched as part of the County Lines mechanism, really are unique. They deserve to be respected as such – and resolution won't be found in one

---

[4] https://iea.org.uk/media/uks-illicit-cannabis-market-worth-2-5bn-a-year-finds-new-report/

turn-key act of broad policy or one sweeping generalised 'insight'. While the symptoms and the outcomes of County Lines are repetitive and recognisable – the personal stories have to be respected as different every time. Young people lament the inability of people to see them as individuals and only view them as a homogenous group.

I have spoken to, and spent time giving undivided attention to many young people who are on the fringes of County Lines activity. No more than one person away from – or often in direct contact with – a County Lines drug dealer. Having built meaningful rapport and trust based on consistency, transparency and honesty - I have been told repeatedly that cannabis is 'everywhere'. "It is so easy to get hold of. It is cheap. It is sociable." As a product it has flooded communities and a generation are growing up making a choice as to whether they use it or not.

Many more people in previous generations *would* have used it, if they could get their hands on it – "...but who could get hold of cannabis in a rural village like this?". That is not a problem today – and perhaps an older generation fails to appreciate such, or struggles to believe it. Like a 'Just Eat' service – the product is always on the road and available to meet at any time (and incidentally, for those who use, the temptation is huge). The choice is a very real one.

Pepsi or Coke? Xbox or Playstation? iPhone or Android? These are all the common choices that every teenager makes. *"Do you smoke weed?"*

This is where we get to the juxtaposition of two massive social problems – what is causing more harm to our children or young people? The violence and the threat of organised crime and criminal exploitation, or the health and social impact of psychoactive substances?

As the IEA themselves suggested in their June 2018 article:

> *"A commercialised market which capped THC levels at 15 per cent would virtually eradicate the black market. If licensed cannabis made up 95 percent of the market and if cannabis was taxed at 20 percent VAT plus a 30 percent excise tax it would produce annual tax revenues of £690 million per annum."*

In the course of this book we consider what 'County Lines' actually is and who is behind the 'County Lines' phenomenon. We will look at the tactics that have been employed to control it and why they aren't working.

We will look at how we diagnose risk in our communities and how our major agencies work together to share what bare resources they have to prevent the spread of County Lines and child criminal exploitation.

I want to talk about the core products that are being sold – the drugs that are the mainstay of the County Line business – how they are used and perceived by young people particularly. We will give thought to the idea of 'gateway drugs', and how and why drug abuse escalates. This will include the steps that ought to be taken when supporting a young person who genuinely wants to reduce their dependency or 'get clean'.

It is my intention to look carefully at the young people who are most susceptible to exploitation and abuse. How they behave and how we interpret their behaviour. What does that behaviour look like and how do we commonly respond to it?

It is opportune to consider cultural influences and the aspects of commercialism and art that motivate and help our young people to identify themselves. In recognising these factors we can identify what draws them towards criminal behaviours and why they don't invest the same time and energy in more legitimate and promising career and lifestyle options (a question often asked by desperate parents).

I feel that it is necessary to revisit the messages around 'trauma informed' approach that are clearly so vital to the situation around the character of Kylo. *What is a trauma informed approach anyway?*

We are going to look at the Pupil Referral Unit (PRU) or Alternative Provision (AP) system, Youth Justice, and the other key mechanisms and constructs that become relevant to the life of a child drawn towards or trapped in the County Lines framework. *How much of this interaction is productive and positive?* How much of it is meaningful? How much of it is actually counter-productive? I won't be shy in saying this – PRUs are holding-pens and filing systems for our 'too difficult' or 'too dangerous' to handle teenagers. Most educators and school Principals shudder at the thought of consigning a young person to such a future. Many of the private operators who control these facilities abdicate the key responsibility of their role by suggesting that the children and young people they support and educate *'were broken before they arrived'* and by suggesting they are *'doing the best we can'* - which allows a highly subjective and defensive presentation of what success actually means.

Let's also consider the effect of austerity – government policy – and the immediate government strategy that dictates how the Home Office views the problem of County Lines drug dealing and Child Criminal Exploitation. Promising words have been reiterated by a succession of Home Secretaries – but what meaningful steps have been taken? Where has the investment been placed? In real terms – where does dismantling the County Lines machinery sit on the overall scale, when compared more recently to Brexit, to the COVID-19 pandemic, and to the day to day political fire fighting of newspaper headlines? Who owns this problem? Who do we hold to account for delivery? What are the targets? What are the deadlines for delivery?

Perhaps it might be considered a cynical view to suggest that just the bare minimum is being done – the token of resistance – the political equivalent of 'thoughts and prayers', when it comes to protecting a generation of young people. Has the government been getting away with knowingly allowing a situation to manifest where County Lines continues to prosper, children and young people are harmed, and generally people – *parents specifically* – go uninformed and unsupported?

In writing this book I will propose a series of steps and measures that could be taken – and undoubtedly need to be led by a government genuinely determined to eradicate any organised crime that targets children and young people. I will suggest to you that a cohesive, 'joined up' strategy could bring the County Lines model down in a relatively short timescale. This is not 'crack down' rhetoric that recommends more proactive policing, search warrants, under-cover operations, convictions and penalties. This is not about scorched earth, zero tolerance policing. *This is not about confronting young people with severe consequences.* This strategy has to be altogether different.

Consider this: every commercially successful company that operates in the UK could be closed down through adjustments to market conditions. By affecting supply, by altering buying habits, by reducing the profitability, by increasing the risk of bankruptcy – even the most determined international organisations would look to withdraw from a market.

Looking abroad to the United States – Detroit Michigan was a powerhouse economy all of its own. It was unthinkable that it would ever decline. It is now largely a shell of its former condition – and a watch word of caution to every other city. *Detroit is a notorious lesson in economic collapse and implosion. Empires can fall.* This includes criminal empires.

My recommendations in the course of this book come from two main directions in a pincer movement on the County Lines model. Neither direction will focus particularly on enforcement as a disruption or a deterrent.

Instead I will focus in the most wholehearted fashion upon the victims, and the market itself, and the steps that need to be taken around those two pillars of this economic model that we call 'County Lines' – and the recommendations that I will make aim to break those pillars and bring the whole thing down.

Chapter One: What is 'County Lines'?

To begin with, we need to know what County Lines is – more or less. Referring back to the words of Inspector John Hallworth at Essex Police – *we accept that precise definition does remain flawed*. In creating an understanding of what County Lines is, we then need to shift our thinking on County Lines quite drastically – from criminal venture, to business venture.

I will begin by offering an opinion (not a particularly controversial one)*: **County Lines is possibly the clearest threat posed to young people in the UK aged from 11 years to 14 years.** Of all the things that might impact on a young life, an entanglement with County Lines could be the very worst. The outcomes can be fatal – and for those who are not killed or suffer serious physical injury – the life-long impact on mental and physical health can be exceptionally severe and impossible to repair.

While many might argue that the greatest risk of serious injury or death is to be found on the roads (driving or travelling in cars, moped use and so on) – we know that broadly speaking the threat to children and young people on the roads remains more or less static or falling in the UK[5], whereas the challenge of County Lines is a dynamic,

---

[5] The UK death rate on the roads has a growth rate of 0.17%. A 2015 report from the UK government Department of Transport suggests that the number of young drivers and passengers killed or seriously injured between 1979 and 2013

growing and predatory one – which deliberately seeks them out. There is a much greater psychiatric threat posed to young people and children through the County Lines phenomenon.

As early as 2009 the NSPCC was calling for a government response to gang culture that was more holistic in its approach, and less focused on punitive actions[6].

The Children's Society[7] suggests (from research compiled in 2018) that four thousand children in London and forty-six thousand children in England are involved in gang activity. While most of these children do end up committing crimes (sometimes very serious offences) – these children are exploited and they are also victims. I personally do not believe in the 'scare them straight' agenda – standing up in front of an audience of young teens and scaring them with stories of prison sentences, or deeply negative outcomes, or even pictures of physical injuries and consequences – this stuff tends to last until the end of the assembly itself (possibly the end

---

has fallen 79% - while the message on drink driving is finding traction as the youth demographic accounts for only 25% of all drink driver fatality collisions.
https://assets.publishing.service.gov.uk/government/uploads/system/uploads/attachment_data/file/448039/young-car-drivers-2013-data.pdf
6

https://www.nspcc.org.uk/globalassets/documents/research-reports/teenagers-at-risk-report.pdf
7 https://www.childrenssociety.org.uk/what-is-county-lines

of the day – the week if you are lucky). I have been asked to do this – *and I have done this* – but I can offer little evidence that it has made a meaningful difference to any specific individuals who heard what I had to say. It is a hugely superficial and problematic approach. Although admittedly, it is easy enough to find horror stories about the phenomenon of County Lines activities.

What *is* absolutely crucial is that we know and we understand what County Lines *actually is* and how this model operates. Like knowing what the magician is doing, deconstructing the process is the key to diminishing the impact and reducing the overall effect. There is no uncertainty on this question – we *can* make environments less hospitable to the County Lines model and I believe that it is our responsibility to do this.

Primarily, let's start referring to County Lines as a business model, because that is what County Lines is. This is not controversial or novel – it is a commonly accepted perception. *County Lines is a business model for serious and organised crime – and it is exceptionally successful and highly lucrative one.*

The term 'County Line' refers to a mobile phone number. It doesn't have anything to do with a boundary at the edge of the county or district area. Police and law enforcement agencies are also very preoccupied with 'cross border criminality' – but this is a very different thing that happens to have an element of overlap (we shouldn't conflate the two subjects).

'Cross border criminality' is a term that makes reference to travelling criminals that enter one police force area from another, commit an offence, before returning to their own area or another. In doing so they exploit the limitations or deficit of communication and information sharing between Constabularies and they make it more difficult to coordinate resources against them (hence the birth of the National Crime Agency and regional teams known as ROCUs or Regional Organised Crime Units). Such offenders tend to use vehicles that are registered as being 'off road' (statutory off-road notifications or SORN being in force) or 'in trade' on false number plates, that are cheap and disposable. They might use secondary high powered (stolen) vehicles and hide their identities and make themselves as difficult to find as possible. The classic example of cross border crime would be a cash machine theft, where an organised team arrives in a location that has a cash machine (usually a standalone) – they rip it out of its foundations or fixings and make off with the contents. You see such stories on BBC Crimewatch regularly because such events really suit that nature of a programme. *By simple comparison 'County Lines' cannot be captured in individual events in such a way.* The profitability of County Lines doesn't depend on one big hit or a single payoff.

Many people confuse 'cross border criminality' with 'County Lines' because there is some overlap between them. For example, the County Lines business model does exist to move drugs out of metropolitan and built up areas into smaller and rural communities to facilitate the street level distribution of the controlled drug(s) in question – often between counties. It is sometimes called 'going County' by perpetrators. This regularly involves trafficking drugs, cash and even juveniles across a district or Constabulary border. The methodology for County Lines is *entirely different* to our cash machine theft though. It is about establishing a subversive network – setting down roots and becoming entrenched in a locality. It is about operating under the radar of law enforcement for as long as possible.

I compare the business model to that of a parasite. Not for emotive reasons – but on a purely factual, logical basis. A parasite is successful for two reasons – on one level it sustains itself by syphoning off resources from a healthy chosen target. On a second level, it either goes unnoticed and hides while it does this, or it makes the process of extracting it too painful and costly to be proportionate or reasonable as an option to go through with.

Here is 'hot take' number one: **I think that government is aware of what is needed to extract this dangerous business model and protect our children and young people – but the cost is considered to be too expensive and/or not politically or ideologically comfortable or expedient.**

There is no question that government is aware that 'County Lines' exists (numerous Home Secretaries have referenced it) – but dismantling the effectiveness of this model will take time, resources and money – I will venture that somewhere along the line a decision has been made that a coordinated, meaningful and effective response is too expensive or politically not popular enough (not a vote winner or not in line with other ideological aims or objectives). Perhaps other concerns have been placed at a higher priority by the big decision makers.

On the 1st October 2019 the Home Office published information on its own website declaring a 'new £20 million investment... [to] disrupt county lines'[8]. Inevitably this involved some of the tired phrases that we have heard before – including 'crack down' and renewed emphasis on the enforcement strategy. It also promised to develop an expanded national specialist support service to help young people and their families – *this support service is not something that ever appears to have materialised and is not referenced elsewhere in key Home Office guidance such as 'County Line Exploitation – Practise guidance for YOTs and frontline practitioners' (also dated 1st October 2019)[9]*. It is telling that this

---

[8] https://www.gov.uk/government/news/home-secretary-announces-a-package-of-new-measures-to-tackle-county-lines
[9]
https://assets.publishing.service.gov.uk/government/uploads/system/uploads/attachment_data/file/839253/moj-county-lines-practical-guidance-frontline-practitionerspdf.pdf

'national support service' came as the final declaration on the 1st October press release – because it is very much at the bottom of the pecking order and seems to be a token afterthought - a bolt on. Speak to any genuine 'front-line' practitioner working with troubled young people and they are only likely to roll their eyes at the idea of coordinated government support on welfare. *As we continue this book I will talk about the personal experiences that I've had trying to help some very desperate parents.*

County Lines is certainly a business model that is built on the parasite principle, but it also exists to insulate the key decision makers and the major beneficiaries from prosecution and losses. We, as a society, are distracted from the source of the problem when young people can be prosecuted and vilified for effectively having become exploited teens from vulnerable backgrounds. It is hugely reassuring to society to hear that 'drug dealers' are being prosecuted – but this is false reassurance in so many ways – we are not winning any 'war on drugs'. Headlines are made in tough actions that celebrate 'front line' enforcement – not in the finesse that is actually required under such circumstances to support young people on a long term basis. Indeed, often teenagers receiving support, and certainly families receiving support, are vilified for being on 'benefits' or for asking for the help that they need. This is particularly the case if we are helping young people who have made the mistake of carrying or moving controlled drugs, knives, monies from crime, or doing other things under criminal influence or exploitation.

As we have stated, the 'County Line' itself is a reference to a mobile phone number – a 'burner phone'. A cheap handset or sim card that, if needs be, can be disposed of in a hurry. This phone number is an order hotline for any type of drugs that the 'customer' might need. Business is usually transacted by text message – and in some circumstances – through direct messaging using social media accounts as a smoke screen.

While the government promise of £20 million to disrupt County Lines sounds wonderful, it is the promise of a £20 million solution to (speaking in the most conservative way) a £500 million problem. On 29th January 2019 The Guardian newspaper reported on data from the National Crime Agency[10] suggested that they were aware of *two thousand* mobile phone numbers being used to support the distribution of illegal drugs in the UK – estimating that each line could be worth as much as £800,000 in revenue (more than a £2 billion market). This report also made mention of the fact that the number of recognised telephone numbers was increasing significantly – indeed the previous paper from the NCA, written in 2017,

---

10

https://www.theguardian.com/society/2019/jan/29/county-lines-criminal-drug-networks-rapidly-expanding-national-crime-agency

suggested that they were aware of seven-hundred and fifty mobile telephone numbers at that time.

Please keep in mind that law enforcement agencies will always be in possession of an incomplete picture of how many numbers are actually in operation.

Additionally an increasing number of County Lines operatives are cottoning on to the fact that mobile phone providers in the UK are obliged to hand over text message (SMS) data courtesy of Regulation of Investigatory Powers Act 2000 (RIPA). Many people remain oblivious to the fact that in most circumstances the main social media providers – including Facebook, Instagram, SnapChat, Twitter and so on – are not bound by UK regulations, such as RIPA 2000.

The reason these companies can circumvent such responsibilities is that they are based in California, USA. To force these companies to comply with the provision of data you actually have to arrive in that State, and raise a subpoena through Californian state legislation, which has to be delivered in person, at the corporate HQ of the relevant organisation. You can imagine how frequently UK law enforcement agencies (with budgets that are dwarfed by the value of companies such as Google and Facebook) actually do this – and where it has been done, how slowly that process could move and how expensive it was.

Instead most social media providers engage on a 'good faith' agreement and cooperate to a greater or lesser extent with UK police investigations. Few turn information requests around very quickly, and rarely will they actually go to the extent of sharing messages for evidential purposes – this even includes threat to life situations. Twitter – for example – refuses to betray the content of a direct message (DM) to UK to police at all.

The usual line from social media providers is to give 'subscriber' details (the name given to them by the account holder) – and possibly an IP[11] address – which might help to track down the identity of the person controlling an account and possibly a user location. If the user is particularly careful and accesses the service through a VPN[12] such data can be easily shrouded or attributed to anywhere in the world. The pace of technology has certainly helped to promote and insulate 'County Lines' as a business model. While the National Crime Agency can publish data on how many active telephone lines it is currently aware of – it is unlikely that that it will ever be aware of a significant percentage of the social media accounts being used to front end such transactions. End to end encryption and mobile phone password and security services have defeated international government organisations – never mind local Constabularies.

---

[11] Internet Protocol
[12] Virtual Private Network

The traditional manifestation of the 'County Line' however is for a young person to offer a telephone number out to people who are clearly interested in buying drugs. It is not difficult – *and it has never been difficult* – to identify the drug taking community. Hanging around in the morning commonly outside of a night shelter, or the local custody block will reveal a number of people actively looking for their first fix of the day. Hanging around the local pharmacists will identify people turning up to take their methadone prescriptions. Pressing a telephone number on a piece of paper into the hand of such a potential customer puts it immediately into circulation.

This is the corporate equivalent of targeting the existing market – like an Android mobile phone provider going after the Apple iPhone user.

Protecting market share is a brutal business. Part of the attraction for organised crime groups (OCGs) to want to operate through the County Lines model is to find and dominate fresh new markets without the constant competition and rivalry that exists inside London (for example).

'Postcode wars' have become a lethal consequence of the drugs market[13] in the capital and in April 2018

---

[13] https://www.irishtimes.com/news/world/uk/how-postcode-wars-have-made-london-a-murder-capital-1.3460692

London's murder rate reportedly exceeded that of New York. Sadly, not because of some remarkable breakthrough in the Big Apple that led to a reduction in crime – but because of very worrying events in our capital city.

Denis Staunton, reporting for The Irish Times quotes Lorraine Jones, an ordained minister whose own son Dwayne Simpson was murdered follow a knife attack in London in 2014:

> *"Drug Dealers have to be really thankful for a society that has been created where you have so many disaffected youth."*

Be that as it may – London is overheated with competition. Murders and woundings are committed to protect territory ownership. Drug dealers want monopolies because monopolies increase profitability. They don't want 'Dutch auctions' where higher purities and quantities have to be offered for less and less money. True market conditions strangle the risk to reward ratio that makes drug dealing a worthwhile enterprise for any criminal – so the answer is violence, protection of what you have, and a ruthless determination to keep on growing your supply chain to reinforce your means.

'County Lines' is also preoccupied with growing the market and finding new users – this is what brings our handlers and sitters out to rural, inconspicuous places.

They colonise. They bring their franchise. They setup and embed themselves and then they fight to protect it.

Consequently the recruitment policy for such organisations is exclusively focused on young people. This is very simple and easy to understand. Young people are cheap, easy to impress, easy to intimidate, naïve and they are usually more easily tricked or conned. A child with minimal parental influence, few role models, and very little face to face adult time is ideal for this. Additionally – the old fashioned image of a very scary looking drug dealer turning up in a BMW, Mercedes or another high powered car – sticks out like a sore thumb in a school environment, outside the school gates or down by the playing fields. *That isn't going to work*.

If you really want to infiltrate a school community you need to move through it without being noticed (parasite principle one – be discreet). A key part of infiltration is being unseen or unrecognised. Our schools are a filter for all our young people – on a statutory basis all of our children, irrespective of their background – will pass through a school. Building your drug distribution network into the fabric of that filter is the goal or objective that preoccupies the County Lines management. To succeed in this way will boost your distribution and profitability on an exponential basis for years to come – *providing that you protect and maintain your presence.*

What you need to do is beguile a young person to take your product into the school – or to become your outlet, or your agent within that community.

How would you go about doing this?

To begin with you need to find the young people who are susceptible to your influence. These, commonly, are young people who are seeking something – have an absence of something in their lives – and that gap, that need, or that neglect, becomes an opportunity for a subversive influence.

This takes us to commonly understood psychological theories – such as Maslow's 'hierarchy of needs'[14]:

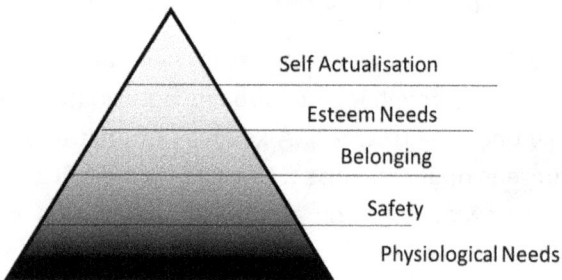

Maslow has given us a very effective way to look at the vulnerability of our children and young people across a spectrum of their different needs. While this has been used in the corporate context to assess what can be done

[14] https://psycnet.apa.org/record/1943-03751-001

to make employees happy, loyal and productive – it works equally well to consider which of our young people would be more or less susceptible to criminal exploitation.

We will return to this for a more substantial exploration of this conversation later on.

At this stage I just want to highlight that a County Lines model depends on young people that have a gaping hole somewhere on this hierarchy of needs – and it invites the handler to step in and offer them an immediate and painless solution. An easy way out. Perhaps even some fun and excitement along the way – but ultimately a reward.

The County Lines handler or dealer is a supervisor – of sorts – the shop steward. This person keeps things ticking over on a localised level. They themselves are probably not very old, perhaps in their early twenties and in all likelihood, they themselves are not that well rewarded – even if appearances suggest otherwise. The idea is that all of the money – or as much as possible – goes upwards through a criminal network. Nobody will be rewarded with financial independence because that equates to freedom.

The 'handler' function is to identify the vulnerable, to seduce them, and to keep them selling. This is done through a variety of means. Commonly this will include friendship (initially), positive inducements (to begin with), the establishment of a debt, the threat of violence, the targeting of loved ones, and more than anything else by making the young person feel like they have little or no option but to continue.

The handler does not need to have any prior psychological training or any particular awareness of (for example) Maslow to be incredibly effective. There are countless young people who exhibit the signs and symptoms or personal insecurity that such a talent scout is looking for. A handler will know quite exactly and with split second efficiency where they are likely to make some in-roads. In many regards, they are looking for someone who closely resembles themselves – or the person they used to be at the same age.

It begins with a beguilement – gift giving, and a process of grooming. This person will be the big brother figure that the target always wished they had, the surrogate parent missing from their lives. It comes with compliments, warmth, a sense of belonging and camaraderie – an arm around the shoulders. It is likely to include - over time – introducing the target to others, being described in a particular language that is contemporary, cool, and incredibly flattering. This might be the very first time in the whole life of this 14 year old that they ever felt this way – this special.

"This is my boy Rob – I'm telling you, he's young but he's streetwise, man. He's one of us yeah?"

This is likely to come along with a little bit of money, maybe a gift here or there – *"Don't worry about it, I've got you"*. But overall you might be surprised at how cheaply this trust and rapport are bought.

It is not difficult to predict what these gifts are likely to be – designer clothes (particularly trainers), mobile phones, technology, computer games. The recipient isn't inundated – they just receive a taste – enough to make them want more. A sample.

Invites to parties are a natural next step – bringing that young person inside the fold. Introducing them to the edges of permissive drug abuse, underage sex, alcohol (if they haven't already encountered it). The whole scene is designed to disinhibit and initiate gradually – edge the young person inwards to a place where their comfort zone can tolerate and embrace what they are being presented with. The entire business model depends on this being successful on a regular basis – *and it is*. Getting a young person to enjoy this scene is something that is corroborated culturally in fashion and music broadly. Cannabis – as a drug – is a huge staple of the County Lines business model. Cannabis is also perennial marker of being cool and anti-establishment. In youth circles few things are as uncool as speaking out against Cannabis, and a massive lobby – often painted as being of a grassroots nature (forgive any pun) – is creating huge amounts of pro-cannabis media on a daily basis. While heroin, MDMA, cocaine, crack and other drugs have clear and accepted warnings attached to them – cannabis revels in the image of being soft, organic, having health benefits and so on.

Importantly the young person isn't suddenly presented with the opportunity to stand on a street corner and sell drugs. It might begin with a very simple problem that they could solve – *a trick or a trap*. This handler who has been kind and generous and introduced this young person into this whole new world has a problem – if only someone could help them out? *"I need to get this package from here to there – I just need someone to carry it across town and leave it with a friend. Someone that nobody would even look at."*

Getting a person to take that first step into the world of supply – just carrying a parcel containing drugs from here to there – and possibly accepting a modest reward for doing it, gets them into the machinery. It establishes a business relationship. It might be sold as a partnership – and initially the rewards might be disproportionate. £50 or £100 here or there could seem very significant, particularly to a 13 year old from a disadvantaged background. Suddenly they are showing initiative – getting out into the world – being entrepreneurial. Mum is very hard up and she doesn't want to know where the money came from and she doesn't want it to stop either. She might work hard to persuade herself that her son has 'got a little job'.

On a macro scale the drugs – a combination of coke, heroin and weed commonly – are coordinated in a major city. Most commonly cannabis is being manufactured on an unregulated basis in converted houses and industrial units across the country. Bland, out of the way locations can be turned into cottage industries that churn out hundreds of thousands of pounds worth of crops on a monthly rotation – short term setups that ruin buildings and get closed down only to pop up again somewhere else.

Coke and heroin remains an import business – a game of cat and mouse with the Border Force, the Royal Navy, the police and National Crime Agency. When a shipment of coke or heroin gets through (plenty does) it will not hit the street unadulterated. It will be diluted with everything from powdered baby milk (if the end user is lucky) to rat poison and cheaper substances that induce numbness to simulate cocaine like effects.

The County Lines model is the distribution strategy. The people organising the serious and organised crime networks need those children and young people at the front end – managed by their handlers – to carry those drugs, and ultimately to supply them.

The handlers will bring drugs into an area – commonly in a 'g pack' – meaning £1,000 worth of street value drugs. These drugs are divided up and put out to the market through the runners at the front end. The County Lines children and young people don't buy the drugs – they don't 'own them' – *but they do possess them and they do supply them*. They are expected to deliver them, to take monies in for the transactions, and to get that money back to their handler. Failure to deliver is met with severe consequences to ensure that such a child is fiercely determined that it will never happen again.

What begins with the friendship and the artificial social scene that happens to have financial and material benefits, will rapidly become a nightmare relationship of an extremely coercive and intimidating nature. The iPhone that was given as a gift is just a method of tracking that young person as an asset. Let's revisit the mechanisms of control: debt bondage, for example, is an extremely common method. The handler is not going to get this business done by asking "Please, go on, be a pal" etc.

Gianni's Story

At this stage I will introduce another fictional character – Gianni. Named after the iconic fashion designer Gianni Versace, Gianni is not Italian. Unlike Kylo, Gianni has been seduced by the County Lines model. He was picked up hanging out with friends near a local shopping centre late in the evening. It wasn't difficult to do – he was already drinking, he was already disinhibited, he already had a false sense of how formidable he was in the streets of his local area.

At 15 Gianni smoked weed, and 'looked after' friends on a social basis. That means that he shared his weed, he cut people in, he coordinated the process of getting enough money together so that they could smoke together. On a legal basis he was supplying, but it was very, very low level indeed – five pounds here, ten pounds there. In his own eyes this made him 'a player' – he looked ahead to a time where he might even buy fifty or maybe a hundred pounds worth, score a little discount, be clever about it. He listened to music that rapped about dealing – hustling – making it. He looked at pictures of supercars and hypercars and he already imagined himself in mansions and helicopters.

His school career was broken between temporary exclusions. On one occasion he mocked a teacher for not earning enough money – and not being ambitious enough and having 'no life'. He rounded on the teacher, showing an ability to be a ringleader as he got his peers to laugh and join in before a more senior teacher had to intervene to restore order in the classroom. It was cruel and disrespectful – he didn't recognise his teacher as a human being with feelings or as a figure of authority - nor did he care.

All these qualities were ideal for a County Lines seduction. What he saw as his strengths were actually his weaknesses, but he lacked the fundamentals of self-awareness.

So when he was approached by a guy who gave the name 'Jordan', who spoke with a London accent, and delivered a confident fist bump and 'dot five' of weed – *for nothing* – Gianni was well on his way.

As previously stated this relationship started off feeding the ego and sense of identity that Gianni needed.

Gianni needed a sense of belonging, he needed self-esteem but was highly referenced on an external basis, and he felt that he needed financial rewards to flaunt in order to feel secure and cool.

Gianni's family were not poor or disadvantaged. Quite the opposite. Without being 'rich' he had two professional parents who were still together and provided a large detached house in a leafy rural area. The family had two cars – one was a large BMW. Gianni had fashionable clothes, the latest computer games, his own bedroom and a degree of affluence that other people envied. His hair was fashionably cut on a regular basis and he chose to adopt the style and identity which amalgamated urban American and London styles. When he was with his friends he adopted a faux London accent of sorts (South London) placing emphasis on certain recognisable words and a distinctive intonation. He was a rap music fan – and like any self-respecting contemporary rap music fan this meant the evolving 'grime' music culture. It alienated his parents – but they figured that their music alienated their parents when they were the same age, so this was nothing new (and to some extent – that is true).

Gianni's room was more or less off limits to Mum and Dad, his phone was *definitely* off limits – but he was the one setting the boundaries.

Both parents had professional careers of their own – full time employment – salaries, management responsibilities, preoccupations and Gianni had two other siblings (of which he was neither youngest nor eldest).

Fundamentally Gianni got little time with his parents – unless they were on holiday – and their situation was then quite awkward and stilted due to a lack of familiarity or rapport. He demonstrated resentment towards them, and they rewarded him further out of guilt to try and find a way around that.

Gianni was not a fighter – but he could be confrontational – he picked on and bullied others verbally. He underperformed at school and had a cynical attitude about school being a mechanism to hold him back; program him to accept the boundaries of society, and to prevent him getting out in the world to make an inevitable fortune.

This young man did not look older or younger than his years. He didn't cut an intimidating figure in the real world (outside of school). Tall and thin, he had a very over inflated sense of self-worth and importance due to a frankly quite indulgent up-bringing that silenced any tantrums with rewards.

When he got scooped up by 'Jordan' he accelerated quickly into the new lifestyle. He went to parties, he lied naturally to his parents, and he happily transitioned from carrying and moving small volumes of drugs, to hiding quantities in his parent's disused garage and garden shed. When the opportunity came for him to sell a little bit for himself he enjoyed the adrenaline rush of looking over his shoulder and confirmed his identity as a rebel and a 'do anything' entrepreneur.

He was clever enough to avoid using from the amounts he was given to sell, but he couldn't resist bragging about his activities or playing 'the big man' around school. He threatened peers that he 'knew people' and did a very poor job of keeping a low profile. He made enemies and he was disliked by classmates who feared him. He knew the Machiavellian code 'it is better to be feared than loved' but never learned the rest of this famous advice:

> *"A wise prince should establish himself on that which he controls, and not in that which others control. He must endeavour only to avoid being hated."*[15]

---

[15] Niccolo Machiavelli – The Prince; Chapter 17 'Cruelty vs Mercy'

The volumes of drugs and cash entrusted to Gianni spiralled with his enthusiasm. Until one day he was carrying £500 in cash and £500 worth of heroin, coke and weed. He took a wrong turn and ended up face to face with three people he didn't know at all. They challenged him for dealing 'on their streets'.

Gianni was given a warning – *a generous warning by way of street justice* – which consisted of a thorough beating, and he was robbed of the £500 and the drugs. He arrived home with a very swollen black eye, bloodied nose, swollen jaw (which thankfully was not broken) broken ribs and bruises up and down his torso and legs from being stamped on.

His dismayed and acutely anxious parents took him to A&E for X-rays and treatment. The doctors and nurses could offer him little more than the reassurance that he would heal up, and some pain killers. Police were informed and Gianni had to go along with the charade of cooperating with that process. Lying to the police, Gianni did a poor job of hiding his disdain for the officers. He showed no gratitude for their efforts to support him or find out what happened. He gave a false account of his movements and this was proven when he appeared on CCTV elsewhere – he fudged his excuses – and it was very clear that all was not what it seemed and this put him on the radar for local services and agencies, corroborating fears already held inside his school (that frankly hadn't been listened to).

He had not been 'mugged' – at least not in the conventional sense that the average person expects where a stranger or strangers pick a victim at random and look to take their wallet or phone.

The worst was still to come for Gianni though. He went back to Jordan expecting some solidarity and concern for his welfare. Some reassurance. Some sense of "We'll find out who did this and…"

Instead Gianni was met with a very different demeanour – like a totally different person.

"You owe me a grand!"

"What? I was robbed – it wasn't my fault?!"

"You fucking owe me a grand – and you're going to come up with it".

"Fuck off. I am not…"

Before the words even fell out of his mouth Gianni got his second beating. Already in acute pain from his initial injuries Jordan focused his attention on Gianni's body and it was agony inducing. He pulled out a knife and held it in front of him – not two inches from his bruised face.

"If you ever disagree with me again I will fucking finish you off mate – do you understand? Now if you don't come up with a grand, and an extra £200 for making me lose my temper, and for making me tell people that I haven't got their money, I'm gonna slice your pretty face, cut your

knackers off and feed them to my fucking dogs. Believe it. You've got until Saturday".

And that was it. Jordan ghosted Gianni for several days – amplifying his desperation and paranoia. He felt completely trapped. Always in control of his boy, Jordan did him 'a favour' and didn't use the knife on him. He broke two fingers "You know I don't want to mate – but I have to – those are the rules out here". Gianni even apologised to Jordan because Jordan had to do it.

They agreed a repayment rate with interest (a ridiculous amount of interest that swallowed up any money that Gianni *thought* he was making).

The interest rate was designed to keep Gianni on the hook – but the twist was what Gianni never saw coming. The people who beat him up were sent by Jordan, he was robbed by Jordan, and Jordan was never out of pocket in the first place.

The three lads that beat Gianni up were brought up from London for the job. They carried the cash and drugs faithfully back to Jordan. They got rewarded and they disappeared back into London. *Gianni would never see them again and he wouldn't dream of supporting a prosecution against them even if he did.*

The whole situation left him entrenched in a situation he couldn't recover from – with daily phone calls coming from people who wanted to buy drugs, and from Jordan who wanted to know where his money was. This was a day and night situation – sneaking out at all hours – always looking over his shoulder with increasing levels of paranoia.

To calm himself Gianni smoked more weed – perpetuating his debt further still – but he was convinced that it was the only thing that could calm his nerves and deal with his anxiety. He self-medicated in a cycle of drug abuse that actually made his paranoia and his mood swings more and more severe. He became increasingly inaccessible to his parents, closed off to the world around him, he failed at school and he lived his life from one day to the next. There was nothing aspirational or entrepreneurial about where he found himself now – and he couldn't bring himself to trust anyone enough to help him out of it. The oblivion of drug abuse looked like quite a good way out – sometimes he thought about suicide.

Comparing Gianni to Kylo you can see the remarkable difference between being *in* the County Lines system, and being hurt by the County Lines system. Without any mistake being made – both boys were brutalised as a consequence of the existence of County Lines – but Gianni became trapped inside it. *He came to realise that he was trapped inside it* – that he was subject to a form of debt slavery and physical coercion – but he had no idea how he could ever climb out. That is a guiding principle of the business model – you make your 'employees' fear you, and you ensure that they cannot walk away.

The structure and organisation of a County Lines enterprise can vary – as Dr Jack Spicer, a lecturer and researcher in Criminology at the University of West of England, Bristol has written in his own published thesis[16]:

> "From what little is known about the operations and inner workings of those that utilise this drug supply methodology, those involved can generally be considered well organised. With regard to structure, it would appear that fundamental to how they successfully operate is part of a relatively well-structured group, organisation or network"

Spicer makes reference to three predominant levels in a relatively flat hierarchy:

---

[16] 'The policing of County Lines in Affected Import Towns: Exploring Local Responses to Evolving Heroin and Crack Markets' (2019)

Top Boy

Sitter

Runner

The 'Top Boy' or 'the Boss' controls the operation. He will be based in a large city –and he sends his satellites out to colonise profitable less contested areas in soft suburban and rural locations. The physical distance of the 'Top Boy' from the market is a good form of insulation from being prosecuted – and if the boss has to come into a local area it will need to be for a good reason (which means an exceptional profit – or, more likely, something has gone quite wrong).

The 'Sitter' is usually younger than the 'Top Boy' – he (*and it predominantly is a 'he'*) will take shipments of drugs out to the colony and he will recruit, cultivate, and manage his runners in that area. It is his role to keep those runners in line and to keep the supply of drugs going in one direction, while cash flows reliably in the opposite direction. From our previous illustration, Jordan was what Dr Spicer describes as a 'sitter'.

In years gone by the 'Sitter' was associated with the processes of 'cuckooing' addresses: this involves moving in on particularly vulnerable residents (particularly drug users or recovering addicts) and those on the edge of not being able to live an independent life. Cuckooing an address involves taking over a house and using it as a base. It might involve a pretence or a cover story about being a relative or carer. The occupant of that address will be kept in fear, and probably rewarded or silenced with some small quantity of drugs (which are plentiful). This makes for cheap accommodation and a strong presence in a local area. More recently the 'cuckooing' tactic has become less popular and more trouble than it is worth – so instead the significant profitability of the County Lines model makes using motels more desirable and less conspicuous. For me personally, I recognised this most remarkably around 2015 – when measures to prevent and deal with cuckooing had really stepped up and were beginning to compromise distribution. Around this time, cuckooing in East Cambridgeshire dramatically fell into decline – but motel use went in the other direction.

Child runners are an expendable part of the machinery (the merchandise and cash that they carry is far more important than they are). They are picked up and prosecuted regularly, they are harmed physically and mentally by the people who exploit them. They exist at the beck and call of the 'Sitter'. They are taught to swallow significant quantities of dangerous substances (lethal doses inside condoms and baggies) to hide what they have on their person and reduce the likelihood of apprehension.

Beguiled – as previously described – through the illusion of friendship and promises – they are held in place through fear, through debt, and not uncommonly through drug dependency. They are juveniles. Children. Targeted and harmed through the 'County Lines' process. Runners are very often looked at as offenders – and not enough people understand the importance of regarding them as victims. Kylo was never a runner – *Gianni was*.

As with most things related to both organised crime and drugs, the structure has become glamourised and enshrined in common language. 'Top Boy' is the title of a BBC crime drama series running successfully on Netflix and being shown all over the world. Descriptions of this take on South London drug dealing are described as 'combining elements of tense gangster thriller with subtle social realism'[17].

'Top Boy' is also already a part of the fashionable social lexicon in the teenage world meaning the hardest, most competitive, most successful alpha male in a peer group. It is often used in a context that has nothing whatsoever to do with drugs or county lines, and the origins of the terms have blurred as to whether it started with the drugs or was just amplified into common usage by drug slang.

---

[17] Google Reviews

William

The story of William – or Will – requires no alteration of identity. Will is an adult now – but still only 19. He has a new life as a gentleman's barber and in the course of three years went on a rollercoaster ride that blasted him through several schools, the County Lines system, the police, YOS, and the Crown Court.

Will was dealing drugs and highly active in East Cambridgeshire at the age of 13. He got picked up by a sitter and enveloped into a world that we have already discussed and described in some detail. I dealt with and arrested Will myself when he became 'wanted' for several offences, some of which were quite serious. He was becoming a thorn in the side for the police and had been known with increasing profile for some time. The most concerning thing about Will was his trajectory – which was stratospheric.

At 13 he went through an alarming succession of very good schools – one after the other – repeatedly triggering the PSP process[18] and ultimately ending in a 'managed move' to restart somewhere else. Exhausting three very good schools locally in quick succession he entered the local Pupil Referral Unit (PRU).

---

[18] System of personal report administered by the local authority usually resulting in a change of schools.

Will was then kicked out of the PRU for threatening one of the staff with a knife. When I went looking for him he was wanted for a street robbery. I'd spoken to him on the phone and I'd made an agreement with him, which I usually tried to do:

"If you can behave like a gentleman and come in by appointment I will treat you like a gentleman – no handcuffs, no messing you about – we'll get everything sorted out..."

He had agreed to come and see me in Ely police station. Nine times out of ten that worked very smoothly and helped to facilitate an immediate rapport. It usually ended up with these young offenders – who wanted to be respected like some type of mature gangster saying things like *"You're alright – I'll deal with you – you're ok, I like you, not like that c*nt over there."* (etc).

We'd get to a point where I could – at the very least – reach the last solicitor they used while they were in custody, convey a message through that person, and get them dealt with by an appointment. Either the evidence was strong enough to charge them or it wasn't. *It was never personal* – gather the evidence, assemble the facts of the case – and if you can, put it before the court. If there was a reasonable likelihood of a successful prosecution at court – they would be charged. Neither side would do either any favours – but on a pragmatic level attending by appointment made sense to both, and both showed a measure of good will and appreciation. It was business like and civilised. The wannabe gangster didn't get bundled by police officers in public, embarrassed in front of his mates or his girlfriend, his mum didn't get her door banged on at two in the morning, or smashed in under a Misuse of Drugs Act warrant. It was civilised and appealed to some sort of Don Corleone image of dignity – the solicitor playing the consiglieri and we all had our place in this pantomime.

For the police it meant that fewer people were likely to get hurt, the time management side of things was more convenient and organised, and let's be honest – who wants to be out running in the streets trying to round up teenagers? Not many people join the police to do that. It could actually be quite embarrassing if that thirteen or fourteen year old looked like they were one or two steps ahead of you.

So I had made an appointment with 'Don' William and he was going to be cool and come in and get sorted out. *Only he didn't*. He was the one out of ten people that changed their mind. So myself and a colleague had to ditch our plans and go looking for him on a rainy, squalid, miserable, dark evening. We had some reasonable intelligence about where he was likely to be and we trekked out to Will's mate's house in North Cambridge and locked him up. Needless to say, it wasn't the mansion of a drugs cartel.

Will wasn't apologetic about missing his appointment either. Quite the opposite. He was full of it. He was ready to play up in front of everyone.

I continued to appeal to his sense of "We're cool right? Ok – you missed the appointment – but we don't have beef – we're good?"

"Yeah but I don't like him" (pointing to colleague) – you can add your own expletives and insults to that remark because there were plenty of them. My colleague had done nothing wrong – he was just the token, arbitrary target.

And from there Will directed his frustrations and apparent determination to have a fight upon my colleague. No amount of conflict de-escalation was going to avert this it would seem. In this situation Will couldn't be seen to just get in the van. Eventually he got what he wanted – but not before the tired *"Is there anything I can reasonably do or say that will get you to comply with my directions"* was issued. This is one of the robotic phrases that often gets used in policing more or less because we think it sounds good in court and apparently it means that we did everything we possibly could to gain compliance before the situation got physical (particularly with a child).

We really did try to avoid it, but nevertheless the situation did get physical.

Will – not the most intimidating figure at less than 5'6" tall and all of thirteen or fourteen years old – was restrained physically, handcuffed, and was bundled into the back of police van literally spitting insults as he went.

His choice of language was deliberately abusive, provocative and confrontational. We knew that he was trying to get a rise out of the cops.

One school of thought is that he deserved to be manhandled – and probably needed to be shown who was boss. He was a cocky little street thug and he would probably benefit from a good hiding.

The more rational position is that actually such behaviour just ingrained his only psychological hierarchy that was based on the use of physical force and violence. You find out where you are in the pecking order by provoking a confrontation and seeing who comes out on top.

Additionally – he was a child. Yes, he was mimicking the behaviours of a full grown man looking for a fight – but he wasn't a fully grown man. He was a child – a vulnerable, damaged example of a child who had already been radicalised into a world of a criminal misbehaviour to suit the profit motives of a more sinister network of people. He was, in every sense, a proxy. His arrest, his confrontational street behaviours, his presence in a community – was little more than an avatar for persons sat miles away who counted the money that resulted from all this, but they risked little in terms of being identified, arrested or prosecuted.

Giving William a 'good hiding' or a 'kicking' in this situation would be exactly what the County Lines management structure wanted. What could possibly make Will hate the authorities more than being hospitalised with a dislocated shoulder or some other painful injury? They would like nothing more than for Will to have a story to tell about the time he got sprayed with PAVA incapacitant, hit with a baton, punched or otherwise physically mauled. *"See, you can never trust a cop"* or *"All coppers are bastards"*. At that point you have lost Will – he would never see you or any other police officer as a way out of his situation. You become the enemy.

In any regard, Will got away with little more than being restrained, hand cuffed, told to shut up – and was put in the back of the Ford Transit van cage. Anything that he might then say on top of that would be nothing more than hyperbole – him making it up to impress his mates.

Personally, I was disappointed that we couldn't talk him into the back of a car – to show him the benefit of treating people with respect and dignity – but it doesn't work with everybody.

Fast-forward now approximately five years in time.

I get my hair cut in the same barber's shop – month after month – and I've been going there for about ten years.

It's a traditional Turkish barber's shop and they treat you like family. Sometimes my son would be given £5 for sweeping all the hair off the floor while we waited. My son flatly refuses to go elsewhere – *they have groomed him in more than one context*. I like and respect the owner a great deal. He is one of the hardest working men I know and he always stops to say hello when you see him around town.

On this particular day I sat down in the chair and the young man – who had cut my hair once before – put the gown over me and began tucking it in around my neck. He asked me what I wanted doing – as is always the routine – and I explained. He got on with it. There was general chat between the barbers – sometimes the customers who knew each other too. One of the other barbers asked me how I was.

That was when Will said to me *"You're that copper, right? From out in Ely?"*

This is usually an awkward question. Getting recognised off duty is a generally an uncomfortable thing. Witnesses who are curious about how *that* case is going (when you're working on so many). Victims who want to relive their experiences with you. Offenders who are a bit disgruntled. *You might even get heckled*. You generally want to just have some time off when you're not at work, and I think that's fair enough. One of the most misunderstood things about being in the police is the constant weight you carry – that sense of responsibility.

If something happens in front of you, you have to do the right thing and snap back into work mode.

As it happens I had already left the police by this point – but I wasn't long out of the job. Weeks, maybe a couple of months. I replied "Yeah, well I used to be – I'm not any more…"

"You don't recognise me do you?"

I genuinely didn't.

This is actually quite unusual – most times you do recognise people and it's part of your job to recognise people in abstract circumstances. He told me who he was and I then immediately *did* recognise him – but in that way that you squint and tilt your head and look, and look harder. You *realise* more than recognise. "No! No way?"

You might think that I'd be perturbed by what I was presented with there – but it wasn't like that at all. He looked good. He'd obviously filled out a bit – wasn't that much taller – but his whole demeanour was more laid back, happier and he seemed to be in a good place.

Before I could say a word he launched into "I just want to apologise to you for what I did. I was a horrible person then, I'm really ashamed of who I was and how I acted and behaved towards people. I was so out of order with you."

I can count on one hand how many times people have come up to me and apologised like that – it just doesn't happen (I actually think it has happened to me twice in seventeen years). Naturally we talked about everything that happened – his arrest – my coming out to find him, how he behaved with my colleague. What was more interesting was to talk about what happened *after* that.

Will found himself being charged with serious offences – not necessarily in relation to that arrest, but he eventually ended up in Crown Court.

"I pleaded not guilty. Not because I didn't do it – but because I just wanted some time to try and show something better about myself. I had nothing positive to offer the Judge at all. My solicitor told me that I was going to prison for two years. I'd been told to get myself ready. I couldn't face it. I knew that if I went to prison my life was going to get really nasty in a way that I couldn't deal with."

Will pleaded 'not guilty' and he got bail – largely because he was a juvenile. The case was prolonged for quite a while and Will persuaded his Mum to send him to Turkey temporarily, where he had family. Will was born in the UK to Turkish parents – his Mum and Dad were separated. He didn't have a strong and consistent male role model during his teenage years – although his mother was/is a hardworking and well respected woman (who I have met). Will had an uncle with a barber shop in

Istanbul – so he was sent there to get himself straightened out a bit.

"I didn't have a single qualification. No GCSEs nothing. I had nothing."

He also had a criminal network surrounding him and his involvement – by his own admission – had escalated into him making journeys into London to collect packages of drugs that he brought back out to East Cambs. He was ambitious.

"I thought I was big time. I was carrying a knife and I was ready to use it. I was ready to fight anybody"

Flying back to Turkey his extended family were well aware of the trouble that he'd got himself into and nobody was impressed. His Turkish uncle took immediate control of Will and subjected him to a job in the shop that involved six or seven straight days, long hours for nothing but food and lodging. Long hours were combined with physical consequences if he stepped out of line. In many regards he was treated like an exploited child again.

Something inside of Will made him want to change. He started watching motivational videos on YouTube and he decided that he needed to learn how to be a barber properly – it was his only option. Talking to me now Will is full of ambition and a sense of direction:

"I don't just want to 'cut hair' though. I want to move up – I want to be doing £20 hair cuts, and then £50 haircuts, and then I want people to be coming to find me because I'm the best and I'm doing £100 haircuts"

He talked to me with enthusiasm about skin fades and other techniques. He showed me photos from his Instagram account of cuts that he had already done. He talked to me about his tools – he had now traded in his knife for a very expensive set of clippers, multiple pairs of professional grade scissors, and a cut throat razor that he used with remarkable precision.

"I just worked day and night for weeks learning and learning and learning."

When he came back to the UK a few months later he appeared before the Judge at court. He dismissed his solicitor and asked if he could speak to the court himself in his own words. He pleaded guilty to all of the charges in front of him, without throwing anyone else under the bus.

"I begged him not to send me to prison. I told the judge what I had done – that I had found a skill, that I was talented about something that wasn't crime. That I was sorry, full of remorse, and that I just wanted to be the very best at my new trade. I knew that no amount of prison would make the difference to me that letting me find a job and getting on with cutting hair would make. I

promised him that I would never go back in front of a court and that it was all behind me".

It's fortunate for Will that the representations worked. The Judge convicted Will, issuing him with a suspended sentence that allowed him to carry on with his new ambition. If he had stepped out of line, Will knew he was immediately going to prison – that was made abundantly clear. It was a huge relief and a new start. Will told me what life was like when it had got completely out of control:

"At its worst I was completely paranoid. I was smoking so much weed. I would walk down the street and cross the road repeatedly because I thought people were following me and were after me. I couldn't sleep at night. I carried a knife on me all the time. I was involved in horrible things and saw horrible things. I beat people up – I was violent. I was just a really horrible person. My life was awful."

Will is now a very endearing person – he doesn't touch cannabis. He has an acute sense of self-awareness – he is self-conscious that he has no education and feels 'stupid' for lacking what other people take for granted. But he is proud of how he has turned things around.

I offered Will the opportunity to come into schools and to cut the hair of some of the boys who openly talked about how gangs were cool, and had started using drugs-slang, and that distinctive, affected South London twang *"You get me yeah?".*

There is something about Will when he talks about what he went through that is utterly convincing and clearly very real. You immediately know that it isn't synthetic or assumed.

When one of the boys started talking about 'trapping' (dealing) Will immediately switched into a tone and a language that was no less distinctive than when he starts speaking Turkish. Culturally, in terms of being easy to understand, in terms of body language and everything – it's recognisable, different and opaque.

All of the boys realised they were immediately out of their depth – they couldn't impress him with it like they might impress their younger mates. It's like watching someone who can't speak French offering "Ca va?" to a French person because they learned it in class. When that French person speaks back there is a bewilderment in their eyes and overwhelmed confusion *"No, you're suppose to say 'Ca va' back like they do in the text book?"*.

"Let me tell you something – if you be trapping, you an idiot. Someone is taking you for their idiot yeah? Don't be someone's idiot"

There is a palpable air in the room – a sense of intimidation – a fear that some of the plastic and artificial 'gangsters' who affect a gangster limp around the school corridors are about to get found out.

I am very grateful to Will because he came into schools, talked and cut hair for nothing – just because he felt that he needed to make good on some of the things he had done wrong in society. He also didn't want to see young people going down the wrong road, making the same mistakes and not being able to get out of it.

So what was different about Will and how did he escape from his nightmare?

When confronted with prison Will realised that he couldn't cope with it. He's a reasonably quick thinking guy and he scanned his options. He had more than most.

First of all he could relocate in a hurry – abroad. Putting distance between himself and what he had got wrapped up in was a very good thing. It removed any temptation. He had the *means* to do that and he was in a place where he *wanted* to do that.

Secondly, he had got to that place – like Gianni – where he knew he was being used. He was tired of constantly having to prove himself, of existing in circles and hierarchies of people who could never trust anyone or each other. He was tired of being misused, and he was constantly paranoid. He knew that he needed rehabilitation from over dependency on weed – and after a few years of being in the County Lines machine his life was getting worse, not better. He was sensible enough to recognise that.

Thirdly, when he got to Turkey an alternative role model came into his life. It wasn't an ideal one – it was still quite violent at times – but it was fiercely honest, and the honour code around him changed. He received outside objective judgement – and that was something that he couldn't escape from or wriggle out of. He had to confront things there. Additionally this place gave him an honest way to make living – a practical skill that appealed to his natural creativity and still embraced his enthusiasm to become an entrepreneur. These pieces fit into place and satisfied his need for safety, belonging and self-esteem. That 'fit' was right for him individually.

When he came back to the UK he was galvanised in a different way – deradicalised from the County Lines programme – and his day in court committed him, and initiated him to a new life. He had to beg for his freedom and it was uncertain that he'd get it. When he did, the suspended sentence remained with him and weighed on his mind.

The Turkish community forgave and supported Will. He got a job in a barber's and continued to work incredibly hard to improve his position – *and he evidenced that there is a way out of the County Lines network.*

Will's personal triumph contrasts against the tragic situation I was confronted with in Ely, a couple of years before that hair cut, when I cut a young black man down out a tree who had hung himself in absolute desperation – at the nadir of a mental health crisis.

Surrounded by intelligence related to drug dealing, including frequent visits to an address that had been cuckooed, found with multiple mobile phones – his suicide note was laced with convoluted lies about a place in life that had clearly been programmed into him over a period of time. This desperate young man found another, altogether less positive, way out. He hung himself with bailing twine and his body was still warm – indicating that he had committed the act perhaps only moments before we arrived.

Air ambulance doctors and local paramedics fought for thirty frantic minutes, with the kind of heroic determination that is somehow amazingly common within that service, to save this young man. His passing was a tragedy.

I met his mother and his family at the Coroner's Court in Huntingdon some months later – he was of second generation African heritage – and the situation was horrendous. Naturally everyone was completely heartbroken. You can't possibly remain untouched by that.

This young man was not unknown to police and other services – but there was no effective mechanism of intervention to reach out and save him. Nobody established that he got to the stage of knowing that he needed a way out – he lacked the means and the guidance to do what Will had done.

We have to be pragmatic when we consider Will – we cannot congratulate ourselves as a society for the way things turned out for him. He was, in part, lucky, but his success is certainly only down to him and the steps he took. None of it really came from a statutory partner, from a material intervention – there was little or no support for Will either, no process of re-education. It was certainly nothing to do with me.

As a Detective Chief Superintendent (Head of Crime) once explained to me when I was a Detective Sergeant:

"If the criminal justice system is a hammer – then all our problems have to be nails"

Funnily enough this takes us back to Maslow – because it was Maslow who coined this phrase (not my Detective Chief Superintendent – although I think he liked us to think that he was responsible for it, he certainly never mentioned or credited Abraham Maslow).

Perhaps the problem with Will *was* 'a nail' and all we needed to do for him was to utilise the Criminal Justice system – he certainly seemed to do the rest for himself. Statistically there will be such cases.

What then, for people, such as that unnamed black boy, who are not nails? Are the typically exploited teenagers who come under the influence of County Lines mostly nails? Do we really believe that we need to hammer them through the criminal justice system?

Returning to the words of the current Home Secretary, Priti Patel:

"We are coming after you… We stand for the forces of right, and against the forces of evil" [19]

Is that a dialogue that would tempt Will, or our unnamed fatality, to put down their knives and ask for our help?

We have to look long and hard at the lies that our exploited teens are sold – the lies that help to seduce and radicalise them towards violence. The question 'What is County Lines?' is not only about the mechanisms and structures of the business model – it is about the lies perpetuated by those who support it, and it is definitely about the place in modern youth culture that it has made for itself.

Understanding 'County Lines' is also about detecting its camouflage. If County Lines is a cancer in society, how many of us know and recognise where the healthy flesh finishes and the disease begins? Nike trainers – for example – a highly desirable pair of Nike Air Max '95 Essential' in black will cost you in the region of £140. 'VaporMax Plus' in white more like £180. Of course Nike are not making and marketing trainers to support the County Lines model – but the County Lines 'sitter' will use these things to seduce and convince a young target to become a runner (not the type of runner usually associated with a sports brand). Either in presenting them as a gift, using them as a goal, or by wearing them

[19] https://www.theguardian.com/uk-news/2019/oct/01/priti-patel-unveils-county-lines-crackdown

himself to impress that youngster. This doesn't mean that every child wearing Nike Air Max is implicated in County Lines either.

The poet Will Self, somewhat infamously declared on live television *"Not all Brexit voters are racist, but all the racists voted for Brexit"* (so contentious is the whole Brexit issue that I have to reassure the reader at this point that your own view on Brexit and indeed my view on Brexit is irrelevant here) – the point is that *'Not everyone who owns Nike Air Max trainers are County Lines drug runners or sitters but it's a safe bet that all the sitters and runners do own and wear Nike Air Max trainers'.*

It is not clear whether County Lines is actually changing cultural tastes or simply following them to increase popularity and for its own marketing and branding. Lazy broad stroke generalisations here are unhelpful and distracting. The point I am making is (and this might be my second hot take for the book as a whole) that County Lines drug dealers are very, *very* cool – at least in the eyes of the people they are trying to seduce or intimidate. There is a very determined and deliberate use of branding and brand association.

BMW, Audi and Mercedes cars. Apple and Samsung phones and technology – but definitely and specifically Apple. You cannot go wrong with a teenager and Apple electronics. Nike footwear is unimpeachable – very safe territory indeed. Gucci, Louis Vuitton, Superdry, D&G,

Prada and others at the ultra high end – uncommonly available in most high streets and reassuringly out of the reach of the vast majority of fourteen year olds – again provide easy choices. I didn't even know about the brand 'Supreme' who have partnered with Louis Vuitton to make a limited edition run of clothing and luggage - £750 for the hoodie, £40,000 (yes forty-thousand) for a large piece of luggage. I was made aware of this by a 13 year old boy – and of course, initially, I didn't even believe him. *He knew about it though.*

And they don't want to be subtle with it either – if you're going to dangle that bait and flaunt that stuff, you really want to put it out there and make it 'bling' – show it off.

You don't have to make children and young people want to be part of County Lines, if you can simply make County Lines synonymous with cool brands. The children and young people we are talking about are already bombarded with advertising and marketing exercises that work with metronomic predictability. Running an OCG, you just get behind that work that has already been done – it's not like one of the brands can find and sue you.

Likewise the phrase 'County Lines' is not used by the groups operating under such models – *the devil doesn't introduce himself as 'the devil'*. A sitter doesn't introduce himself with a business card that says:

As this book continues we will discuss how we can learn from the County Lines model, and *what* we can learn from them. They have and they use numerous tactics and strategies that *we* do not employ on a 'hearts and minds' level.

One thing that I will reiterate is that there is a marketing war that we are losing – that we are a million times worse at – as one professional has confided to me *"They are just much better at grooming our kids than we are, and we have to be better than them"*. It sounds awful – but it is true.

One of the instrumental and pivotal advantages that the County Lines machinery has – that schools and colleges, social care teams, early help teams, youth workers and countless others have been deprived of over the last ten years - is cash. This has been a government decision – the rationale for that decision is probably to be found in another book – but definitely, certainly – and with one hundred times emphasis, it has made it much easier to recruit and seduce runners.

If you want people to drink your water – and one hundred other people are offering water, you need to have the coldest, purest water. The 'Evian' option. The glass bottle with the condensation running down the side, served by a model, in a crystal glass – cheaper than everyone else, closer than everyone else, more thirst quenching... and so on. If you are in a desert, confronted by an orderly queue of thirsty people, and you are the only person with water – a thimble full of diluted poison that doesn't taste *that bad* is going to be enough to impress everyone. We should make no mistake about it – with schools resorting to crowd funding computers during the COVID 19 crisis – we are in that desert. It is another part of the organised crime monopoly – they have the money that nobody else can offer.

I've previously illustrated how County Lines isn't just about exploiting children who are affected by poverty – and it doesn't just harm children who are 'poor' – but my goodness, it does thrive on poverty, and childhood poverty and County Lines are the very best of friends. County Lines has boomed while child poverty has increased. County Lines is not causing that poverty – it is feeding on it.

We must look at society – *modern society* – and understand that we are either knowingly or unwittingly allowing our children and young people to participate in a huge experiment. Most adults today can remember the pre-internet world – only the youngest adults have no recollection of what that was like (because they weren't there). The next generation and going forward, will be a generation that has come up through the proliferation of social media and we don't know how this is going to turn out in the long term. The internet and social media is the new wild frontier – there is very little policing of online content and social media providers are becoming more and more influential in how governments are chosen, and consequently how these spaces are (self) regulated.

Facebook was founded in 2004 and it is not a cool brand with teenagers – *it is already old hat for young people and the place where their parents hang out* – few of the children and young people I speak to will admit to having a Facebook presence (don't worry for Facebook – they also own the far more fashionable 'Instagram'). Despite having annual revenues of around $70 billion and a CEO with an estimated net worth of $86 billion at the relatively tender age of 36 – at 16 years old, Facebook isn't a cool teenager. But it is one of the oldest and most prevailing of the social media outlets and it is incredibly powerful and influential. In the time that Facebook has been around, Myspace, Friendster, Google Wave, Google Buzz, Google+ *(Google has been trying to succeed in social media a lot)*, FriendFeed, and Vine (remember any of those?) have failed. Even in its death rattle Myspace changed hands for $580 million. Before Facebook happened 'Friends Reunited' was born and it died. In this vibrant, volatile, dynamic context we are bringing up and raising our first generation of social media children.

This involves two key strands that are an absolute advantage to the County Lines phenomenon – first and foremost children are being given their own mobile phones and tablets at younger and younger ages. The second strand is that children and young people are being targeted in a far more direct and deliberate way by specific advertising content that is based on the naivety of their internet choices. If a generation of kids grew up through the 1970s, 1980s and 1990s were seeing or hearing advertising content on billboards, television and radio shows – it was comparatively 'broadsweep' delivery. Football crazy boys interested in the latest Transformer toys happened to be watching the same adverts as their sister when the Barbie and Tiny Tears doll adverts came on.

Social media, and the success of an incredibly specific, targeted and ultimately successful Brexit 'Leave' campaign has shown: advertisers are not wasting time delivering messages to people who haven't already shown the early signs that they are interested, susceptible and/or sit within a demographic that they want to reach. *This is advertising on steroids.* Our children today have a much stronger degree of brand awareness, and they relate much more closely to brands as a method of identity than ever before – they are being shot at with absolute precision. If the 1980s advertising industry was a blunderbuss of grape shot, the modern social media platform has sniper rifle accuracy, and assault rifle repetition. How much do our children and young people want these brands? So much that they feel that something is wrong with them if they *don't* have them.

Previously owning the equivalent of Louis Vuitton at the age of 13 (what even was the equivalent of Louis Vuitton at that age – did that exist?) was a life goal. *"When I'm grown up I would like to own a house with a swimming pool and a Ferrari"* – it was an early example of how children and young people referenced themselves to the Maslovian concept of 'self-actualisation'. Today it is about *self-esteem* or even (further down the Maslovian pyramid) *belonging* – much earlier in the hierarchy of needs, and far more crucial to their sense of self-worth and ability to fit in at a much younger age.

If Facebook is sixteen years old, it was only about five years old when the national austerity project began in the UK. There has been more time spent *in* austerity than out of austerity during the life of Facebook. Quite a sobering thought. For that entire period advertising has become more effective, compelling, more direct and more targeted through all social media channels. An inverted relationship to means and income exists throughout this time – as standards of living fell, and we discovered definitions that had to be adapted to include new concepts such as 'poverty' and 'absolute poverty'.

To our collective shame The Institute for Fiscal Studies has warned that almost 40% of children in the UK will be living in poverty by 2022.[20]

Multiple sources have given disclosure that the most successful social media channels are mimicking reward and dependency methods found in pharmaceutical and illegal drugs to make their products more compelling[21]. We are already 'drug dealing' the social media and the advertising cycle to our children – affording unrivalled access to whet their appetites. Previous fears that cannabis was a 'gateway drug' – certainly on a pharmaceutical level – seem to be unproven, but the addicting qualities and the dependency relationship with social media is right there in front of us – and we're pretty cool with it.

To loop back around to County Lines then, this is an open goal and an incredible opportunity. They don't need to do any market research to know that a generation of impoverished children want access to both the technology (to enhance their multimedia engagement) and the golden branded images that they are fed once they are online. They also know that there is little or no

---

20

https://www.theguardian.com/commentisfree/2019/may/16/tories-children-poverty-britain-austerity

[21] https://www.businessinsider.com/facebook-has-been-deliberately-designed-to-mimic-addictive-painkillers-2018-12?r=US&IR=T

likelihood that this generation will lay hands on these designer items by any legitimate means in their immediate lives (a child version of immediate is very literal). All the criminals have to do is bait the hook. This is a crucial part of what County Lines is and why it is so incredibly successful right now.

102

Chapter Two: Radicalisation & Criminal Seduction

Radicalisation is a term that has entered the common vocabulary over the last twenty years and broadly since the '9/11' New York terror attacks on the World Trade Centre in 2001. The concept and fear of radicalisation was particularly ingrained in the British psyche following the '7/7' bombings in London in 2005 and a subsequent host of vicious and apparently religiously motivated attacks that have been witnessed across Europe, including Norway, France, Germany and in North African holiday destinations such at Egypt where large numbers of European visitors are likely to be found (Sharm El-Sheikh was also bombed in July 2005, and several times more in the years that followed).

In truth this is a very Eurocentric timeline because even cursory amounts of research into the terror attacks that have been inflicted on North Africa and the Middle-East reveal a catalogue of events that barely got mentioned in the media, if they did at all.

Perhaps the scariest aspect of the rise of radicalisation has been our growing awareness that the human brain can effectively be 'reprogrammed' so thoroughly, indoctrinated so heavily, and in such a remarkably short period of time that a person can be persuaded to give their life to some horrendous and hateful cause.

Suicide bombings in the twentieth century were a largely unknown affair in Britain – the IRA bombed British cities but the offenders tried to escape. If asked, most people would stretch to recall that Japanese pilots in the second world war adopted such extreme measures – crashing their planes into the decks of American aircraft carriers. As extreme and exceptional as this was, it was framed inside the context of a much broader war scape and it generally involved soldiers killing soldiers. Nevertheless when my grandparents told me stories about it, tinged with a generally anti-Japanese overtone, it was with an inability to comprehend something so strange and vicious. They could only attribute such behaviour to Japanese people being so strange, foreign or cruel.

Extremism and radicalisation – in the most orthodox term – is of course generally associated with the most serious forms of violence. The willingness to give your life to take a life, or lives. Killing without any regard for whether you are going to die. This might be in the form of a political assassination where a specific person is targeted as a figure head – or (as is more commonly the case) it might be in the killing of a number of innocents in a political statement and for the spreading of fear and terror.

Radicalisation doesn't always rely on the fact that the radicalised party is willing to die or wants to die either. The shocking death of Jo Cox MP on the 16th June 2016 was the lowest moment of the whole Brexit Referendum

– and the inhumanity of her killing ought to remain with us all. She was murdered by a radical neo-Nazi, Thomas Mair, who shot her three times, and stabbed her fifteen times while reportedly shouting "This is for Britain. Britain will always come first"[22].

It will always remain impossible for me to understand why Nigel Farage spoke in the early hours of Friday 24th June – *just eight days later* – and declared that independence had been won "Without a single bullet being fired". It was not the first time that Farage had been accused of dog whistle politics or stirring tensions for his own political gain. The day before Jo Cox was murdered Farage unveiled what is now an infamous and reviled billboard poster declaring *"Breaking point: the EU has failed us all"* (against a backdrop of international refugees apparently making their way towards the UK). Eighty-nine minutes before Jo Cox was shot, UKIP – Farage's political vehicle of the time, released an image of the same billboard[23].

It is clear that such behaviour is legitimately dangerous and does feed into and support the ability that people have to radicalise others. So it is also logical to say that in any case where radicalisation and/or criminal seduction is happening there must be at least two parties – the person radicalising or seducing, and the person who is

---

[22] https://www.bbc.co.uk/news/uk-37978582
[23] https://www.newsweek.com/brexit-eu-immigration-ukip-poster-breaking-point-471081

being subjected to that behaviour. Very often when an atrocity has been committed – such as the murder of Fusilier Lee Rigby in May 2013 – there is a rush to ascertain whether the offender(s) were connected to a political group or cause – or were acting as what we now commonly refer to as a 'lone wolf'.

Although Jihadism is probably the most commonly presumed 'cause' of radicalisation today, we have seen extreme behaviour in many forms – both before the turn of the modern century and since, but we usually associate extremism and radicalisation with Jihadism and the Jihadist movement. This is generally about military and terrorist activity that is perceived to be rooted in the Islamic faith. It is important to underline the concept of *perception* here – because of course many millions of moderate and peace loving followers of Islam would reject such an idea vehemently, and quite rightly feel incredibly and indescribably distressed that their fundamental identity has been subverted for such political and military reasons.

In truth we can recognise that the human mind has been deliberately subverted to extreme measures of violence and self-destructive behaviour for many, many reasons – some we might even be broadly sympathetic to (women's suffrage, and racial equality both being examples) and many less so. *I clarify carefully here – and insist that we observe – that you can be sympathetic to a cause, while you still reject extreme violence and such methods of supporting that cause. I am not writing this to provoke a utilitarian debate on justifying means to their ends.*

On a deeply personal level I turn my attention to Ireland. I am half Irish – on my mother's side – born in England and I admit that I have a somewhat confused and unsettled view of politics in Northern Ireland – it is a genuine identity struggle for me. The honest history of the British Empire is at the very least a racist and unsettling one that has – within itself – involved a huge amount of bloodshed and loss all over the world. For many people in different parts of the world the British Empire is only associated with oppression, inequality, famine and bloodshed. I can only summarise to say that sectarian violence is an awful thing that has cost far too many lives – in Ireland, in the Northern Ireland region and in Britain. The shadow of 'the troubles' is never that far away and the fragile peace that was brokered through the Good Friday Agreement was an essential and a priceless one. We must never go back to the way things were in the 1970s and the 1980s. Families were pitted against each other from within, children were exploited, parents were murdered and radicalisation was an essential part of getting communities to pick up guns and bombs and do abhorrent and heart breaking things to each other.

Radicalisation is not, therefore, simply about connotations of Islamic terror.

An incredibly pertinent article in the Irish Probation Journal (volume 14, October 2017)[24] by Dr Orla Lynch at University College, Cork offers the following:

> "A failure to account for the diversity of pathways into terrorism is a weakness in how we think about radicalisation and terrorism, because, as with any other complex human behaviour (e.g. crime), we cannot causally link one isolated factor to the behaviour itself. This article advocates that there may not be a single identifiable cause for an individual's choice to engage in terrorism and instead we should consider that focusing on a range of psychosocial risk factors may be more appropriate"

Dr Lynch continues to consider how radicalisation uses identity as a method to pursue ideological and organisational goals – the consequence being something that 'is constructed as both a security threat to the West and an existential threat to national and regional values'.

It is the existential threat – as Dr Lynch phrases it – that preoccupies me.

Radicalisation occurs for a number of reasons and by many collective methods. It is not a singular event (one billboard) – a light switch in the head of the exploited

---

[24] https://www.pbni.org.uk/wp-content/uploads/2015/11/OrlaLynch_IPJ-13.11.17.pdf

person – that is thrown on by a Svengali figure, a hypnotist, or an arch manipulator. Actually, it is a tapestry of causation, interwoven to the same big picture. It involves controlling what information a person consumes, it also involves restricting access to conflicting sources of information, and it is about denying a person the value of independent critical thought. Reinforcing this with a range of apparently corroborative social circumstances, hardships, rewards, and other factors begins to build a world in which radical thought and behaviour is possible, conscionable, and even to some extent, inevitable.

I have met very few criminals, who having been caught, have experienced an existential crisis, have blamed themselves, and have there and then expressed disappointment in their actions and behaviours. I have lost count of the number of criminals that I have encountered who would angrily offer *"Why aren't you catching burglars / rapists / paedophiles"* or instead *"Go out and catch some real criminals"*.

If you catch a shoplifter he wants to know why you aren't catching burglars, if you catch a burglar he wants to know why you aren't catching rapists and child abusers and so on...

The human ability for self-justification is quite staggering. We can enable and permit ourselves to do quite remarkable things – and sometimes even horrific things – without being pathologically predestined to that mindset.

Let's look at something altogether more trivial though – *how we go shopping*. Taking a psychological approach to the processing of making major buying decisions, Neil Rackham wrote his book 'SPIN selling' (McGraw-Hill). SPIN is a simple acronym that helps to take sales professionals through the process of influencing buying decisions by creating logical paradigms and outcomes.

Rackham's rationale is simple and logical. The larger the buying decision, the stronger the justification needs to be – but aside from this – the more reasons the buyer will need (i.e. numerous justifications). *So for example* – if you are tempted to buy a new television, you probably won't buy it just because you like it and it's cool. For most people televisions are too expensive and the costs are too prohibitive. However, if you convince yourself that your TV is on the blink, about to die at any moment, that you'll save yourself money overall because the old TV can go in your son's bedroom and that will prevent you from having to buy two TVs overall, that there is a good deal in front of you right now in this store, and that actually... You are adding up the justifications. Rackham argues that most people have to come up with three to four fairly decent, plausible justifications to tip the overall balance and part with their money. This might include a process of extending the justification by making the negative outcome of *not* parting with the money worse. *Imagine being stuck at home during a COVID19 lock down with three kids and no TV... (shut up and take my money).*

Have you ever come home with a spontaneous purchase that you thought was a bit extravagant on reflection? 'Buyers remorse' is what happens when those justifications melt away by the time you get through the front door or you suddenly recollect that you actually needed that money to get the car serviced and MOT'd.

Retail behaviour is a classic example of how we can talk ourselves into things/give into ourselves for indulgences that in a more rational and objective moment we would think to be really silly. Surrounded by the attractive environment of the store, the buying experience, the salesperson, the general excitement of the product – *we part with our money*. We have all done this. We have an entire economy built on this.

Let's scale this up a bit. Look across to the casinos of Las Vegas – many people have gone into such environments believing that they were too strong to be seduced by them, that they'd only gamble what they had in their pocket ("I'll only gamble $100") – but entering an environment where you cannot tell whether it is night or day, where there are no clocks on the walls, where there are flashing lights, sounds and free drinks to disorientate you – beautiful, courteous and obliging people serving you, feeding you, flirting with you and keeping the party rolling – somehow (within an amount of time) you could be the person who has spent hundreds, thousands, or if you are wealthy enough, even millions of dollars. Vegas is the known playground of the world – obliging the consumer with anything they have an appetite for, sex, drink, gambling, drugs and of course *secrecy*. Perhaps the biggest part of the brand is the ability to divide your identity – leave your sensible state at the door – and go wild knowing that no matter how shameful your behaviour might be (when compared to your daily value system) you'll never have to confront that, and nobody need ever know about it. Cheat on your husband or wife? Sure. Cocaine for the first time? Sure. Lost five grand? *The guy at the next table lost twice that amount...* (in actuality a lot of people are very proud of how wild they got when they visited Las Vegas, and how out of character their behaviour could be).

Knowing that we all operate in the shallow end of seduction and radicalisation is something that a lot of people don't want to confront. *There is a very strong argument to say that nobody is immune.*

The situations that I have discussed thus far (within this chapter) are *broadly* to do with adults. Adults operating with fully formed personalities, values, and cognitive function. The human brain does not stop developing fully until you are into your early twenties. Children are far more malleable, impressionable and susceptible. The saying goes *'You can't teach an old dog new tricks'* – and while you probably *can*, it is much easier to train a puppy.

I began with the term 'radicalisation' in this chapter quite deliberately - and it wasn't to shock or to sensationalise.

Of course there is a massive difference between being seduced by a big screen TV in John Lewis' or even a glamourous lady in Las Vegas, and becoming a fully radicalised, determined, murdering tool of a political movement.

One of the major differences that I would cite is that the former choices are – you would hope – short term, not life changing, and you probably make them with every intention of not disrupting your larger life plans. They are a break from the norm or a holiday from yourself. Sure those temporary choices might be completely incompatible with your bigger ambition in life or even inconsistent with your identity (if you are, for example, a Trappist Monk or a Buddhist convert) – but you enter into that scenario of seduction for a *temporary* purpose.

A huge part of radicalisation is about sacrificing your entire identity, surrendering your future, and going into something that is going to be your life and potentially (with a strong emphasis on the potentially) your death. *At the very least it is an open-ended situation.* Consequently, radicalisation is often associated with initiation ceremonies and indoctrination celebrations – something that symbolises a rebirth or a new beginning.

Many atheists would look at my being brought up in the Catholic faith in exactly this way. There is literally a process called the 'Sacraments of Initiation' which take a child through Baptism, through understanding and taking Eucharist (the body of Christ) and finally Confirmation. Confirmation is the literally the 'sign on the dotted line, I am a Catholic' moment. Baptism generally involves a commitment by a parent to give their child/baby to God, Christ and the Holy Spirit. Baptism also includes a process of exorcism which rejects the devil and all his false promises. So effective is this whole process that Irish comedian Dara O'Briain quipped *"You might decide you no longer believe in god, but you'll always be a Catholic"* (and the Catholics laugh because we know it's true).

Drawing on such profound imagery (particularly Catholic imagery) the notorious organised crime movement of Italy and Sicily – the Mafia or 'cosa nostra' (which translates literally into 'our thing') has the same hugely symbolic and emphatic method of claiming a person as their own.

A man named Joe Valachi, an American Mafia gangster of the Genovese crime family (one of the 'five families' of New York) offered possibly the most famous witness testimony of this type of ceremony. Valachi gave break-through evidence under oath to the US government at a time (1963) when people were even debating whether the Mafia actually existed or not. The following version of events is attributed to him:

"I sit down at the table. There is wine. Someone put a gun and a knife in front of me. The gun was a .38 and the knife was what we call a dagger. Maranzano [the boss] motions us up and we say some words in Italian. Then Joe Bonanno pricks my finger with a pin and squeezes until the blood comes out. What then happens, Mr Maranzano says, 'This blood means that we are now one Family. You live by the gun and the knife and you die by the gun and the knife.'"

Selwyn Raab has written an extraordinary and very detailed account on the Mafia in America and specifically in New York. 'Five Families: The Rise, Decline and Resurgence of America's Most Powerful Mafia Empires' was published in 2005. In a highly compelling, page turning account, he gives further details of the 'oath of omertà' – the vow of silence that forbids initiated members from speaking the secrets of the organised crime group.

Other accounts of the initiation are more florid and ornate – incorporating the drinking of red wine (symbolising blood), drawings and pictures of skulls, and even pictures of saints being set on fire. The LA Times reported with fascination in 1985 – a time point at which such things were still broadly very secretive:

"He said the initiation rite involved pricking his finger, rubbing the blood on a small picture of a

saint, and reciting an oath of silence as the saint's picture was set on fire.

I had to pronounce an oath whereby I was to say that should I betray the organisation, my flesh would burn like this saint"

[Let's be fair – this is somewhat stronger that 'What happens in Vegas, stays in Vegas'.] This account was printed on the 31st October 1985, written by Bob Drogin, reporting on the testimony of Tommaso Buscetta a high ranking Mafia officer giving testimony against Gateano Badalamenti – a man he (Buscetta) said had risen through the ranks of Underboss, Boss, Member of the Commission and eventually to become Boss of the Commission 'capo di tutti i capi' or 'boss of all bosses'. *If ever an effort was made to throw a powerful man under a bus – this was it.*

Somewhat remarkably – despite his testimony – Buscetta lived out the rest of his days under assumed identities and died of cancer at 71 years old. He was even buried under a false name – apparently in Florida. The Mafia never found him.

The behaviours and actions of initiated Mafia foot soldiers are no less extreme than Jihadist terrorists – with honour codes, systems of rank, behavioural models, and exceptional levels of violence that include murdering people, making statement killings, causing fear and intimidation, and ultimately being ready to give your life to that code and that identity. It evidences that criminal radicalisation is 'a genuine thing'.

For the Mafia the intrinsic religious symbolism and racial overtones (you had to be Italian or of Italian parents to start with) are part of that woven tapestry too. Italian children brought up in the Catholic faith are taught to revere and submit to such religious structures. For the Mafia to utilise that foundation to build absolute obedience to a criminal empire is both logical and effective. To overlap and blur the lines around sacred symbolism by using red wine (the blood of Christ) or by burning saints – such super powerful statements are being made.

Who on earth has the power to burn a picture of a saint? A saint is a consecrated and selected representative of God? It's a confusing act of heresy and sacrilege – but an overt statement of power and control at the same time. It works primarily because it bleeds into the pre-existing structures of a particular community. *Burning a picture of a saint means nothing to a life-long atheist who has no knowledge or regard for the church.*

Dr Lynch in her paper on radicalisation identifies that the process of becoming radicalised is still a topic in debate and it is unlikely that there is one pathway towards it. Lynch identifies three predominant theories on how radicalisation is achieved:

1. A key psychological moment or identity crisis that causes someone to reach out and seek it;
2. Contagious transmission between peers, or group leaders to followers (cult like seduction);
3. Progression through slow degrees of increasing increments or stages – gradually strengthening resolve or adherence;

Radicalisation does not have to be religious and does not have to be underpinned by ideology – there is even such as a thing as 'non-violent radicalisation' (i.e. radicalisation without violent aims or outcomes). So while our mainstream image of radicalised behaviour rests upon both a religious and political purpose, combined with a violent methodology and outcome – this is not necessarily true at all.

Lynch herself cites the work of Akimi Scarcella – an academic who co-authored a paper at the University of Stirling[25] which drew upon twenty databases across the fields of law, medicine, psychology, sociology and politics. It resulted in an ambitious twenty-six item checklist utilised in an attempt to measure susceptibility to radicalisation, ostensibly to further our understanding of this subject and to help us deal with the threat of terrorism and suicide bombing.

The conclusions reached were unclear and Scarcella reckoned them to be unreliable. They appear to only

---

[25] https://www.stir.ac.uk/research/hub/publication/537905

underline the gaps in our knowledge and appreciation of this strange phenomenon:

> *"...it is recommended that a multi-disciplinary working committee is established to find a way to help identify individuals at risk of participating in terrorist and extremist acts of violence in a fully comprehensive and evidenced based manner."*

In short, what Scarcella is saying after a hugely detailed study, and with some sense of disappointment – we don't know how to screen for the early signs and symptoms of people more likely to be radicalised, but we do need a reliable method. I would add to that, that being able to do so with child criminal exploitation would be equally invaluable.

I am convinced that – within the context of any political, religious, or criminal movement – that such a golden measure would be eagerly sought by the offenders. It is almost akin to discovering the military secret of rocketry, splitting the atom, or code breaking your enemy's transmissions. In the wrong hands such a formally recognised methodology for being able to screen and identify your potential foot soldiers is a terrifying idea. You can only imagine what it would be worth to organised crime.

So *does* County Lines involve a process of radicalisation? I would certainly recommend that we look upon it in such a way. Disregard previously held connotations of religion, of bombing people, or running away to join a war in the Middle-East. All these things are *versions* of radicalised behaviours. They are outcomes cultivated to particular causes. The version of radicalisation involved in County Lines is far closer to that of the Mafia and 'cosa nostra' – social and criminal radicalisation, a step further from the religious or political.

Primarily, I would suggest that it involves not merely one of the types of radicalisation methods suggested by Dr Lynch – *but all three*. That is to say that there is evidence that the young people who are more susceptible to County Lines are young people in crisis, young people seeking defining identity, and young people with an absence of support structures around them (I intend to discuss adverse childhood experiences in a later chapter). In addition to this, we know that peer influence and ring leader behaviour is incredibly important in childhood and teenage social circles – and any professional working with these age groups will corroborate such. The idea of 'peer contamination' is becoming far more pressing. Methods of coping with negative behaviours are far more focused on separating and creating sterile spaces between young people exhibiting such problematic and antisocial behaviours, and young people who aren't. This is considered a matter of fact method of regulating school environments. *Finally*, we know from speaking to young people who have been involved in County Lines that they were incrementally brought into the criminal structure. *This serves two purposes: to establish if they are reliable, but to also gradually broaden their comfort zone so that they don't immediately run away from the threat that is posed.*

Speaking to Will (who we introduced in the previous chapter) – a person who has successfully recovered his life from County Lines – it began with just doing little things. Things that seemed trivial and innocuous in a process of acclimatisation. A very soft delivery of a package from point a to b, for an apparently disproportionate reward and a lot of gratitude with a sudden sense of belonging to something. This is such an intoxicating and heavy mix of excitement and reward.

For other young people that I have worked with who have admitted to acting as low level couriers or 'runners' – it just seems like very easy money and they don't actually feel the sense of being caught in some form of criminal tractor beam.

Graduating up to bigger things is baited with larger material rewards, greater status and recognition, improved popularity comes with notoriety in the peer group and the community broadly. The exact same code of silence is explicit and pervades – the 'oath of omertà' – it might be unspoken in this context, it might not come with a burning picture of a saint or a blood promise, but that is not to say that the threat of the gun or knife is not as explicitly on the table.

Radicalisation is all about the consumption of identity – throwing off an old version of self, and the adoption of a new persona. Literally taking a new name or moniker is not uncommon at all.

One of the most telling signs that a young person is being seduced into County Lines, or has been seduced into it, is the changing behaviours that they exhibit (we are going to talk a lot more about behaviour as a reliable form of communication as this book continues).

I have sat down with numerous parents who have told me the same story:

> *"I don't recognise him any more. He's not at all like he used to be. He talks differently, he dresses differently, he is hostile towards me, he is so angry, I can't trust him"*

One distinct aspect is the proliferation of a faux South London accent and the use of slang terms that originate from that area. This is just one of a number of tell-tale signs – the 15 year old South Cambs gangster might seem ridiculous and worthy of being laughed at or looked down upon – but he is shaping his vision of what he wants to be, he just hasn't grown into it yet (and he is growing quickly). He is also seeking vicarious experiences through his choices in art, music and culture.

One parent that I spoke to explained that her son was almost schizophrenic in his presentation towards her –

'Jeykyl and Hyde' is the common expression that is presented to me.

> *"One minute he is my son, and he's lovely and fine – then he has changed his clothes, he puts on the tracksuits, and he's talking like he's black and from London, and he's onto his mates on the phone with all this slang"*

Why do middle class boys from the villages in South Cambridgeshire suddenly adopt alter egos and even names?

In one instance where a parent reached out to me it was explained that in about six months her son has changed in ways that she just couldn't comprehend. He didn't eat with the family anymore, he used their home as a base that he touched down in at unusual hours, his movements and whereabouts were erratic and secretive, his moods and his appetites were unpredictable. He had become confrontational, angry and aggressive. He started stealing from family members and the family home. She no longer knew his friends and associates.

The thefts began with family members seeming to 'lose' things – but the items became more significant and more valuable – and the coincidences too obvious to ignore. She ended up putting combination locks on internal doors and bought a safe for her bedroom to keep precious items. Her own home started to resemble a hostile environment. She even tested him by leaving bait out to see how long before it would go missing.

Young people going through this process are often seen to become remarkably more manipulative in their own habits – apparently shifting with deliberate ease in and out of their previous and more childlike identity to get what they want. Cover stories become more elaborate, counter arguments more difficult to disprove, and they line up witnesses and alibis in advance – they simply get better at it very, very quickly. The evidence of being 'schooled' is obvious. They become cocky and self-assured particularly so when they are advised that certain things are going to happen – *"so when that happens, you tell them this…"* – if such things are fulfilled it gives the young person even more confidence.

Every time the young person does something and they don't get caught, punished or harmed they convince themselves all the more that someone has been lying to them, and that their new found friend is absolutely right. They smoked weed and they *didn't* collapse into a psychiatric condition – in fact they really enjoyed it and they felt really cool.

Yeah, they punched that kid after school, but now they are in this group nobody is going to snitch about it – not even the victim. Nobody saw it. Nobody can prove it. You can't touch me. The feeling of being more clever than the authorities is both thrilling and addictive. All the radicaliser has to say is *'I told you so'*.

I've seen fourteen year old boys modelling gang behaviours – targeting vulnerable and isolated peers in public spaces, for the offence of apparently showing disrespect. "Get down on your knees and beg for forgiveness" the victim was chillingly told in one confrontation. Working with the young man who issued that demand, I was asking him what he enjoyed in his life, what he aspired towards, when was the last time that he had a sense of pride and fulfilment? He struggled to respond, he stared at me blankly – but with utter honesty he told me after a moment *"I felt good when I told him to get down on his knees and beg me"*. It was the only point of reference for such an emotion that he could find in his recent memory.

The young people that I have spoken to includes a fifteen year old girl who steadfastly told her parents for months that she had only smoked weed *"Once at a party, and I didn't really even like it, it was months ago"*. Parents were absolutely convinced that this wasn't true. When I got the parents to put a simple THC urine test on the table – it was clear that she could only either refuse the test and thereby tantamount admit that she was using, or take the test and you would probably know with a decent degree of certainty.

Initially she offered mock outrage – the classic "I'm not going to dignify that with a response" – answer that in every other form of her communication admitted that she was using. When the parents then insisted on the test, it came up positive for THC. The girl admitted that she was using *"probably two or three times a week"* and the frank conversation went on to reveal that she was also sexually active with the older male who was supplying her and she thought that he genuinely cared about her and they were in a 'proper relationship'. In reality though, how else could she afford the cannabis?

Everything that she was drawing from this source/older guy was teaching her to look down on her immediate family – to hate them and to redefine what was important to her. Her behaviour in and out of school suffered and her attendance dropped. She was getting into violent confrontations on the street with other girls. She had a job lined up that promised a post GCSE apprenticeship – but inexplicably she *just stopped going*. On some days she left for work, in her uniform, but when parents checked, she wasn't on the roster at all that day and instead she had gone somewhere else secretively.

Eventually this fifteen year old girl moved out of her parent's home to go and live with her more indulgent and more trusting grandparents. She rejected the boundary setting that was being placed upon her in one location – and sought another where she found it easier to be manipulative and to get what she wanted.

Her identity was shifting before the eyes of the people who knew her best – she rejected previous family pet names and nick names – and she sat in stony impenetrable silence when her confused parents asked her what it actually was that was making her so unhappy, why she was so angry, and what it was that she wanted.

As grandparents grew exhausted she began to stay for long periods of time with this new influence – in his mother's house – smoking weed in the house with permission. She had adopted a new lifestyle – it had by that stage grown to include elements of confrontation and violence, it included frequent drugs misuse and reliance on cannabis, it included under age sex where an older male (himself not yet 18) was engaging in penetrative sexual activity with a child under the age of 16 (statutory rape, as such a person cannot offer true consent), and her new lifestyle included a rejection of education, school or work. She was becoming NEET (Not in Education, Employment or Training). She embraced all of this within six to eight months – and with a sense of headstrong determination and absolute confidence. She was unrecognisable to the shy and quite sheltered girl that she had been just a year before – and she managed to retain and exude a 'butter wouldn't melt in my mouth' good girl impression that was mixed with increasingly manipulative personality traits. This is how she thought she wanted to live now – she was streetwise and edgy all of a sudden and completely over confident in her ability to survive on her own wits. What became very clear and very worrying to everyone connected to this case was that this girl was now at the beck and call of this young man (himself only 17). Above all others, she did as he asked, and whatever he wanted – and she had absolutely no concept of what she had sacrificed in putting herself in such a position.

It is not uncommon, in this situation to then see parents trying to exert their power by threatening to cut ties with the child or young person in question. To disown them both financially and emotionally. Furious and hurtful text messages fly back and forward and the threats escalate rapidly from *"I'm not going to pay your phone bill anymore"* (usual response "I don't care and I don't need you to anyway") to "I don't love you any more – you're not my daughter".

If the parent hopes, believes or is desperately trying to get that daughter to come running back at that point in a state of anxiety saying "I'm sorry, I'm sorry, please forgive me" – generally speaking this is *not* what happens.

First of all, pride forbids it in most cases. Stubbornness overrules even the genuine hurt and pain. The daughter probably will cry – but in her anger she will persuade herself "Fine I don't even need them anyway, I hate them". The seducer will be presented with the open goal *"We'll be fine just you and me"* – and any time he needs it he can play the *"They don't even love you, I love you"* card. They form an all-the-more romantic 'Bonnie and Clyde' pact.

In this situation the daughter is only likely to respond out of anger and pain – and what she will direct back to her parents will be hurtful, probably abusive, and will be unlikely to heal any wounds. The situation tends to give way to long term silence – anxiety, distance and uncertainty.

Isolation only places the daughter at greater risk of abuse – physical, psychological, sexual, emotional and financial (usually involving criminal behaviours of an incrementally more serious nature).

Parents are left expressing confusion and hurt – a sense of grief and loss, even bereavement, hangs over the family and their home. Both in terms of boys and girls I have heard the phrase many times:

> *"I feel like someone has died. I feel like I've lost a child. How could somebody steal my child from me like this? Will I ever get them back?"*

If you feel that radicalisation is too strong a term for this phenomenon, you only need to speak first-hand to such a parent who has suffered through this or a similar experience (I have cited three different parents in specific examples through this and I could have offered more sadly). They talk about a sense of their son or daughter being 'brain washed'.

In the case of the daughter that I outlined above the risks of her becoming a courier/runner are substantial, the likelihood of her moving through the lower stages of supplying to friends are obvious, but there is huge danger of her being pushed into sexual exploitation too.

While she has ventured into sexual activity within what she is convinced is a 'grown-up' and loving relationship, based on trust, and mutual interests and wanting the same things – there is a strong probability of her being introduced to other people, sexually objectified, trafficked and exploited on that basis too.

You might think this is just extreme teenage girl behaviour – the change in male behaviour is not remarkably different, although the method of gaining that all pervasive influence is likely to be.

As a uniformed police officer I had a fifteen year old boy try to bail out of a moving police car because he was asked to hand over his mobile phone. The relationship between the child/young person and their mobile phone is absolutely pivotal and another crucial indicator around some quite extreme behaviours. A young person involved in running will endanger their physical safety without a thought or consideration if they think that they are going to be separated from that phone.

There is a common acceptance in counter terrorism that where the signs and symptoms of radical behaviours have been spotted, an intervention and preventative strategy is necessary – and an intervention that is specific to the person in question (irrespective of whether they are an adult or a child). The agenda for intervening on radical behaviours that demonstrate extreme ideological sympathies towards political and religious causes is known as 'Prevent'. This is a Home Office initiative delivered at a local authority level and it is a strand of the national counter terrorism strategy.

A really useful guide to Prevent is available from 'Let's talk about it'[26] and a great deal of the available resource is about spotting signs and responding to it as early as possible with appropriate measures.

From a professional perspective I have referred a young man who was being radicalised towards neo-nazi thoughts and behaviours. In his example he began to openly espouse far right beliefs in school, and his bedroom had begun to accumulate SS imagery and memorabilia. In that context I was able to flag that young person to the Special Branch / Counter Terrorism service who have trained professionals to intervene in an appropriate way over an extended period of time.

De-radicalisation is *not* an overnight process – if it takes a person weeks and months to get to a specific position in their thoughts and behaviours, it is likely to take weeks and months to untie that connection and help them back out of it again.

Dr Keiran Hardy at the Griffith University in Queensland Australia authored and published content on this subject in February 2020[27] he places emphasis on the fact that

---

[26] https://www.ltai.info/about/

[27] https://blogs.griffith.edu.au/gci-insights/2020/02/11/when-does-someone-radicalise-and-deradicalise/

radicalisation to deradicalisation is, logically, a reversal process that is invested in reshaping a worldview. He also emphasises a different strand of this work which he introduces as 'disengagement' – *the process of getting someone to stop acting on their beliefs.*

> "Disengagement is primarily a process of behavioural change, deradicalisation seeks cognitive adaptations"

Hardy also highlights the overlap with criminal behaviour – underlining that disengagement might be referenced as 'desistance' within the context of crime (that is when someone ceases their involvement in criminal behaviour). As Hardy himself identifies:

> "As many terrorism researchers come from a political science background, fewer criminological concepts are used to understand the behaviour, even though there can be significant overlap in the ideas and approaches".

As with the work of Scarcella, Hardy acknowledges that defining concepts and measures are imprecise and difficult to grasp – which is definitely problematic. Certainly - if we believe that a person has been radicalised, be it for political or criminal purposes – we need some effective means to know when they have *actually* been 'de-radicalised'. In the plainest of language – how do we know that it has worked? Taking it from a perspective of the parent, the question that I'm often asked is "When will I ever be able to trust him/her again?".

Returning to the research of Dr Orla Lynch, she underlines that the existence of numerous methods of radicalisation tends to suggest the existence of numerous methods of *deradicalisation* (which is a logical hypothesis).

Her work predates that of Dr Hardy – but she agrees that a line has to be drawn between de-radicalisation and disengagement as two separate concepts. The absence of an effective measure of the existence of radicalised thoughts and intentions makes the objective assessment of de-radicalisation practically impossible or at least very uncertain. Citing disengagement as evidence of de-radicalisation is not sufficient – if we are being strictly honest with ourselves.

At this juncture I would probably argue that this is where we witness a significant rift between radicalised political behaviours and radicalised criminal behaviours, and specifically within the context of County Lines.

Looking once again to the Mafia – a foot soldier was (perhaps is) signed up for life (and death). In County Lines – generally speaking – a child is signed up for life (and potentially death) *but only if their life is tragically short*. County Lines and these organised criminal gangs are not genuinely seeking lifelong affiliates in the same way. They are looking to use children and young people through a window of their life – if they get out of that window of high risk it is unlikely that they will continue to be of any use to the business model whatsoever, or perhaps only a few of them will. You can't stay a child drug runner for ever.

While the 'thug life' or 'bad boy for life' mantra is sold on the basis of a whole and permanent identity change – and a new fantasy future (which also hangs somewhere alongside the vague concept that many teenagers have of being ageless and forever young) – the cynical reality within County Lines is that runners are completely disposable and have a finite shelf life. The people who radicalise these young people and twist their world view don't really care too much if that is shattered or that child dies, is significantly harmed or is extracted by some means. If something else takes them in a new direction (such as an eventual sense of maturity and a better grasp of independent critical thought) – they don't have to murder the child. The process is designed – factory like – to keep scouting these children, keep recruiting, and to manage that turnover.

This is partially why Will was able to escape. He didn't go to the court or tell the police everything about who he was working for – he took his punishment for what he did – and there was almost a severance agreement about that situation. Even now, and even to me, he has never told me who he was handled by or a great deal about the fine details of it – just that he journeyed into London and met some very scary people. It might have been very different for Will if he *had* supplied information leading to actions being taken against the people who were managing and handling him – but we can only speculate on that. There are obviously circumstances where enforcement violence and revenge violence is part and parcel of the County Lines existence (I'm not saying young people can just disengage as easily as they might wish – but disengagement can be achieved). The fact is that particular organised crime groups know (without the same rigorous academic certainty sought by Scarcella, Lynch or Hardy) how to identify, locate and radicalise another Will, and they are willing to play a numbers game until they do. Strictly speaking this is for criminal and financial purposes, not for ideological or political reasons, and it is just easier to get on with that as an almost corporate function of their business model.

By comparison people who leave the Mafia – having taken their blood oath – are likely to be killed if they try to walk away. In Russian organised crime a 'vor' (as they are known from the full title 'Vor V Zakone' or 'thief in law') will be punished with death if they even *deny* they were involved or had become an affiliated organised crime member. Their bodies are marked permanently with significant gang tattoos that denote their membership, their role and their rank. Social media feed Pinterest actually has a section which simply shows Vor tattoos, and their significant meanings[28]. They can be as ornate and fascinating as they are disturbing.

As far as County Lines is concerned, affiliation is a double-edged sword of course. On one hand the children and young people trapped within it are potentially going to transition through it – they might not see it for themselves, but it is a dark tunnel of sorts and they can get out the other side. *They are likely to suffer traumatic experiences on numerous levels – psychological, sexual, physical and emotional* – but the people who seduce and radicalise them are eventually going to cast them aside when they are broken and no longer of any use. On the other hand – because the investment in them isn't genuinely long term – there's little disincentive to not treat them as a disposal resource or in a thoroughly inhumane manner. As we are talking about a business model that is imbued top to bottom with the effects of abuse and harm – there is a certain inevitability within all of that.

Very sadly, without the correct intervention, and not providing an effective recovery programme to these children – they are likely to face criminal conviction, a ruined personal record prohibiting employment, they are going to have few legitimate qualifications, possible issues with drug misuse and addiction, haunted by

---

[28] https://www.pinterest.co.uk/velinow/vor-v-zakone/

traumatic experiences of violence and/or sexual abuse. Few people will offer them any sympathy.

In the context of political/ideological/religious radicalism we recognise and implement a process of intervention as a consequence. 'Prevent' is an example of how the Home Office has acknowledged the need to do this on a consistent basis across the country. There is an implicit understanding that without 'Prevent' a number of children might be converted to extremist views and scaled up what is referred to as the 'staircase model'.

The 'staircase model' is a graphical representation of how any person – young or old – can be escalated from a sense of injustice or inequality to a place where enemies are actively identified, and the targeted use of extreme violence is thereby justified. There are six 'floors' on the model – and it is noteworthy that as early as the second floor (the third tier) people are being segregated, reprogrammed to hate specific individuals or groups, and by the fourth floor isolated from previous friends and family. The final floor is where extreme action follows. The model was originally proposed in 2005 by Professor Fathali M. Moghaddam of Georgetown University.

Clearly 'Prevent' aims to intervene, counsel and mentor a person out of this state of mind – or to help them find healthy expression and non-violent solutions to the original causational issues. It might help them to understand through critical and reflective thought how they have been misled, have misperceived the issues, and have probably targeted people wrongly, or been encouraged to develop a hateful mindset.

The young person that I referred into 'Prevent' was being very actively groomed and managed by a hard line Neo-Nazi outside of his family unit. The offender had cultivated a trusting relationship with parents, and there were some signs that the young person's own father was on a similar path towards holding sympathy with extreme right-wing views also.

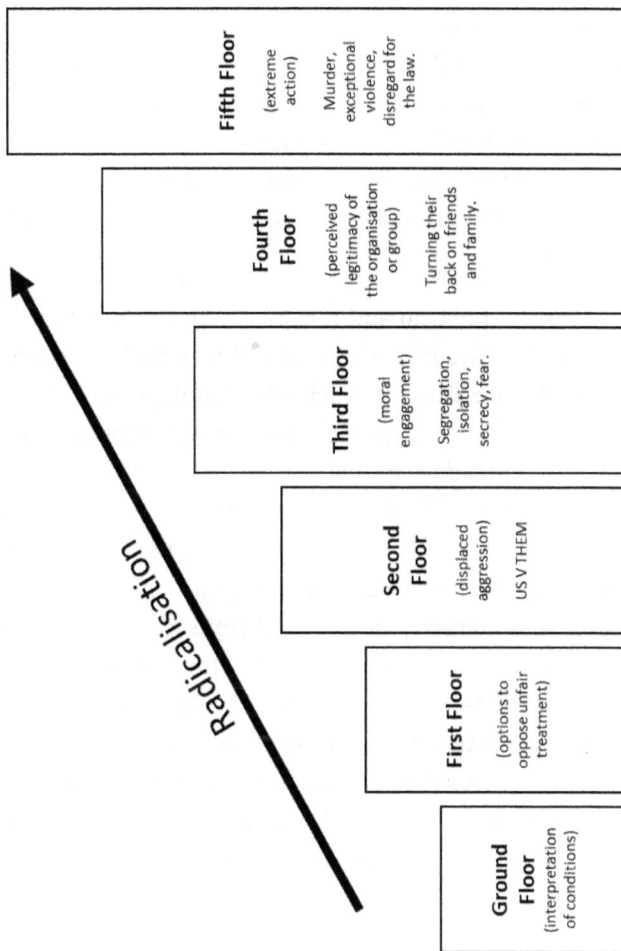

Radicalisation

Ground Floor
(interpretation of conditions)

First Floor
(options to oppose unfair treatment)

Second Floor
(displaced aggression)

US V THEM

Third Floor
(moral engagement)

Segregation, isolation, secrecy, fear.

Fourth Floor
(perceived legitimacy of the organisation or group)

Turning their back on friends and family.

Fifth Floor
(extreme action)

Murder, exceptional violence, disregard for the law.

What is very obviously missing from the tool kit we use to engage with County Lines, is the same consistent and invested approach in de-radicalising young people, supporting families, and extracting victims from such pathways to harm, abuse and exploitation. In protecting *them*, we also protect entire communities and broader peer groups.

In terms of political and religious radicalisation the risks are fairly obvious – when we fail to identify a Thomas Mair, or the likes of Michael Adebolajo and Michael Adebowale, catastrophic and violent events follow. Salman Ramadan Abedi was a twenty-two year old British born Muslim from Manchester. He was radicalised at an early age, fought for Islamic State/ISIS/Daesh in Libya before returning to the UK. He became apparently *disengaged* from radical behaviour for a period and slipped under the radar of British intelligence services but on the 22nd May 2017 attacked the Manchester Arena on the night of a high profile pop music concert killing twenty three people and wounding eight-hundred. The attack was a suicide killing and Abedi detonated an improvised explosive device (I.E.D.) for the purpose.

All of these cases underline that without intervention horrific and wide scale consequences do follow. In terms of the terror threat there is clearly no debate about the need for the Prevent programme and ongoing early intervention and de-radicalisation of high risk individuals.

By comparison – in looking at the relative harm that is presented through County Lines and Child Criminal Exploitation we witness an altogether more quiet, secretive and insidious thing. The fear that surrounds it is not as publicly prominent, and without argument, the risk of wide scale immediate death, injury and destruction is not in the same bracket. Having said as much, the political and ideological radicalisation of children and young people is not on the volume or scale that County Lines and Child Criminal Exploitation is. It is very difficult of course to quantify a comparison between the two – but the National Crime Agency are aware of more than two-thousand 'County Lines' telephone numbers in active use – which is by no means the full picture of exactly what type of activity is going on out there. *We can only make educated guesses at what sort of percentage that two-thousand phone lines represents in comparison to the actual number.* Criminal Exploitation and drug supply is absolutely everywhere offering the type of commercial reach and penetration that most legitimate businesses can only envy.

I am not about to prop one against the other and draw a verdict on where the greatest amount of harm comes from. There is no merit in doing something like that, the measures are likely to be unreliable and it is frankly an offensive exercise. *I empathise massively with anyone affected by either form of criminality.*

There is – however – an inescapable fact, that at the heart of this business model is a form of criminal seduction and radicalisation that is essential to its success and prosperity. The scale and the impact as a national priority – in terms of protecting the vulnerability of children - is absolutely at the highest end of the spectrum. Finally, while we do have a range of de-radicalisation and intervention programmes and resources on a nationally coordinated scale, we do not have a comparable programme being delivered nationally and on a consistent basis to tackle County Lines. Instead, what we do have, are independent groups, organisations, charities and resources delivering separate messages, in different formats, to different audiences, with varying degrees of undocumented success. We certainly don't have a de-radicalisation programme that equates to 'Prevent'.

Chapter Three: The Product

This is very much the chapter where we talk about the drugs.

We've already discussed how County Lines is about selling a lifestyle – a lifestyle that is edgy, cool, streetwise, well connected, entrepreneurial and ambitious. County Lines is about being street smart – not stupid enough to stay in education for years, get onto the debt ladder, working hard for little reward. It's about a fast track way to real money – in your hand – and escalating dreams of designer clothes, cars, holidays and all the things that children and young people vicariously consume through the influencers they follow on social media. That in itself is a product of sorts – of course – it is a lie, without doubt a huge deception – but it is one that is sold.

Let's put *that* 'product' to one side. The product that I want to discuss in this chapter is narcotics County Lines is a method of delivering drugs – psychoactive substances – into softer rural markets from main metropolitan super-hubs like London, Birmingham, and Liverpool so that profit margins can be held at a much higher rate. Urban turf wars in South London, fighting to the death for low end margins due to massive supply over demand ratios – is not palatable for any criminal organisation.

For any criminal organisation – for any business – a high risk investment can only be contemplated if the rewards are highly lucrative and fairly immediate. This in itself is a toxic, but addictive combination that is difficult for any gambler to walk away from (and will make a gambler out most of those who experience it). The first initial rush of 'easy money' is a hard one for anyone to ignore. *We are all greedy*. Soft rural areas – calm little villages and Cathedral cities offer plentiful opportunities – albeit we have already seen violence escalating in these areas as the competition gets more confrontational.

The drugs commonly supplied through County Lines absolutely includes cannabis, heroin and cocaine. These substances are very common – and of course they are made available at rates that are easy to understand. £10 is the common going rate for a 'hit' regardless of what you're getting into.

Cannabis

Cannabis is a controversial topic. Where heroin and cocaine are concerned – there is little doubt that these substances are incredibly dangerous, lethal actually, and very addictive. Striking a dark comedic tone, the famously rehabilitated addict and comedian/raconteur Russel Brand said with a typical flourish:

> *"The trouble with heroin is that it's very more-ish"*

I think everyone knows that you can overdose and die using coke (for example), and more broadly there have been horror stories about things like MDMA (the Leah Betts death) and acid/LSD is linked to 'bad trips' and terrible cases of long term psychological impairment.

Despite being frequently linked to psychosis including schizophrenia, depression, insomnia, suicidal thoughts and more – Cannabis survives as one of the most popular illegal substances that holds apparent health benefits and 'no downside'. There is a very strong legalisation lobby – and internationally there has been a sweeping process of decriminalisation that has reached across North America, including the USA, Canada, and on towards Europe. The market for cannabis is vast – and the *legal* value of cannabis is now a multi-billion-dollar international market which focuses on both the recreational and medicinal consumer. Regulation of the cannabis market is being considered as a proportionate step towards managing any risk (to the user and to society) and dealing with the social cost of enforcement tactics which run into the multi-million bracket themselves.

There are some significant messages that I have to convey through all this though:

First and foremost cannabis in the UK – despite the unofficial marketing – is not an 'organic' product. Yes it is a plant – but so is Water Hemlock and Deadly Nightshade – and they are both clearly very poisonous. When it comes to the term 'organic' this usually denotes a product that has been raised without unnatural or chemical sustenance and in ground that hasn't been polluted for a certain amount of time prior to the harvest. Two key points of understanding are that first and foremost, there is virtually no[29] cannabis being grown in organic conditions in the UK, secondly you would have no way of ever knowing whether the cannabis you were sold on the black market was grown organically or not (other than to understand statistically that it is highly unlikely).

Cannabis has evolved as a product over generations and is very different today than it was even ten years ago. The truth is within the THC content, and the ratio that exists between THC and the CBD.

We'll begin with understanding what THC is. 'Tetrahydrocannabinol' is the principal psychoactive substance – this is the substance that interacts with the brain and stimulates a variety of reactions commonly on the spectrum of hallucination. In low doses THC 'tickles' the brain and stimulates it – commonly making people laugh, feel light-hearted, slightly animated. Heavy doses of THC takes people into a place where they see and hear things that aren't actually there, and can leave them (over prolonged use) mentally impaired with long term,

---

[29] I would say that no cannabis is being grown organically but I can't prove it.

incurable consequences (which may include paranoia and panic attacks).

CBD is 'cannabidiol' – a counterbalance of sorts to THC. The commonly perceived effect of smoking weed is that it leaves you feeling chilled out and relaxed, blissful or euphoric. Broadly speaking this comes (at least partially) from the cushion that is provided by CBD. The THC and CBD counter each other. Cannabidiol is the crash barrier to the THC ride – and generally the presence of a generous quantity of CBD is something that acts as the air bag and safety belt. CBD is associated with a warm, slightly sleepy feeling – and it is used legally on sale in the UK by people who suffer with insomnia and other anxiety issues. It is a recognised anti-psychotic[30].

Traditional cannabis product would include a balance of THC/CBD. A bit more THC generally than CBD. If the ratio might have been 5:3 or something of that nature, over time THC has become more and more prevalent, and CBD less so. That ratio has broadened and got wider. The effect of THC has become the defining factor of the cannabis experience – and THC values have spiralled into the teens of percentages and higher. New experiences became prevalent with separate defining terms such as 'cheese' (strong cannabis/THC delivery with a very distinctive smell), 'chronic' and 'shatter'. Synthetics (lab based creations) have taken this only further still.

---

[30] National Elf Service - CBD as an Anti-Psychotic 2018

'Shatter' is actually a cannabis oil product or 'hash oil' which can contain THC content above 50% - the effects of which are all about the impact of the hit, rather than any warm chilled out feeling. The name is a pun on the appearance – which looks like a brittle caramel, clear toffee or spun sugar and which would 'shatter' if you dropped it. The name is also an effective promise of the impact and effect that consumption has on the user. The implications of high THC abuse are very clear – as compelling as the experience might be for some, it can be terrifying for others, and the long term risks are very real.

As THC levels have been on the increase, CBD levels have been declining. Cannabis plants grown in artificial circumstances are far less likely to produce substantial levels of CBD – and from a market perspective, removing that CBD creates a product that users are immediately likely to find more stimulating and compelling in the short term. Overall, however, this is a dangerous and unhealthy trend in the cannabis market. For drug dealers, having a THC heavy, CBD light product to offer is going to give your consumer a 'hit' – they will feel it more quickly and in a more substantial way, offering the likelihood that people will confuse this experience with it being 'good shit' that is both strong and pure.

In a peculiar loophole of the law in England and Wales it is perfectly legal to buy and sell cannabis seeds – owning them is no problem – but as soon as you cultivate them, you commit an offence. Take a trip to the London Seed Centre online and you'll be presented with an array of names like 'Quick Satan' 'Bruce Banner' (named after the anger management and split personality icon – 'The Hulk') and 'Savage Hulk', 'King Kong', 'Crystal M.E.T.H.' and 'White Widow'. There is a definite market out there for the scare ride, and the threat of an experience that is less than blissful.

A broad comparison that I would draw is between personal tastes in chocolate. People have different favourite brands and cocoa contents. You can consider the spectrum between white chocolate and dark chocolate. The blend depends upon the cocoa and milk ratio (I'm sure chocolatiers will correct me that it is slightly more complicated than that). Think of cocoa as THC and milk as CBD. If I go to a shop to buy my favourite brand of chocolate – I can consistently buy that brand knowing what is in it, or failing that, if it is sold out, I can buy another brand with the same equivalence in cocoa/milk to suit my tastes. Bottom line – production is consistent, it meets a government standard, it is approved for distribution and I absolutely know what I'm getting.

Not only is it impossible to do this when buying weed (because you never know what you are buying or how or where it has been produced) the market has shifted hugely towards almost exclusively offering a THC heavy product that is broadly CBD absent or CBD minimised.

Very often people – including a large number of children and young people – buy into the cannabis experience with expectations of a very chilled out 'hippy' experience. In actuality what the cannabis market is delivering is something quite different and it is much more likely to result in dependency and long term misuse problems. Many cannabis users balk at the term 'dependency' or 'addiction' – but the National Institute on Drug Abuse makes it very clear[31]:

> *"Marijuana use disorders are often associated with dependence – in which a person feels withdrawal symptoms when not taking the drug...*
>
> *People who begin using marijuana before the age of 18 are four to seven times more likely to develop a marijuana use disorder than adults."*

Let's consider why cannabis *is* a risk:

First and foremost cannabis is the product that is most likely to be adopted by teenagers. Fewer teenagers are smoking traditional cigarettes – but opt instead to smoke 'blunts'. A blunt is a cannabis 'cigarette' that is purely cannabis and not mixed with tobacco. Blunts are definitely more popular based on the mistaken belief that while tobacco is unhealthy, cannabis is *not harmful*.

---

[31] https://www.drugabuse.gov/publications/research-reports/marijuana/marijuana-addictive

Additionally, the teenagers that I work with have told me repeatedly that cannabis is available 'everywhere' – "It's just so easy to get hold of". It would seem, ironically, that it's easier to get hold of cannabis than it is to get hold of alcohol and I've been told "I'd rather not drink".

One girl based in Cambridge, aged 15, told me why she prefers cannabis to alcohol. There is a ritual that she enjoys in being with her friends and rolling up a joint, the preparation, buying it together and then using and sharing the drug. It is – at least initially – a deeply sociable thing. You become disinhibited together and while you are high it's a great place to be for many people. Speaking to drugs counsellors and a consultant psychiatrist I have been warned of how this creeping use of cannabis is disturbing on multiple levels:

Dr Dicken Bevington, consultant Child Psychiatrist with the NHS CASUS service at Mill Road, Cambridge told me:

> *"When the drug itself begins to be more important than the friendships the problems really begin. Needing more and using more cannabis can mean an inability to share, an inability to be able to afford what you need, arguments between friends over how much they are using and who owes what to whom. This can result in young people retreating to their bedrooms, with the curtains closed, becoming more reclusive and living lives that start to be scheduled around their use of the drug."*

In explaining the dependency issues to me Dr Bevington was clear that we weren't talking about the traditional physical addiction that is associated with heroin or cocaine. Statistically it might only be one in ten or two in ten people who become addicted or dependent in the most traditional sense to cannabis. *There are a number of drugs with much more addictive qualities and without doubt nicotine in the common cigarette is definitely one such substance.*

Adolescent use of cannabis is often about finding an easy way out of difficult stages of the most awkward phase of personal, emotional, sexual and psychological development. Commonly – without drugs and psychoactive substances as a crutch – we learn healthy ways to manage stress and anxiety. As our brains develop different parts of the brain grow and 'come online' in a sequence of ages. We gradually become more self-aware and self-conscious. Our ability to empathise and see things from other people's points of view starts to mature, and quite critically the part of our brain that manages anger and helps us to control our temper or our emotional reactions certainly starts to develop later in the teenage years. It probably won't reach maturity until our early twenties.

Introducing cannabis as an emotional crutch – as a way of defusing an immediate sense of inhibition, anxiety or stress – prevents the brain from having to address those needs. A different route is carved out in the neural network of the brain. Like neglecting regular exercise – if you don't use certain muscles regularly they become weak and ineffective, they are easily exhausted and overwhelmed at the critical time. The parts of the brain that helps our teenagers to function successfully and confidently in the world is absolutely undermined by frequent abuse of cannabis which acts to 'take the strain' instead. *A coping mechanism is setup where the young person develops a learned behaviour – that in times of stress you light up a joint or a blunt.* This is a type of dependency that isn't quite the same as a heroin addict waking up in the morning in a state of withdrawal – but nevertheless, it is a real and very meaningful state of dependency. I have spoken to numerous teenagers who complain that they cannot sleep unless they smoke weed – and when they do smoke weed the quality of sleep improves, they *enjoy* the quality of the sleep much more.

Furthermore we know that cannabis is linked to an increase in mental health problems – what we call neurosis or in the more profound and long term category – the psychosis. These things are likely to include anxiety, anger problems and panic attacks, paranoia, and even schizophrenia. *This isn't about cannabis implanting these problems in the brain* – but in cases where there is susceptibility to such issues, perhaps where hereditary links already exist – abuse of cannabis is far more likely to open the door to such life long problems. It is a door that we don't know how to close – *we cannot put that toothpaste back into the tube*.

Despite all this, cannabis enjoys a remarkably positive reputation. It is unfashionable to criticise cannabis and indeed very outlandish claims are made daily in different discussion groups, social media channels and other unmoderated forums that it cures a range of life limiting and terminal illnesses, and galvanises the human condition against a whole measure of nasty but more trivial ailments.

One conspiracy theory is that if people were allowed to grow their own cannabis, and smoke or otherwise consume 'weed' the pharmaceutical companies would be massively out of pocket selling the alternative treatments and drugs that we consume over the counter. The suggestion is that 'big pharma' is working with government to deny the people in protection of share prices and profits. Why cure a person – goes the reasoning – if I can sell them a remedy for the rest of their lives?

When speaking in school assemblies I will commonly ask how many people have heard suggestion that cannabis cures brain tumours? Regularly ninety percent of the assembly will put their hands up. *At least five percent wouldn't raise their hands for an immediate cash reward.* A substantial volume of people have come to believe that there is *some* relationship to be found between cannabis and curing cancer. It is an often repeated lie – and we are told, repeat a lie often enough, and people will begin to accept it as the truth. This is called the 'illusion of truth effect' and is often attributed (for a touch of additional menace) to the propaganda Nazi, Joseph Goebbels.

Few understand that in reality cannabis is being explored as a method of making palliative care more successful – versus the use of heavyweight painkillers like morphine – and that the manner of the medical trials are very often based on isolated forms of CBD, *not THC*. Cannabis might offer a step forward in the treatment of cancer, and chronic conditions like M.S. – but only in the context of other treatments – and not to such an extent that doctors and experts are recommending it to people who *don't have cancer or chronic conditions like M.S.* Cannabis is not a vitamin supplement and there is no medical condition that recognises the absence of cannabis or THC in the human body as a health problem in its own right.

Checking out the legal supply of cannabis – these being the producers of cannabis and the retailers/dispensaries of cannabis in legalised markets - you can tell a couple of things fairly immediately: commercial outlets are not selling cannabis as a cure for cancer (and of course if they could, *you know they would*). Secondly they are very clear about how cannabis should be consumed, if it needs to be consumed. Bedrocan[32] – a Dutch company producing cannabis exclusively for the medicinal market – makes it very clear that cannabis should only be used

---

[32] www.bedrocan.com

following prescription and *never used with tobacco*, and furthermore, never in conjunction with alcohol. They also recommend strongly that it isn't used by children or young people, nor by the elderly.

Additionally, looking in the most cursory way at the value of pharma companies that are producing cannabis for commercial applications (medicinal or otherwise) – take for example 'Arena Pharmaceuticals Inc.'[33] of California, USA (an exclusively medicinal and highly scientific pharmaceutical operation) – the share price was listed at above $60 per share and the total company value above $3 billion[34]. It seems unlikely that 'big pharma' (as an industry) is worried about the opportunities that broader decriminalised access to cannabis is providing – it is just another market that they can move into and make profit from.

Regardless of all this, cannabis, as a product enjoys an anti-establishment image – which makes it only more cool, urbane, and hip. The fact that it is also illegal and illicit makes it more desirable – like getting into a speak-easy, being inside a circle, in on the joke, up on the rumours and well connected. Nothing is cooler than that – and nothing ever has been. It is what we are all seeking

---

[33] https://www.arenapharm.com/#
[34] Yahoo.com '25 Biggest Marijuana Companies in the World' - August 2019

– and in the context of Maslow, it is a massive in terms of both 'belonging' and 'esteem needs'.

The media presentation of cannabis is more and more towards the liberalisation of the drug and the popular use of it. We are often confronted with the meme of the teacher who tells the kids 'don't do drugs, just say no' – before going home to smoke weed and let the stresses of the day drift away. In 'Bad Teacher' (Columbia Pictures) the uber cool and hyper desirable Cameron Diaz (playing the 'bad teacher') sneaks off to smoke weed in her car in the middle of the school day – just 'because'.

There are very few Seth Rogan films that don't star him as a loveable, happy, functional stoner that everyone would like to be mates with. In many regards you can argue that cannabis is the element that changes him from being a bearded, overweight middle-aged jobless loser parody, towards being someone who is hip, funny and actually a bit cool. He is at his worst when he is irritable and strung out – but always so much better after a hit of the bong. This is pretty much the message that we are conveying regularly and it is being consumed by our teenagers with the consent of most parents.

What harm then – in carrying a parcel of weed from A to B in return for £50?

Most teens would balk at the idea of being roped into a world of 'hard drugs' – cocaine and heroin – people know that these substances ruin lives and entire communities.

But people who do cannabis don't go out mugging people or breaking into cars or burgling houses (and genuinely – I haven't met any).

There is the often argued question of the 'gateway drug'. As Dr Bevington himself told me – there is little evidence that people who smoke weed are going to gallop onto an appetite for crack or meth – there is no physiological reason to maintain that this is the case, but – *and there is a big but* – most people who are in treatment for heroin addiction or cocaine addiction *did* start on their journey with cannabis, and have or do use cannabis still. The autobiography of Mike Tyson 'Undisputed Truth' (HarperSport) makes a pretty good attempt at explaining his relationship with drugs, as does the autobiography of Anthony Kiedis 'Scar Tissue' (Sphere) – for two very different but quite iconic men, getting clean didn't really include or prioritise cannabis. In the Netflix comedy series 'Loudermilk' Ron Livingston portrays an emotionally dysfunctional alcoholic in recovery who organises a support group programme for a local community. *'When your life is a mess, getting clean is the easy part'* it suggests. They don't miss the opportunity to have a cannabis addict as the butt of the joke in one episode, who comes forward to say that he is hooked on weed – only for the show to invite you as the viewer to think "What really? Get out of here! This is a recovery circle for *real* addicts". The character might have confessed to being addicted to chocolate or cloud spotting – carving a line between 'proper drug addicts' and, well, people who smoke a bit of weed.

I struggle to counterbalance any of this content with a portrayal of a real life cannabis dependent. It doesn't offer the truth about struggling with being stuck in a cycle of cannabis dependency.

"I feel really edgy – really angry – and I just want to use weed and make it go away".

I have been told this so many times – both by boys and by girls. The loveable, harmless cannabis high is never examined when the morning after 'hash hangover' has hit and the incredibly irritable personality comes out that can be venomously unkind towards immediate family members and others. There is a raw nastiness for *not being high* that creates confrontations and violence in families. For a child or young person who already possesses an inadequate or incomplete ability to deal with frustration, anger, awkwardness and vulnerability, to be hit with these mood swings – is really no place to be. Their comfort comes from getting more weed and feeling fine – and most parents, if they know that this behaviour is coming from an abuse of cannabis, of course they will attack the drug. *"It's the weed – you smoke too much of it and it has changed you".* You can only expect a very angry backlash to that assertion and the situation escalates.

I have worked with a young man over the past year – and sadly the outcome wasn't a particularly good one. He did end up being moved out of mainstream education and into a pupil referral unit. He was very open with me that he was smoking weed heavily – *daily* – rationalising that he didn't use before or during school though. So he was in control of it by his own estimation. His normalising of cannabis use was exceptional.

What he *was* exhibiting in school though was uncontrollable rage – what they saw of him in school was always on the backswing of the previous night's use.

He raged to such an extent that he had to be sent home – collected by his mother – on multiple occasions.

"You treat me like a dog!" he shouted illogically towards teachers who had made exceptional efforts to look after his welfare and provide him with additional opportunities and reasonable adjustments. He offered fury that the Principal didn't treat him – a 15 year old student – as an equal.

He swore at teachers, he threatened peers, and he physically attacked another student for a perceived slight. His triggers became impossible to avoid. His rages took longer and longer to calm down – not hours, but days. He would sit on his anger and brood on it, focus on it, relentlessly unwilling to forgive anyone for what he perceived to be signs of disrespect.

While we worked on relationship dynamics and how interactions between himself, his teachers and his peers could be more positive (and why they weren't working) – and the reasonable steps that he could take – he leapt to the animated defence of any suggestion that drug counselling could help. He was steadfast against any suggestion that reduced use might make these things easier over time. His anger flared and flashed in a very unmanageable way around any explanation that extended abuse of cannabis was actually undermining his ability to cope or work with anger.

Speaking with his mother she acknowledged that the weed was a massive issue – but she was terrified to challenge it. If he was to choose between her and the weed she believed that he would choose cannabis.

So if you want to buy weed, who do you go to? *A drug dealer*. A person who wants to sell you onto more expensive, more compelling, more addictive substances. If they can get you into ket (ketamine) of course, that's their job. If you can't afford it, creating a debt that they can agree to 'work off' is something that can be sorted out.

Cannabis is still the drug that nobody has died from taking – as most loyal cannabis users will tell you fairly immediately. Users and devotees find it *particularly unfair that cannabis remains unlawful but smoking and drinking remains both legal and socially acceptable.* Aside from the psychiatric and developmental concerns that we have already considered – many of the risks associated with cannabis are particularly interwoven with the County Lines threat. Put a line of cocaine in front of an uninitiated thirteen year old they are likely to blanche and try to get out of there – the illegal supply of cannabis does have a role in helping to bridge the uninitiated from being drug wary to drug permissive.

When discussing and presenting on the subject of knife crime with the Tactical Firearms Unit from Beds Cambs & Herts Police – we took real handguns (Glock) and semi-automatic (Heckler and Koch) rifles into schools. The guns were made safe – no ammunition – and offered no threat. They were placed on the table at the front of a pre-COVID19 hall so that young people could crowd round and get a close look at them. Despite having room full of (particularly) boys that could name a surprising number of guns (with enthusiasm) from their 'Call of Duty' experiences online, few wanted to touch them or felt comfortable handling them. The *idea* of a gun was cool and yes, everyone had seen them in the films, but an actual hand-gun? No thanks. Everyone was uneasy.

Are you surprised by that reaction? For many the reaction to cocaine and heroin – hard drugs – is the same. Speak to the boys who like to talk up how cool it is to be in a gang, who adopt the mock South London accent, and experiment with all the things they see and hear about the culture – talk to them and the attitude towards heroin and coke and you get quite similar responses. *"Weed is different – it's just weed. I'm not stupid, I'm not gonna get into coke. I don't want 'nuffink to do with it blud"*.

Cannabis is definitely inside the comfort zone of many of the most vulnerable young people in our communities and it affords a wonderful opportunity to criminal exploitation and County Lines drug dealers. The gateway is real – but it's probably not the gateway that you thought it was. It's not about the drug itself – it's about how it enables the dealer to start the conversation on drugs.

The withdrawal effects of pulling back from cannabis abuse can be profound and difficult for a teenager to manage alone. The worry of getting into trouble or being prosecuted is a reason why some choose to go it alone *if they try*. The availability of counselling and support is another.

You can expect to see a number of consequences from an unmanaged withdrawal – these can include anxiety, depression, insomnia, irritability and anger management issues, flu symptoms, and weight fluctuations. For a teenage girl an episode of weight gain – for example – can be an absolute deal breaker, and if a girl (particularly) comes to associate not having cannabis with weight gain this in itself can be a trigger for eating disorders or quite simply a sense of 'not being able to do without' cannabis itself. Withdrawal symptoms are generally expected to last between one or two weeks – but they are usually tougher and more severe than the user expects. One young man that I have been working with for the last year came in to see me looking ashen pale, hollow eyed, with dark rings – he admitted that he was feeling irritable and was finding it difficult in class because the smallest things that people were doing (intentionally or otherwise – pen clicking for example) were absolutely 'in his face'. What was very noticeable was that this young man who was usually quite slouched and low in his chair, somewhat zoned out and foggy, was now paying attention to things happening through the window and on the road beyond – looking at the haulage trucks that rolled past the school to see who they were and so on. It was hard for him to adjust to the stimulus that his brain was processing. His brain had learned to function in the impairment and fog of chronic misuse – and now it was like he had come out of a darkened room into the bright sunshine.

Generally any withdrawal should be managed with expertise and advice – CASUS (Child & Adolescent Substance Use Service) – is a definite referral that should be made. This young man did manage a number of days of 'cold turkey' but relapsed, and this is quite typical of this type of approach to not using weed. A gradual reduction of any drug (titration – the careful and monitored reduction of a drug to minimise and monitor side effects) – combined with counselling and appropriate mindfulness and other approaches to mitigate unwanted impacts is definitely a better route to success, but this also takes courage and honesty to succeed. This young man did accept a CASUS referral – and the combined support of his counsellor and other people who took an active interest in his recovery had much more successful results over the longer term.

Other drugs

The two most popular drugs in adolescent communities are – *with absolute certainty* – alcohol and cannabis. Both of these psychoactive substances (psychoactive being any substance that interferes with or influences a person's mental state) are a common meeting point for people who choose to use or 'dabble' in other things at a developmental age.

While heroin and cocaine are the parental nightmare there are few children and adolescents that I work with talking about or showing curiosity towards these particular substances. It's a massive relief to be able to write that. When I first began in policing in 2003 there was a very definite heroin epidemic and working in York, North Yorkshire, I knew a number of teenaged heroin addicts and it was horrific to witness the consequences.

I'm not going to devote a substantial amount of time referencing heroin and cocaine as a consequence – but traditionally we know that widespread heroin abuse does lead to increased levels of serious acquisitive crime (basically, theft in bulk or high value). We are talking about burglary, we are talking about vehicle crime, cycle theft, theft from shops – anything that really offers the opportunity to realise enough cash to immediately go and score some drugs.

Most heroin addicts are *not* trying to chase the warmth and the bliss of their very first hit of heroin. Replication of that feeling is only about larger and larger doses of a frankly adulterated and questionable product. For most it is just about trying to stay 'straight' and not entering into the tormenting pain of DTs (detox or withdrawal). This is particularly painful for needle users, for whom chronic addiction is an inevitability on an almost immediate basis.

Speaking to numerous heroin addicts I have found that these people – and they are, and always will be people, (as much as they are generally hated by society) – have been stripped of their humanity. They tend to hate themselves when they reflect on their behaviours, and they feel trapped. One heroin addict – as close to sober as he was ever likely to be on a cocktail of booze and heroin – told me as I took him into police custody that he'd do anything to never have taken that drug. I have seen amputees who hobble back to their dealers on crutches for more 'gear'. It's not about being clean – *it's about never having met heroin in the first place*. Once switched on, that switch is never off.

Sabine is a recovering addict who I worked with recently who offers her life experiences with both heroin and

166

crack addiction to children and young people. She speaks with courage and candid honesty about what she has been through – which includes custodial prison time – and perhaps most movingly when she describes the death of her father from cancer:

> *"He was dying from a painful cancer and I was stealing his painkillers. When he died – he wore a number of rings that were a beautiful thing to remember him by – I removed his rings and I thought that I'd keep them to always remember my dad by them. But within a minute I realised that I could sell them for another hit, and within ten minutes of him dying I was taking them down the road to sell them so that I could score."*

Heroin addiction is an evil disease. Meeting a heroin addict is the closest you might ever get to meeting a real life zombie – particularly if they are in the acute state of craving and they are seeking a hit – or just after a hit when they are 'nodding'.

Thankfully 'heroin chic' – a mode of fashion from the early 1990s has fallen into decline. The 'nihilistic vision of beauty' referenced by the Los Angeles Times in 1996, is – we hope – in the rear-view mirror[35] and perhaps like smoking cigarettes, is gathering far fewer victims from the teenage demographic. I'm not declaring that heroin

---

[35] https://www.latimes.com/archives/la-xpm-1996-08-08-ls-32243-story.html

is over – but right now there is a lull in interest, it's not a fashionable drug, and fewer teens are curious about it.

Coke is the ying to the heroin yang. A stimulant, and a party drug. An instant boost to self-confidence (to the point of obnoxious narcissistic self-belief and self-importance). This white powder (white to heroin's 'brown') is definitely still circulating in clubs, raves, parties and concerts and is probably slightly more appealing to young people than a heroin fix.

Cocaine – by comparison – is a quick hit drug, with a short half-life. Users' exhibiting dependency have to keep using steadily through the day and have to keep the hits coming to maintain the high. Very often tolerance – like with most drugs – builds up, so greater volumes are needed to keep that high running too.

Francis Rossi of the highly successful rock band 'Status Quo' writes about his own cocaine addiction in his autobiography 'I talk too much'. At least for Rossi, the cost of cocaine (financial, not personal) was met by his exceptional earnings. He confirms the pattern of getting to a point where it was his first thing to do in the morning – and the dehumanising physical and psychological damage of persistent use (I encourage you to buy and read his book – it is incredibly frank). It is associated as a rock star drug, or a stockbroker drug, and a recent round of politicians came out to confess their own abuses (including cabinet ministers).

Individual hits are usually not exceptionally expensive and availability isn't generally problematic – but the cycle of use can make it prohibitively and ruinously expensive if someone gets locked into a misuse cycle. There are functioning 'weekend users' out there – far more likely to be the case than with heroin – but as with any drug, the addictive properties of coke are going to encourage a greater use over time that is likely to become problematic. Additionally, most drugs promote tolerance in the human body – so greater quantities are eventually required to achieve the same impact.

Cocaine is a highly addictive substance – and as with anything of an addictive and physically rewarding level – prolonged abuse promotes the likelihood of forming a solid addiction.

As cocaine is a 'party drug' it seems to be more appealing right now than heroin – but heroin and cocaine seem to occupy a particular place in the teenage psyche where generally use of these drugs is a knowing level of self-harm that puts the vast majority off. Nonetheless cocaine and heroin are a big part of the County Lines product. While County Lines is a threat to children and young people – this is not the exclusive focus of the County Lines operation. Returning to our early assessment of what County Lines is – it is a business model – used to make money. There is still a huge market for cocaine and heroin which needs to be moved about and sold.

I have already referenced the National Crime Agency official Intelligence Assessment 'County lines drug supply, vulnerability and harm 2018'. In this document the NCA estimated that 69% of County Lines distribution was focused on crack cocaine (the freebase and more addictive delivery of cocaine) and heroin. They warned that the vast majority of supply was heroin – but at that time of writing – crack supply was only increasing:

> *"It is likely that the increased use of crack cocaine is a result of focused marketing activity by county lines offenders encouraging use of the drug, either on the basis that it is more profitable than heroin, or to increase profit through the overall volume of drugs supplied. It is also possible that crack cocaine is seen as a more attractive primary drug than heroin amongst the younger users, likely to form the largest cohort of new customers."[36]*

It is cold comfort then that heroin appears to be less popular than it once was. While heroin is a theft drug – shop theft, burglary, vehicle crime – crack by comparison, is associated with violence: robbery and snatch theft offences on a street level for example. It

---

[36] https://www.nationalcrimeagency.gov.uk/who-we-are/publications/257-county-lines-drug-supply-vulnerability-and-harm-2018/file

results in a level of desperation that is coupled with an aggressive and determined urgency.

A 1998 study[37] conducted in 142 cities across the United States focused on the rate of robberies and burglaries – noting in the late 1980s a decline in burglary versus an increase in robbery:

> *"The results suggest that the emergence and proliferation of crack shift the balance of urban offending opportunities and rewards from burglary to robbery"*

The County Lines model is still preoccupied with selling and encouraging addictive class A drug abuse – whether heroin, coke or crack. The rationale is simple and it always returns to profitability: As unethical as the statement may appear to be – every organisation wants to offer a product that is so pure and so effective that is results in dependency and addiction.

Any company in the world would prefer to have a standing order or direct debit relationship with a customer, rather than a one-off purchase. It's a business model that has surged in every manner of consumption – men's razors, computer game content for children, music and multimedia delivery, mobile phone provision,

---

37

https://journals.sagepub.com/doi/10.1177/00224278980350 03004 - Eric Baumer, Janet L. Lauritsen, Richard Rosenfeld, Richard Wright; August 1998

and even the charitable sector have all jumped on this band wagon. Most charities don't want a 'one-off' donation – they want your sponsorship on a long term basis "For just £2 per month we can…" goes the line.

Addictive class A drugs are always going to be the easiest and most efficient way to achieve the closest possible equivalence to this that a drug dealer can achieve. Repeat business.

Moving on from Crack and Heroin

Notwithstanding our previous discussion, our children and young people are now far more interested in synthetic drugs. Cannabinoids – like the hideous product that is 'Spice' – were at one time sold for a period as 'legal highs'.

The 'legal high' tag is marketing masterstroke – although legislation is working apace to try to keep up with what is rolling out of laboratories (and such substances are not legal any more) the previous suggestion of legality suggests safety and even government approval. Spice is a massively overcharged THC delivery method – with huge THC quantities reaching over and above what 'Shatter' and other products are offering. Remember – 'Shatter' can wade in at 50% THC. Nevertheless, this can be completely overshadowed by what Spice brings to the table – and the outcomes are profound and exceptionally scary.

Spice is linked to extreme hallucinatory experiences, exceptionally aggressive behaviour, and users relinquishing temporary awareness of the reality surrounding them. The impartial drugs advisory and information website 'TalktoFrank.com' is something that I recommend to young people quite frequently. This service gives expert advice on an anonymous basis in response to nameless enquiries. They highlight the major difference between the synthetic cannabinoid versus cannabis: while the pro-cannabis lobby will boast that nobody ever overdosed from weed, we have recorded deaths directly linked to the misuse of Spice and other similar products. Additionally they warn:

> *"use of synthetic cannabinoids can cause psychotic episodes, which in extreme cases could last for weeks."*

The other synthetic drugs (sometimes referenced as 'designer drugs') or perhaps more correctly and formally referenced as 'psychoactive substances' includes a resurgence of LSD (lysergic acid diethylamide) or 'acid'. This has found a place in the teenage appetite along with a recent craze for 'micro dosing' where the user divides a tab up into small sections that are 'drip fed' in small pieces, regularly, throughout the day – in an attempt to maintain and manage an adjusted mental state.

> *"And there is no downside at all. It's absolutely safe. It doesn't do any harm at all. All it does is*

> *open up your creativity and help you to develop*
> *new ways of thinking."*

This particular young man got quite angry with me when I disagreed on the subject that LSD could cause brain damage and long term psychiatric harm. He dismissed the case of legendary Fleetwood Mac guitarist Peter Green (who lost any awareness of who he was and lived in poverty for approximately twenty years after going missing) as irrelevant and "probably untrue". It was quite unacceptable to consider the inconsistent production qualities in differing batches or not knowing who had created it.

This is a worrying contrast to attitudes around both crack and heroin – which young people generally have seen with their own eyes as being deeply harmful drugs. Not one young person has ever argued for 'zero risk/zero downside' when we've talk about cocaine or heroin. Synthetics – such as MDMA and LSD present the same risk as any other drug that come from an unknown source in terms of purity and content, but generally they are considered to be more socially acceptable, less risky, and easier to self-administrate on a reliable basis.

> *"I'll just take half a tablet and I'll know when to*
> *stop."*

Gavin Guy – a retired police officer and an expert witness on drugs who is employed by Cambridgeshire Constabulary – presents regularly to a mixture of audiences. While he gives guidance to the judiciary and to juries in court environments – he also briefs and educates adults, parents, children and young people too. An excellent presentation that I have seen him deliver many times references the work that he does analysing drugs and particularly MDMA ('ecstasy') tablets seized from events such as the 'Secret Garden Party' hosted near Huntingdon annually. MDMA is almost exclusively a party drug – a rave conduit – and a massive disinhibitor that particularly contributes to sexual vulnerability in young women.

Showing a graphical slide displaying a wide array of tablets with multiple different designs moulded into them – including Teenage Mutant Ninja Turtles, Mitsubishi logos, smiley faces, and Playboy bunnies – the variation of psychoactive content is startling. Pointing to the massive projection of the image, Gavin says:

> *"That one has no MDMA in it whatsoever. It's just all kinds of other powder and it could be brick dust or talcum powder, anything."*

Pointing to another one:

> *"That one has three times the amount of MDMA of the average tablet dose. You might take a fraction of that tablet and still be taking a full hit. If you pop two because you're impatient - wanting it to kick in – you've actually taken six tablets."*

Ketamine – an animal tranquiliser generally associated with horses – has also seen an increase in popularity. Compared to cannabis however, I have nobody currently talking to me who is willing to admit they are using it. They will however tell me about *other* people who are supposedly using, and that the drug is popular and definitely in circulation.

> *"Oh I wouldn't use it myself – but I know that _____ is"*

It is always an eye widening moment when we talk about how frequent ketamine abuse can lead to problems with bladder and bowel control. This is just not something that many young people seem to be aware of – as deeply uncool as the possibility of a psychosis is, shitting yourself in front of your mates is one-hundred times less edgy or cool. The unestablished and relatively young nature of the drug seems to mean that fewer are wary of the consequences associated with abusing this substance. 'Ket' is popular though – it is in circulation – and instances of burglaries at veterinary surgeries by offenders seeking ketamine (and often the popular gas, nitrous oxide) have been reported.

Ketamine has taken a benefit from some positive press around how it has been used as a replacement for diamorphine in emergency medicine. Strangely many young people that I have spoken to are aware/hold the opinion that ketamine is a desirable alternative to morphine and opiate drugs.

This is classic gaslighting and selective reporting – we can only guess what the source of such information is or how it so effectively reaches the destination – but I am deeply suspicious about where such knowledge emanates from when it doesn't also include an awareness of some of the severe downsides of ketamine abuse.

Sure, if I was in a motorcycle accident and my leg was a mangled part of the wreckage – I'd be very grateful for a shot of ketamine I'm sure. I probably wouldn't say no to morphine, and I probably wouldn't argue about the relative merits of either at that specific time – but the circumstances of extreme physical pain do tend to make a remarkable difference to whether I can contemplate the two drugs from a consumer perspective. As with weed the health benefits are entirely relevant to the context.

Overall, while the big three drugs are likely to remain cannabis, heroin and cocaine (including crack) – there is a plethora of other substances out there and the County Lines network exists to create channels that deliver anything that anyone would like to part with their money for. Like a friendly barman offering the latest local beer on tap, you can expect your County Line dealer to at least try to whet your appetite with a taste of something new – and that will include explaining the benefits and the up sides and even doing you a favour with a sample to get you going.

Irrespective of the product – when it comes to targeting children and young people with psychoactive substances – the outcomes are predictably difficult to manage.

The protocol for dealing with a trauma wound (such as the stab wound of Kylo in Chapter 1) in an Accident and Emergency setting is to first ensure that the victim is stabilised, bleeding has been addressed and the risk to life is steady. You then move on towards the risk of infection, dealing with repairing the wound, and with cosmetic concerns and on to recovery.

On a psychological level the abuse of psychoactive substances deeply destabilises children and young people making them more prone to negative secondary symptoms like irrational rage, violence, physical threat to peers, self-harm, eating disorders, and other massively risk taking behaviours which may include premature and unprotected sexualised experiences which for many represent becoming victims of statutory rape that they might think (at the time) they have consented to.

Protecting children and young people in such circumstances does mean gaining an honest access to, and understanding, about their (that individual child or young person – not 'young people') misuse of psychoactive substances. Defeating County Lines – and doing much more to impair the growth and proliferation of such drug distribution networks is an essential part of this. The product and the market is evolving and changing – and we must listen to and observe what is going on. We must stay aware of it in a non-judgemental way. If our reaction as parents or as professionals is to fly into our children with high handed judgements, threats, condemnation, and severe levels of emotional rejection we will lose our understanding of the market and we will lose them too. This is not about moralising the situation.

We can do – and we already do – a great deal of work on a covert basis through law enforcement agencies, to infiltrate markets and to build a reliable picture of what is out there. What we can't do is use children as Covert Human Intelligence Sources – we cannot task our children and use them to infiltrate markets. We cannot put them at risk by creating underage test purchasers with alternative identities (for example). We can do something far more simple though – we can listen and pay attention. Even when our children and young people tell us that they hate us – *even if they are burning down the school* – they are still communicating with us. This brings us to our next key topic in defeating County Lines: *all behaviour is communication*.

Chapter Four: All behaviour is communication

In the course of my work, both when I was a police officer, and since, I have engaged with young people in extreme levels of distress – some in chronic (long term) circumstances and some in acute crisis. I have met young people who have destroyed the entire contents of their own bedroom, or even larger parts of an entire home. I have worked with young people in the immediate fall out of them having turned over a school office, or in the wake of a substantial fight with their peers.

Commonly I do see very similar reactions from the adults that surround these young people and take responsibility for them – *we all tend to react in similar and predictable ways* (shock, disapproval, anger, dismay, concern). Primarily such behaviour (from the young person) is classified as 'misbehaviour' of course – that is to say the behaviour and the event is immediately passed unconsciously through a filter where a decision is made as to whether it is positive or negative, acceptable or unacceptable. Most commonly this process appears to happen subconsciously and without an active decision being made – it is a reactive, natural, logical and an immediate process.

Having recognised 'bad/poor behaviour' the adult interprets what this means *to them* (individually) and also about them (the adult, not the child usually). There is very often an a posteriori / after the event evaluation that rationalises that *the adult* behaved only in such a way that attempted to prioritise the welfare and the needs of the child – but in some circumstances, even if the adult refuses to accept it, you can see that a certain amount of ego and preoccupation with self and how that adult felt about what they were witnessing was a prevailing factor in what that reaction or response amounted to. This isn't really about the child – this is about how the adult in the dynamic feels about what is happening or has happened and how it challenged them. You simply cannot eliminate that - it is part of the human condition – and different people do this to differing extents.

Let me say that working with young people in such circumstances is not easy and it can been incredibly difficult to disengage your own emotional response to what you are seeing – *or on a more complicated level* – rather than shut down all emotional correspondence (which can be equally damaging and even provocative for the child) – to actively control which emotional responses you offer in such a crisis. Please understand this – the vast majority of what you communicate to the child in that situation is non-verbal and it's about *what you do* and how you go about it. A great deal of what you say will fall on deaf ears right there as the child in crisis is probably shutting down on a number of emotional, sensory and psychological levels and may be suffering from 'red mist'. This often results in raised voices and shouting – when actually the situation needs to become more calm and controlled.

I'm going to turn, at this point, to a child who I will call 'Zoe' – *naturally this is not her actual name.* The circumstances are entirely factual but I've taken every effort to disguise anything that would tend to identify her.

Zoe (14) came from an incredibly difficult background. Her upbringing was single parent – *and I'm not going to make a broad sweeping judgement on single parents or parents who are separated.*

Let's deal with this very explicitly at this juncture: I have seen some brilliantly supportive and loving parents who work together successfully to parent their children after they have separated (genuinely this is not 'single parenting').

Likewise I have seen circumstances that it is absolutely for the best that the child is brought up without contact with or only highly restricted/heavily supervised contact with one marginalised parent.

In other circumstances one parent may have refused their responsibilities and simply walked away from the child.

I admire the parents doing their best on their own – perhaps the circumstances, which might include abuse, addiction, bereavement or other factors – might make it impossible to do otherwise. Regardless there are some incredibly loving and determined, nurturing parents out there doing it all on their own – we don't see these parents, they don't make headlines – it should not be presumed that they don't exist. I have met several. The prejudice against single parents – and particularly single mothers is very real and it is both harmful and unfair.

Not undermining the admiration I have for such individuals – it is a massive disadvantage to bring up a child alone – or where one parent is significantly disengaged from the process and offers little or no support, financially, emotionally or as a role model.

Zoe had one parent and *that* parent had a massive deficit of parenting skills – a mother who was very determined to filter everything first and foremost through how it made her feel, whether she was happy and whether or not it disturbed her own sense of comfort. Consequently, Zoe received the bare minimum of everything. In the context of Maslow it was bare physiological needs provision only – food and water, sleep, clothing – those types of things. Emotional reassurance was absent, and mum saw her role in her daughter's life only to correct her with punishment and criticism. It is important to be clear – *Zoe's background and upbringing was a source of trauma.*

I have been told that in clean water projects in Africa there is a significant issue when clean water pipes have been installed in villages. Children who have only known dirty water can be known to seek the old polluted water to drink. The reason is the clean water tastes strange, and they don't trust it. You might think that the 'improvement' would be obvious – but it's a huge adjustment, and shifting from something that has apparently sustained you all of your life is not a small thing. So when that clean water arrives it is instinctively treated with suspicion and children have to come to trust it and transition to it.

Zoe was brought up on the emotional equivalent of polluted water. So when she moved into school environments, she couldn't cope with or understand positive engagement with her adults. She was known to literally seek *judgemental* behaviour, reprimands, and confrontations. To her – this was attention. She was confused by, and experienced some degree of pain, when people were 'nice' to her. It seemed erratic but somewhat predictable (a paradox, I apologise) – when you were speaking to Zoe – she would suddenly do or threaten to do something explosive and incredibly harmful. This might include an outburst and a threat to self-harm, an overt threat to a peer, breaking something or even making you apprehend an immediate threat to yourself.

If you didn't know Zoe this seemed incredibly random and you'd look at this as 'bad behaviour'. It would be easy to package her into a box that was labelled 'mentally unwell'. "There's something not right with that one" would be an unguarded observation that any adult might make on an off-hand basis.

Actually though – despite the fact that Zoe was one of the most difficult and confrontational children you might encounter – there was something very logical in it. It made sense. It *was* predictable. She was communicating.

I'm not parent blaming here – it's so easy to say "I blame the parents" – the mosaic is different for every single child, but clearly her home life, with patterns of neglect and emotional abuse were telling for Zoe. Irrespective it seems that Zoe couldn't trigger the thresholds and ceilings that could result in her being taken into care – and being taken into care is certainly no magic wand solution anyway.

Zoe's behaviours escalated to become more and more impossible for those around her. It is easy to dismiss such cases as 'attention seeking' – and she was, but ignoring an attention seeker is not always the great idea that it is often recommended to be. *Reshaping* that behaviour so that they know how to reassure that need in a healthy and positive way, is incredibly difficult and a lengthy and prolonged process.

Great efforts were made at school – but like a child being offered clean water after a diet of only dirty water – Zoe's instinct was to push back against it and revert to entrenched behavioural patterns that continued to be reinforced at home. We were desperate to preserve

Zoe's good character and help her to avoid prosecution – but she resorted to escalating criminal damage offences outside of school which included literally kicking entire fences down, damaging cars, and assaulting people.

When police were called to intervene the officers didn't want to take a hard and physical line on Zoe – if she could be talked into going home so that she could calm down and be dealt with, interviewed on a separate day – so very much the better. Instead – when she realised that compliance meant that she wouldn't be arrested – Zoe would deliberately do something to provoke an arrest. This often included assaulting the officer and she even drew blood on multiple occasions. Less importantly it might also include damaging the police car. Being arrested was seen as a reward and she was seeking it.

It got to the point where she had assaulted most (and I genuinely mean this without a word of hyperbole) of the officers in the local police station and *every* police officer there was warned about her and knew who she was.

If ever a child was perfect for exploitation, it was probably Zoe.

Reactions to Zoe's behaviour included adults asking *"Who do you think you are Madam?"* – which tends to imply that the person saying it felt that they were above her, more significant to her in the social hierarchy, and that it was Zoe's natural place to offer respect, compliance and cooperation through her behaviour. Sometimes tempers were exhausted. People found it inexplicable, exhausting and frustrating (and it was massively fatiguing). When the levee did eventually break, and she was man handled into handcuffs or was placed into a restraint hold, she laughed gleefully and showed signs of celebration that had a manic tinge to them. What you could see in an isolated incident was that Zoe was perpetuating cycles of behaviour that she had learned from an early age – and she was receiving the only type of attention that she ever really trusted or understood. Her behaviour was all about communicating and interacting on this level alone and she had no frame of reference of how to communicate on virtually any other level. Her vocabulary wasn't great and her ability to trust and interact was non-existent. She had a reliable history of being dishonest in what she did say.

No police officer wanted to get into a physical confrontation with Zoe – she was a 14 year old girl – small, and she could be genuinely vicious. I saw the injuries that she caused and they were very real. It was an absolutely no-win situation to try to manage and one prone to incredible levels of escalation with the slightest mistake made.

The breakthrough came with Zoe when I brought my then twelve week old puppy, Bessie, into the school for the first time. I wanted Bessie to acclimatise to school environments and children of various ages and in crowds, so that I could nurture her and train her into a therapy dog role. I was very lucky because this particular school wanted to support and encourage that as a means of engagement between the police and the local community – and specifically with their kids.

I was apprehensive about introducing Zoe to Bessie – and I felt very protective of Bessie – I honestly worried that Zoe might be some sort of cruel pathological case that might evolve to hurting animals. I was very wrong about that.

As soon as Zoe saw Bessie – *and it was a chance encounter in the school office* – something incredible happened. She absolutely reverted to the emotional age approximate to a primary school child. It was like she went back to the place where her emotional development was fractured and she reached back to that place to bond with this puppy.

Of course in school, reaching out and offering physical affection to a child is impossible. For numerous good and appropriate reasons you cannot scoop up children who 'need a hug' and just go about showering people in physical contact. The introduction of a dog – and particularly a puppy – was a very different and surprising dynamic though.

Zoe – who could be, as I've described, bombastic and unpredictable in her behaviours, became quiet, inquisitive and gentle. She beckoned Bessie into her lap and just cuddled her. She kissed her, she stroked her, she rolled a tennis ball for her. I don't think anybody dare say anything to disturb such an astonishing and fragile moment. Zoe literally sat on the floor like you do at primary school with legs crossed. There was a whole different child there – and for the first time she was recognisable as a child – not the *enfant terrible* of the entire district.

There is something so honest about a dog that is impossible to refute. Dogs do things for treats, but they don't *lie* to you. If they give you some affection you can trust it. They have a loyalty, an ability to recognise you, when they form a bond and a rapport it is true and very real. The two of you communicate on a behavioural and emotional level only. Dog owners (and I am no different with Bessie, who is still with me today) convince themselves that their dog understands every single word they say. You can have quite the one-sided conversation with a dog. You sometimes find yourself explaining at length to a dog when they have been 'naughty' and why it was wrong to chew up the post *"Bessie that post had a very important letter in it and I can't read it now, and that means that the council tax is going to be wrong, and I don't know who to phone – what am I going to do?"*.

The communication level with a dog is a few words of vocabulary at best (don't get me wrong – Bessie definitely knows the word 'chicken' – which is a favourite – walk, stop, come here and basic commands) – but mostly dog owners communicate with their pets by observing and offering behaviour, body language, physical affection and so on.

Anyway – Bessie warmed immediately to Zoe and their emotional communication was very pure and very understandable. Without words everyone could see the communication happening. Zoe was absolutely starved of this type of affection and unconditional love. Bessie didn't bring any issues up about Zoe's past, her reputation, her actions – there were no strings attached and no hoops to jump through.

What was more incredible was that while Zoe was with Bessie she remained completely calm – and I could talk to her without any fear of something happening, of an outburst, a flash of violence. The honesty and the candour that Bessie showed to Zoe was reflected in Zoe's responses during these sessions. It was like plugging the missing piece into the computer – and it stopped short circuiting.

Without rushing or pressuring Zoe we would let her sit and pet Bessie – and the two buddies would be together in the most heart warming way. It was actually therapeutic for other people to just watch this happening. For Zoe I became linked inextricably to Bessie and from there onwards she showed me nothing but kindness. It didn't come in a contrived way, it still included emotional outbursts and anger – but she never assaulted me, she never used me as a target or an outlet for any of her pain.

We continued to have incidents with Zoe inside and outside of school. Although inside of school I could sometimes mitigate the threat by saying, perhaps on a Wednesday "Zoe, if you can make it to the end of Friday with [x] number of behavioural points – I'll bring Bessie in on Monday with a tennis ball so that you can play with her".

Outside school, Zoe did continue to get into lots of trouble. She targeted the police station and often came round and sat on the wall outside to see if she could recognise any of the officers that she strongly corresponded with. These would be either those she had assaulted – or those she liked a little bit more. She threatened to damage cars – not police cars – but the officer's private cars, by walking on the bonnets (she could walk along the wall and threaten to step off onto the car – teasing for an emotional response). Very often she was seeking acknowledgement the only way she knew reliably to get it.

The relationship with Bessie meant that I could go out to see her, with no body armour, no personal protective equipment, and we could have a chat. I could talk her down. I could get her to go home. This never, ever included *"Zoe, if you don't get down off that wall, I'll see to it that you never see Bessie again"*. It didn't include 'pay-off' transactions either – *"Zoe if you get down off that wall, I'll bring Bessie to see you".* We both knew that Bessie was a school visitor – although neither of us ever said that explicitly. Zoe knew that Bessie didn't live at the police station and wasn't there – it wasn't why she came around.

Zoe – from her context, from her fractured emotional background, from her life experience – was very poor at communicating. Her communication was highly non-verbal – the times that she was dishonest were always verbal. Her non-verbal communication was always far more honest. She demonstrated her mood, her state of mind, her emotional condition – all though physical behaviours. She wasn't 'stupid' – she wasn't behind the curve on natural intellectual ability – true enough that she was behind her peers on syllabus and reading age and other academic achievements, but she was well within a medium ground that you would expect a girl of her age to have in terms of reasoning, problem solving and other basic indications of mental capacity. She always knew the nature and quality of her actions too – she never claimed to have gaps in her recollections or blank spaces in her memory. She could explain that hurting someone made them sad – that it was not nice to do that to people – that she would get into trouble *and so on*. She could explain the difference between the truth and a lie.

She remains one of the most explosive, yet vulnerable young people I have worked with. We managed to get her through to sixteen years old and into a Young Persons Project where she lived in a supported way with adult professionals around her. She was much happier there. We couldn't save her from a criminal record – although her behaviours improved significantly and became more positive and less antisocial.

When I encountered Zoe in the town subsequently, unexpectedly, off duty, she ran up to me excitedly when I saw her. She was smiling and full of questions about Bessie (who wasn't with me). How is she now? How big is she? Do you still take her into schools? Do you give her treats?

This isn't the happy ending that I'd like to give you – Zoe was still prone to making very poor decisions and gravitated towards people who were also highly vulnerable, people who were alcohol dependent or using drugs. Zoe never will be a success story in the way that you might highlight in a TV show or a movie – this doesn't end with Zoe going to Cambridge University and becoming an amazing mother or a teacher or an inspirational international super figure reaching out to others. This being said, the damage was limited and mitigated in many positive ways and Zoe got through that very dangerous period – like a World War II merchant vessel escaping the mid-Atlantic gap. She was far from unscathed – *but she got through*.

We did find a way – albeit fairly accidentally – to interpret how she communicated with us. We did decipher the messages that she was sending us, and I wish that somehow we had figured it out sooner. Like emotional code breaking we made the worst of it stop by getting very close to Zoe, by listening to her non-verbally, by learning from her, and by implementing and trying numerous different things (many things that didn't work). Bessie was a hugely effective intermediary in many ways.

The difficult thing is that there is no Rosetta stone that is transferrable between different children and young people. As dynamic individuals, each – as I have previous stated – they are unique in their own ways. There are transferrable principles, of course, somethings are perhaps more logical and more *likely* to be true – but some things can be counter intuitive and, until you learn over time it might seem to make no sense whatsoever.

What you can't rely on, or what you can easily over rely on, is the verbal layer of communication. I have met so many young people who would seem to 'cut their nose off to spite their face' (as my mother would say) verbally. So many children lack the ability to trust, build rapport and form appropriate bonds when you reach out to a hand to offer them assistance.

Let us return to County Lines then. A County Lines sitter who is looking for a runner isn't trained in any of this – but is hugely experienced in it. So many are from abusive backgrounds, have suffered neglect or hardship, have networks of contacts that exhibit strange, complicated and difficult behaviours and they can naturally perceive and interpret insecurity as a signal.

Zoe would be very easy to recognise – probably more difficult to beguile – but sitters do perceive that insecurity fairly naturally. Even when it is masked with apparent confidence or over confidence (perhaps more so).

It may seem obvious to say this, but how many times has a young person infuriated their teacher/parent/insert professional with actions that signify "He is so cocky and full of himself" – but really he is communicating "I am crippled with self-doubt and feelings that I don't belong here – please don't make fun of me".

When a young person in this bracket can 'give it out, but they can't take it' – it is often perceived as vanity and pride. Vanity and pride are usually perceived as negative and narcissistic qualities. Narcissistic personal disorder has come into the lexicon commonly thanks to a generation of recent politicians and media talking heads. They are defining the age that we are living through in a way that Hitler, Mussolini, Franco, Stalin and others did during the era of 'great dictatorship'.

We seem to be more vigilant for narcissism than ever – and fairly determined, in many cases, to 'stamp it out'. It is a fascinating topic – and I think people are drawn into the stories of acute selfishness and antisocial behaviours for natural reasons. Narcissism does bring out audacious and bold behaviours that can be very attention grabbing – and to be perfectly honest we all have traits that fit the mould to some extent. *Answer this question honestly* – when you look at a group photo, who is the first person that you look for in it? If an old friend finds your school class photo from years and years ago – who do you look for first?

Ok, so we all have a bit of that in us – but genuine narcissism, as a psychopathic/pathological disorder, is thought to be prevalent in only about 1% of the population[38]. It is far more likely that the child or young person is not pathological and has acquired their behaviours in the short journey of their development. It is not that they are saying "Look at me I'm a raging narcissist" – they're communicating things like "I am incredibly insecure, I am distressed, I don't know how to cope in this circumstance". The ironic fact that they tease others, or subject other people to the same feelings – often to reassure themselves or to try to achieve popularity – may not even occur to them.

As I found out from speaking to Dr Bevington – not all of the pieces in the physical brain of a developing child are in place yet. Certain parts of their actual brain development might be behind their peers or in front of their peers, and the imbalance can result in some remarkable outcomes. Like a high powered car with

---

[38] Theodore Milton – Disorders of Personality (1996)

upgraded horsepower, but poor handling qualities, and no brakes. Stature – height, weight, size – may almost seem to present a young adult. The emotional and cognitive contrast within can be striking.

Most of the children and young people that we are discussing within this frame have little or no access to mindfulness techniques, cognitive behavioural therapy, a non-judgemental mentor or role model figure, and other positive and influential tools, techniques or people. They have learned their own way, to adapt and overcome the obstacles that they encounter – clambering over them inelegantly, falling over, and getting hurt. Naturally – the vast majority are not just going to develop the best way to deal with things organically out of their own creativity and genius. They might mimic a number of negative things that they see from friends or adversaries, from parent or an elder sibling, from watching YouTube content – any number of influential sources. Few build in an opportunity to stop, reflect and review what happened. "How could I do this better – what did I learn?" It is somewhat startling when you actually do encounter this in a child or young person and we label it (for obvious reasons) as 'maturity' because it is so obvious and outstanding when it does happen. It is definitely a trait of more successful children and people generally – but how many of *us* practise it?

So when it comes to interpreting behaviour – where are our expectations? What do we have to reflect upon and challenge in ourselves?

First of all, let's acknowledge and accept that everyone has strengths and weaknesses. Some people are naturally more adept at this type of work with young people. It is also a skill set that improves with focus and reflection and learning. Intuitive behaviour – as defined with the Myers Briggs framework – versus sensing qualities are in the minority, and depending on the source that you look at to verify this, the disparity this can range from just 2% to 25% (Intuitive Personality Types) to 98% to 75% (Sensory/Sensing Types). This depends largely on who you reference and which data you trust.

Sensing people rely on – as the title would suggest – sensory data. What they see, hear, touch, taste and smell – and they prefer it when that data is literal as opposed to figurative or metaphorical. The 'intuitives' are less dependent on that – or they are less steered by that – because 'here and now' predominates less with them. Instead the measure of meaning and interpretation is far broader, but perhaps less precise. In the context of interpreting 'misbehaviour' as non-literal form of communication, it would seem that intuitive personality types would have a definite advantage.

It might be useful to look at the Myers Briggs framework and participate in a personality test. Being classified in either camp doesn't automatically make you fantastic at working with vulnerable people – nor does it preclude the ability to learn and develop the relevant skill set through the application of time, patience and discipline.

Quite separately, if you are prone to be triggered to reacting emotionally – and we all have been/are from time to time (there is no personality type that is not prone to anger whatsoever – we all have an anger threshold) – you would also be at a disadvantage in this type of situation. If you are more likely to interpret a child acting out and struggling with their anger as an afront to you (specifically when they target that outburst *at you*) – or an attempt to undermine you professionally or personally – you may find this very difficult. Getting beyond this, and 'behind' this display is what is important here. Finding a way to remind yourself that you're not the significant part of this is paramount. The situation – no matter what – is about *their* vulnerability.

Getting a child or young person to recognise, talk about or acknowledge where their insecurity resides is a major challenge for anyone. Again – disengaging your ego is critically important because it doesn't have to be 'you' that unlocks that achievement. There are no prizes, there is no league table and we are not keeping scores. No matter how good a professional is, a child or young person can simply reject the best advice or the best attempts to form rapport and trust – even with the very best practitioner.

It might be a natural reaction – when you depersonalise the challenge of a confrontational child or young person – to say *"This isn't about me but I am going to get behind what is causing this…"*. This can be quite problematic in itself. It can lead to – even without the practitioner realising it – to a piling on of pressure that is directed towards that child or young person, and they certainly tend to perceive it. We do need to resist that temptation and not get tunnel vision. We must always try to move at the speed of the child.

I find it beneficial to ask myself "Am I the person this young person wants to engage with?" – we have to retain enough humility to agree that we won't be the right fit 100% of the time with every child. Rapport can't be forced like that. We don't select the young person – in so many regards- they select us and it's actually a privilege to be invited into that level of trust no matter what the age of the other person is. For some of these young people it is absolutely all they have in life to give anyone – and for many they have been betrayed so many times and let down on so many occasions – that giving you that type of connection is the biggest compliment and the most generous thing that they have to offer in the world.

We must always be ready to interpret when to step down and let someone else come in. It's a fine balance – because most of the progress made with young people in challenging circumstances does come through persistence and tenacity – and you don't want them to feel that you turned your back on them either. This is indeed a complex balance.

I want to make reference to another type of professional, a horse trainer (or equine behaviouralist) Monty Roberts. At eighty-five he is a true legend of the horse training profession who specialises in developing trust based relationships with animals incapable of verbal communication. Everything that he does is built on the foundation of behaviour as a communication tool. His 'join-up' approach is about the strength of rapport and trust that comes from finding an instinctive bond that operates outside of the realm of words and verbal language.

'The Man Who Listens to Horses' (Hutchinson) is his incredible book and I recommend it thoroughly. There is one particular aspect that I really want to tease out of it though. The technique is called 'advance and retreat'. I find that this is as relevant to humans (for me) as it is to horses (for Mr Roberts). *I would note here that I do not work with horses.*

> "I was to realise that nothing was done by accident. Every small degree of a horse's movement occurs for a reason. Nothing is trivial. Nothing is to be dismissed... horses are 'into pressure animals'. If you place a finger against a horse's shoulder or flank and push, you'll find the

weight of the animal swing against you, not away from you."[39]

What this man established was that horses exist with an intricate level of non-verbal communication. Furthermore when pushed they tend to push back into the pressure, against the person who is doing the pressing (does anyone recognise this behaviour in confrontational teenagers?).

Additionally, and quite importantly, until you earn their trust, the horse will not allow you to approach and won't be comfortable in your presence. This seems logical and obvious when I write it like that – but prior to the work of Monty Roberts and other people willing to embrace such techniques 'horse breaking' was the alternative. This is the habit of chasing a horse down to exhaustion, and tying it down until its will gives way. This was the accepted alternative method of gaining compliance from such a beautiful amazing animal. Quite inhumane actually, in my humble opinion.

I have been inside schools where the phrase "He has to learn to conform" has been said to me by a Special Educational Needs and Disabilities lead – locked into a battle of wills with a particular child. In my mind it linked horribly to the concept of horse breaking.

---

[39] The Man Who Listened to Horses, Monty Roberts; Arrow Books, 1997 (page 104)

Instead *'Advance and Retreat'* is a technique used in the wild. Which Mr Roberts himself attributes at least partially to Native American tribes who would be willing to follow a herd for days to build a rapport and trust by a steadily decreasing the physical distance between them.

1. At first the approach is made to the herd, and the advance is made. The herd will retreat.
2. The advance halts, and the tracker gradually retreats away in a counter motion.
3. The common herd response is curiosity and the herd will close the gap somewhat (following back) – if not substantially.
4. The advance is made again – and the herd will retreat once more.
5. The tracker will repeat the cycle, and the herd will follow once again – gradually closing the gap further.

With this swaying back and forth motion those following the herd will eventually move into it, will sit on the edge of it, and will patiently build a bond of rapport and trust. If they move away from the herd, it will be likely to follow. They show that they offer no threat, and they coexist together.

With children and young people we cannot tap our watches and tell them to get on with it inside the hour – this is only likely to cause resentment. You have to have the time and patience to work within 'your areas' and 'their areas'.

Walk into a one to one session with a child or young person, and launch into asking them if they have been offered drugs, if their friends have been approached, if they drink alcohol – what can you expect? *A hasty retreat* – they might offer dishonesty, they are likely to evade, they might change the subject – anything to avoid a reliable engagement.

Instead, my experience has taught me to be ready to venture into a topic which is sensitive *very gradually* – but back away from it immediately when signs of discomfort are shown. You have to be ready to build rapport around things that they like – and become at least somewhat knowledgeable on those topics to engage in a sincere way. If you start by establishing that the young person is keen on boxing – use that as their safe area and talk about that. The fact that you are talking about boxing is irrelevant in many ways. It is just giving you the opportunity to observe the body language, facial expressions and other non-verbal communications they offer when they are being open and sincere in a safe space. Use these lessons to compare how they engage with you subsequently when you advance again into something more sensitive or contentious from your agenda. Compare and contrast the change.

It could be something simple as *"How are things at home?"* – when you already know that things at home are difficult. You are not asking *"How is your mum doing with her drink problem?"* – but the hint and the implication is enough. If you get a monosyllabic response it is possible that the child or young person maybe doesn't trust you yet, or alternatively doesn't know how to verbally respond and explain what they are going through (and need your help to learn).

I recommend that you use the contrast in responses and rely upon it just as much – if not more – than what the child or young person is actually verbalising (their response might be entirely non-verbal).

As you 'advance and retreat' – slowly and patiently moving between your areas and their areas – gradually you build trust and rapport.

Your body language should in and of itself remain open and with them – it's good to smile, to offer warmth – but your reactions should correspond to their non-verbal communication in a meaningful and appropriate way. Mirroring is a technique subject in and of itself – taught to police officers in principle (and others) to help with things like conflict de-escalation. Mirroring means that you tend to replicate some of their gestures or body language (without becoming a parody or a mimic) – perhaps a crossed leg, folded arms – after a period of time you will achieve some measure of joined up rapport here too. As you unfold your arms – watch to see if they do – if they follow you, you are developing a tacit connection.

All of these non-verbal signals are specific messages that should be read and understood. You don't need to ask "Do you trust me?" (or worse "Don't you trust me?") if you are passively monitoring this behaviour and communication. *You are being told all the time*.

It will put the young person more at their ease not to be asked constantly "How are you feeling?", or "Are you ok?" – seriously important lesson here – don't under-estimate the power of those questions, they can in and of themselves be bomb-shell remarks that fracture your rapport and send your young person into a huge retreat. It leaves them thinking *"Why can this person not see how I feel? It is so obvious!"*.

In fact being able to say "I can see that you're feeling unhappy" can be a huge reassurance.

Likewise, I personally recommend that you don't correct, speak over or reprimand your subject when you are trying to gain rapport. If the child or young person swears casually, and you don't draw attention to it, the world will not fall off its axis. In fact the young person is probably not testing you – but they are showing signs that they are growing more comfortable in your presence, less apprehensive, and less guarded. *We don't want them to swear like troopers in front of us* – but if you are one to one, they're not showing off to anyone else, and if you don't register any particular pronounced reaction it's unlikely that it will become a big deal. When you do get to a point where you have got a very secure and reliable form of rapport and understanding, you can probably address concerns about bad language in a constructive and supportive way that emphasises what it says about them, rather than about how it makes you feel.

Interrupting at such a fragile developmental moment is a timely reminder to said young person that you are not one of them, that you are not trustworthy, that you are hung up on things that they don't believe matter. *"I'm here actually telling this guy about all this and he has a go at me because I accidentally said 'fuck'"*. It really prohibits your ability to co-exist there. Be patient, there will be a time when dealing with that language becomes appropriate and so much more effective.

Gradual acceptance might come from them in the form of a "You're alright" or even a "Will you be back next week?" – if you start seeing these signs you are massively on the road to having a very good rapport and level of trust in that relationship. You will probably get to a stage where they clearly demonstrate to you that they are happy to see you – turning up for a session with you early, drawing you a picture, or taking in an interest in you by asking you something about your wellbeing.

Another manifestation of the advance and retreat technique is to lead off the first couple of sessions by asking something that is very much in 'your agenda' "I'd like us to talk about x". In a later session you might just ask *"What would you like to talk about today?"* and see what comes out.

I will usually get an update from school as to how the said young person has been that week – any welfare issues? Stuff from home? Behavioural incidents? Knowing this and then saying *"How has this week been for you?"* is a great 'open' start. Review the non-verbal communication, choose an opportunity, and *let them demonstrate to you how much they trust you.*

Hypothetically let us suggest that 'Gary' has had a difficult week. A big bust up at home – the emotional debris has come into school – he has ended up in a fight. He got a fixed term exclusion – but he has been readmitted now. You ask *"What kind of week have you had?"* – to see what happens. Conventionally I have experienced the following:

1. Gary tells me all about it – from his perspective. What happened at home, how the day in school went, that he did x, y or z. He got excluded and so on. This might not be a full and objective mea culpa – he might still cling to a suggestion that it was all someone else's fault and tell you that a particular teacher 'hates him' etc – but Gary is trying to explain this to you from his perspective. If it's not the version you've heard – his lack of objectivity and reflection doesn't necessarily mean that he is lying to you. This is a great platform to begin doing a review of what

happened with Gary – gently and gradually looking at it from other perspectives, without overt criticism or confrontation. If it gets too intense for Gary, you can retreat into one of your safe topics (football, cars, boxing, art, music) and take the pressure off him.

2. Alternatively, Gary tells you the week has been fine and nothing exceptional has happened. In this situation Gary is withholding information from you for a number of reasons – maybe he wants to impress you/doesn't want you to disapprove or withdraw/perhaps he doesn't trust you completely yet and maybe he just doesn't want to go there. In this situation I'd tell him that I know about the fixed term exclusion – you can see that something has gone wrong there – but you're still there to help him cope with it and you don't think less of him as a person. You can make it a point of mutual understanding that your presence is not a conditional thing, and that you're with him in difficulty as well as success, probably more importantly when he needs it the most.

3. Another scenario involved Gary giving you a full and frank evaluation of what happened from an objective perspective – offering a 360 degree review on his own behaviour, while retaining a proportionate and considered view of what other people did that contributed to it and how

he affected them. His scale of empathy and understanding shows an emotional maturity and he asks you to help him to rebuild any damaged relationships. *No I'm only kidding, I've never experienced this. Gary is a child or a young person and we must adjust our expectations! I suppose the situation is not impossible – so it makes the list – I've just never come across it.*

4. Finally there is a very real possibility that Gary will explode angrily and leave the room. He cuts off from you and doesn't want to work with you in future. The relationship, the rapport, the trust is burned. Yup this *has* happened to me – and it *can* happen – carefully tapering the pressure involved in a sensitive question is vital to the preservation of the relationship, and you have to handle that with great care. Nobody is immune from this outcome. I don't think that chasing Gary down and trying to get him to come back is the right idea. All you can do is get the message across – perhaps by a third party – that the door always remains open, and hope that he comes back. You are, after all, sorry that you caused him any distress.

So what would you interpret from the behaviour exhibited in point four (above)? You don't get a great deal of verbal explanation – you might get some insults and some expletives as he leaves – but generally speaking you need to look at what just happened.

211

Something has exploded for Gary – it might be a minor explosion at a particularly sensitive time (the straw that has broken the camel's back) – *or it might be a very big issue to him*. He possibly doesn't have the self-awareness to know for sure – but it probably is quite painful or he wouldn't have got into such an emotional state – and we have to acknowledge that pain (it is very real).

You might react with a sense of guilt, you might feel professionally embarrassed that you feel you *'got it wrong'*. You might be offended or feel that Gary is being ungrateful towards you for the help that you are trying to give him. All of these things are natural reactions. When working through such feelings it can be helpful to pause and reflect – write such things down in a journal and be honest with yourself about it. Then review them and identify the feelings that are going to help you move forward in a positive way – highlight your best way forward, and above all else apply patience to your chosen response.

What I would say is that *you can't make consistent rules from the reaction of one child or young person*. The fact that Gary reacted in this way does not mean that the next person you are working with would react in the same way if you did exactly the same thing. This is precarious and confusing – *but it's definitely true*. I find generally that using an 'advance and retreat' technique, and monitoring body language carefully (using mirroring in a subtle and appropriate way) is the best way to monitor the pressure in any conversation, and offer a release valve. Generally it is far less likely that the situation will boil over or become something a young person can't cope with. This being said, none of us get it right all the time.

It is definitely true to say that you cannot expect constant ground-breaking progress with any child or young person by pushing forwards at all time. There is always a time to push forward, and a time to hold back and show patience. Professional experience and judgement is the measure of what you choose to do. You should be able to see and feel the readiness of the child or young person in their demeanour, what they themselves choose to volunteer, and how they project themselves. You could – on one day – feel that you have made tremendous ground and that together you have moved forward a lot. The next time you see that child or young person you might even be right back at square one. In that situation you just have to be ready to re-establish that rapport and redevelop that sense of trust – allowing the non-verbal communication to be the guide that you rely on for the actions that you choose to take in building that relationship.

You might evaluate a relationship that is constantly going into a sense of 'reboot' or 'restart' and ask another professional to lead instead of you, to compare how that young person responds. Generally, changing one thing in your approach at a time is the most logical way to evaluate what works and what doesn't.

This book is – overall – about beating County Lines. It is not a full and detailed and text-book on the interpretation of human body language. I can't provide you with the human equivalent of the cracking the *'Enigma Machine'* – although I sorely wish that I could. The purpose of this chapter – however – is to stress the importance of one to one contact with the young people most highly at risk. This one to one contact needs to be pretty adept at reading all of the levels of communication – and not merely what is spoken, or what appears to be obvious on the most superficial level.

That one to one contact will say a lot more through the channels of non-verbal communication than it will through eloquent verbal explanations. In my experience children and young people are more likely to reveal their trauma when you establish a reliable degree of trust that is based on comfortable non-verbal factors. Troubled and vulnerable young people are far more likely to be less eloquent and have the type of vocabulary that helps them to express their trauma without frustration, or without that factor of feeling 'stupid' for not possessing the words they need. Highlighting this, and not being able to communicate with them as a consequence is very likely to hinder the relationship altogether.

Chapter Five: The Trauma Informed Approach

'Trauma Informed' is the approach to any trauma victim that helps and supports them by demonstrating an appropriate level of awareness and understanding about what they have experienced and how it has affected them.

First and foremost it is an extremely positive step to identify the existence of trauma – and understand that 'the trauma' might not be something that you *personally* would recognise to be such – but the effect upon that child or young person is nonetheless very telling.

Getting to a point where a young person can verbalise in their own language what they believe caused their trauma is hugely significant.

You might consider what the police would call 'victimology'. In the death of a person, building up an accurate picture of their life is an essential way to help identify how they died. It is statistically unlikely that a random act killed a person outright *e.g. debris falling from a plane struck the victim in the head and left them instantly dead at the side of the road.* The more convoluted and less obvious the circumstances appear – the less likely it is that you've got the correct hypthosis ('Occams Razor').

For people who cannot speak for themselves – the very young, the developmentally incapable, the elderly in their final years of decline, or (in fact) the dead - having an accurate plan and understanding of the life of the case in question will be exceptionally important. This is certainly true where issues such as post-traumatic stress disorder make a significant contribution to behavioural patterns.

Dr Laurence Knott, in a very helpful article on post-traumatic stress disorder (hosted by patient.info) offers an accessible overview of this much misunderstood condition. For some PTSD is something that effects soldiers with harrowing battlefield experiences, particularly those resulting in injuries or wounds, or having witnessed people receiving such. Thankfully knowledge, awareness and understanding of PTSD is growing and we know that this illness is much broader than this.

> *"It is estimated that up to 3 in 100 people may develop PTSD at some stage in life. One large survey of the general population of England found that 3 in 100 adults screened positive for PTSD."*

Dr Knott identifies other broad groups more likely to suffer with this illness – including firefighters, teenage car accident survivors, rape victims and prisoners of war. Of course there is no exhaustive list.

While three in one-hundred might be the figure for people suffering from PTSD *in general* it is not every trauma victim that develops the disorder. It is important to understand that PTSD in and of itself is a specific diagnosis resulting from trauma – and an absence of PTSD does not preclude the possibility that the person in question has survived or lived through or with trauma without showing such symptoms. One in three adults who experience trauma are believed to develop PTSD as a consequence according to NHS research[40].

The symptoms and the effects of trauma can be severe and they can last a life time. Aside from PTSD, trauma in early life is known to alter the development of the brain – with symptoms including cognitive delays, impaired emotional control and increased problems including anxiety, emotional numbness, or hyper sexualised behaviours. Early years trauma has even been linked to the development of and increased likelihood of cancer.

Nadine Burke Harris M.D. – in her book 'The Deepest Well'[41] – makes explicit reference to how her research has underlined a relationship between childhood trauma and life-long physiological changes:

---

[40] https://www.nhs.uk/conditions/post-traumatic-stress-disorder-ptsd/#:~:text=PTSD%20can%20develop%20immediately%20after,condition%20and%20others%20do%20not.
[41] Houghton Mifflin Harcourt, 2018

"…it can dramatically increase the risk for heart disease, stroke, cancer, diabetes – even Alzheimer's."

Discovering a point of trauma – and bringing a young person to the point of being able to even verbalise it in their own language and vocabulary – is an achievement. You might refer to it as a 'breakthrough' because of the demonstration of emotion that often accompanies that particular moment.

Trauma is usually categorised under three broad headings –

- Acute trauma
- Chronic trauma
- Complex trauma

Acute trauma is used to explain the effects of a single incident. It is sometimes referred to as 'type one trauma' in the United States. An example of this could be a car accident. Becoming the victim of rape or grievous bodily harm gives you a clear single incident you can put your finger on very specifically. Acute trauma victims find it easier to locate the route of their harm and can point to a very defining moment when something changed their life dramatically. A victim of a terrorist act can divide their life between – for example – when they could walk to work, until the day that the bomb went off, and now they are confined to a wheel chair: 'that day'.

Chronic trauma, as you might expect then, is about a series of events over a prolonged period of time. These might be escalating events on a scale of severity that start by conditioning the victim deliberately to accept and normalise a volume of traumatic behaviours. Domestic abuse is very much like this, and inflicts self-doubt and works by instigating neurosis. *"I felt like I was the one who was wrong – I felt like I was going mad"*. As the chronic trauma continues one or two events might stand out more prominently – but speaking to a victim of such harm is a remarkable thing – because they might casually discard one particular event that makes you recoil in horror. I was a Detective Sergeant for two years in the Domestic Abuse Investigation and Safeguarding Unit. I spoke to several such victims of domestic abuse during that time. Chronic trauma victims are far more likely to struggle to say exactly when it started – and timelining exercises can help to clarify and make sense of their past (for them as much as anyone else). I personally find that chronic trauma victims tend to take more convincing and more reassurance that their victimisation wasn't their fault. Chronic trauma is often referred to in the US lexicon as 'type two' trauma.

We also refer to 'complex trauma' as our third category. This category is probably more difficult to explain than the previous two. It references the experience of numerous events (similar to chronic trauma), can come from a broader range of sources and tending to be of 'an invasive, personal nature'. There is a helpful article written by Dr Christine A. Courtois[42]. As she states herself, that article is written as an introduction to the concept of complex trauma for practitioners and therapists.

> *"Complex trauma generally refers to traumatic stressors that are interpersonal, that is, they are premeditated, planned and caused by other humans, such as violating and/or exploitation of another person."*

Worth noting here then, that complex trauma has an element of something deliberate about it – which tends to go beyond neglect or accidental harm. There is a clear overlap here with victims of domestic abuse who may be regarded as having suffered *both* chronic and complex trauma.

It is worth noting here also that trauma is highly relevant to County Lines. First and foremost, child trauma victims are more likely to be vulnerable to the influence of County Lines organisers, and secondly, the process of becoming subject to criminal coercive behaviours is in and of itself clearly within the defined boundaries of deliberate and premeditated trauma, as explained by Dr Courtois. When trapped inside a coercive relationship, trauma is used to gain compliance, and the threat of

---

[42] https://www.giftfromwithin.org/html/cptsd-understanding-treatment.html

further or renewed trauma hangs over the victim at all times.

As you might imagine – when a child does open up and invest in an adult by talking about trauma – the situation can involve tears, grief, and distress (and even self-loathing and guilt). Trauma has a way of taking us back into a moment. Like a specific smell or a sound – we trigger vivid memories in numerous ways. On a deeply personal level my grandfather smoked a particular brand of pipe tobacco – the distinctive smell of that brand, if I ever encounter it, transports me back to a very happy place that is full of nostalgia.

Trauma can be triggered by such sensory stimulation quite easily – and trauma victims quite commonly cannot confront the things that evoke what they went through. Something as simple as hearing a song that was playing at the time of their trauma experience would be a classic example. This is incredibly precarious because such apparently innocent things happen all the time quite randomly. In fact this can be used deliberately by a perpetrator for a harmful effect.

It is also important to realise that trauma in and of itself can also become its own trigger, so seeing some element of a similar dynamic, or talking about it, can take a person right back into the middle of it. When dealing with trauma, one thing that I find very common is a change in descriptive tense. We are likely to shift from talking about the past tense:

"…and when this happened"

Towards the immediate and present tense:

> *"and the next thing I know is that I'm standing…"*

A shift into the present tense definitely signifies a process of re-living the event. Body language is likely to change, the eyes might go into a more glazed or glassy or stare like expression because they're not viewing 'the room' you are in, they are reviewing images and recollections that their mind is presenting to them at that time. They might even recollect something that previously their trauma has withheld from them for some time and then remember something new.

I think that most people have been through a process of 'reliving' for themselves and understand what it feels like to be transported so vividly to a certain place and time – *even if not as a consequence of trauma.* Intensely happy experiences can function in the same way or a similar way if the emotion is overwhelming.

It is also not uncommon to find a trauma survivor showing guilt and offering multiple apologies

> *"I'm so sorry, I'm really sorry…"*

Of course sometimes there is *some* accountability with the person who suffered the trauma – particularly if they (for example) started the fire that got out of control, or if they did something that formed part of a chain of causation – but this is less likely to be true with a child of limited judgement and life experiences. Irrespective of whether their actions were deliberate or accidental, causational or not, and the consequences were subjectively predictable, the self-critique and blame can be quite savage and relentless. One aspect of trauma can be the creation of a fierce inner critic – almost like a second voice – that never really leaves that person and just shadows them with constant blame and disapproval.

It can be very difficult emotionally, and quite exhausting for everyone in that room – and I tend to find that the more people in the room (unless it is a very well established and particular sharing circle) the less likely it is to happen at all. Usually I find such 'reliving' is more likely to happen in quite an intimate, one to one space – but generally when there is broader sharing in a group it is common for everyone to somehow instinctively tune in and a certain silence will pervade. *It is amazing how the emotion of the group becomes shared in a wordless understanding.*

In one such circumstance, where I was mediating between a teenaged boy and a teenaged girl who had been in a quite unhealthy feuding relationship, broadly based on his inability to deal with the maturity of the things that he was feeling towards her – he suddenly brought himself to verbalise that his brother was dealing drugs, and his mother was suicidal, and he just didn't know how to cope with all of the feelings inside himself.

Huge, heavy tears rolled slowly and silently down his face – his body language was head down – *almost between his knees* – it was as if he was simulating the position you are advised to adopt in case a plane is about to crash. He sobbed – but in an absolutely repressed and noiseless way – totally silent. He couldn't bring himself to offer eye contact with either myself or the other person in the room. His hands were shaking.

The girl in question – who prior to the conversation – said she only felt confused, hostile and deeply hurt because of the bullying and criticism and abuse that she had received from this boy over such a prolonged period, responded with *total* compassion, patience and dignity. It didn't feel like anyone needed to say anything to anyone to explain what had happened there – it was like seeing an open wound or the symptoms of a very obvious and serious illness.

I've said before – but I do reiterate – that it is an absolute privilege to be a person who receives such a disclosure or to be present when such a disclosure is made. The disclosure must be handled with the utmost sense of responsibility. Sharing information resulting from a trauma disclosure must only be done for a necessary and valid reason – and the grounds for the necessity have to be based around the welfare of that young person as the first priority.

The issue of confidentiality is a contentious one in some regards. How do you manage that? Obviously if you promise a young person that they are giving confidential disclosure you are exposing both of you to enormous risk. You cannot betray such a commitment once it has been offered – you will never receive any further communication if you do, but worse still, you will forever risk them not being able to offer disclosure or trust anyone else placing them at exceptional risk.

To this end – and particularly where you believe that trauma is going to be referenced or identified – you should be open and transparent about the fact that you *don't* keep secrets. The way that I tend to address this is to explain that I definitely will not keep secret any information that I think is going to be harmful to the person I'm working with – that their wellbeing is more important than anything – and we can find a way together, to talk to the right people.

Sat with a fourteen year old girl, she told me that she would like to tell me *everything* – but only if I promised not to 'snitch'. As tempting as it was to say "You can tell me anything" – it is unethical and you cannot do it. There are only a few professional/pastoral relationships that can offer this type of confidentiality to a child. If that young person does insist on only making disclosures on a confidential basis to build their confidence and to help them start speaking about what they have been through and where they are in their life – it is your responsibility as a professional to help them find such an individual or support service (if you are not one of them) that can genuinely offer them such terms[43].

In this case – *let's reference this girl as 'Kate'* – she got very angry and frustrated with me. She tried to coax and even manipulate a situation in which I, as the adult in the room, could agree that we guarantee that nobody would know about what we discussed in order for her to speak openly. Believe me – I *really* wanted to get through and beyond that issue so that Kate could start talking. I genuinely had significant fears that she was under a criminal and coercive influence, and was using controlled drugs heavily (a mixture of drugs). There is a huge moral and ethical argument – and I hear and understand people when they say that you should take that disclosure and use as much of it as you possibly can to protect the immediate community and the child. Unfortunately to do so would be quite impossible, incredibly limited in effect, and in all likelihood would inflict huge and disproportionate harm on that specific young lady. You just cannot do that.

Instead, it is far better to spend the time developing rapport – offering an open door – utilising time in that steady 'advance and retreat way', but always being very clear: "I am a professional, and my primary responsibility is your welfare, I won't keep secrets that are going to

---

[43] *If there is a drug issue (for example) online and anonymous drug counselling is available through www.talktoffrank.com between 2PM and 6PM every day.*

226

cause you harm. I share information to promote your safety and your long term happiness."

While Kate was angry at me for this – she also demonstrated respect for it and the consistency that I offered. Consistency was not a big part of her life and I think she really looked for that quality. She did eventually make more limited and cautious disclosures, she did agree to meet with a drugs counsellor, and for the relatively short period that I got to work with her, she opened up *somewhat* – if not on a consistent, predictable or complete basis.

'Kate' brings us on to the types of trauma that we encounter – or are more likely to encounter – in children and young people.

I have found that the term 'self-medication' has entered the vocabulary at a teenaged level in quite a broad way. I have had numerous fourteen and fifteen year olds talk to me about 'self-medication' – particularly through cannabis – and how it helps them to cope and feel better.

The types of trauma that I have encountered include:

- Bereavement / suicide survival / suicide attempt
- Parent being convicted and sent to prison
- Witnessing or being subject to domestic abuse and/or violence

- Unwanted/unplanned pregnancy (including miscarriage)
- Sexual abuse
- Violent or coercive behaviour at the hands of a peer, adult, parent or person in position of trust;
- Prolonged and seriously neglectful behaviour
- Parental divorce and separation / parental estrangement / parental rejection
- Coping with the mental illness of a loved one
- Witnessing/dealing with the consequences of drug or alcohol addiction
- Being involved in an accident causing significant injury or harm to self or another (perhaps feeling responsible for it)

Clinicians sometimes use the term 'ACEs' – this is 'Adverse Childhood Experiences'. Northwestern University in Chicago, Illinois, USA is the home of the Centre for Child Trauma Assessment Services and Interventions. They reference a number of key statistics around the effect of 'ACEs', which suggest that 65% of children experience at least one 'ACE' during their childhood years. The percentage falls to 40% for two or more 'ACEs'.

The University College London (UCL) Institute of Health Equity published a paper in 2015 authored by Drs Matilda Allen and Angela Dorkin. That report specifically references ACEs in the form of maltreatment and household adversity. They point out explicitly that the mishandling of trauma can increase the likelihood of death or serious injury under the age of 18, and make specific references to the causational relationship with childhood suicide. A few poignant statistics include the statement that just two ACEs leads to a 57% higher likelihood of death before the age of 50 in males, but an 80% increase in risk to women in the same context (which is frankly very shocking)[44].

When referencing the issues surrounding the health harming behaviours of alcohol misuse, smoking, sexual risk taking and violence, including behaviours that lead to obesity – where *four* or more ACEs are prevalent the child or young person is 11 (eleven) times more likely to go on to use heroin or crack cocaine.

This places a huge responsibility on professional partner agencies to be more trauma informed – and to respond in a more supportive and more appropriate way to help the trauma survivor, to promote their long-term wellbeing. There is a collective responsibility to reduce or prevent the likelihood of them coming to future harm. This is the stated purpose of being 'Trauma Informed'

---

[44] http://www.instituteofhealthequity.org/resources-reports/social-inequalities-in-the-leading-causes-of-early-death-a-life-course-approach/social-inequalities-in-the-leading-causes-of-early-death-a-life-course-approach.pdf

and taking such an approach to the way in which one engages with young people in any formal setting.

The National Health Service in the UK – through the CAMHS service – actively promotes Trauma Informed practises. They publish advice and guidance on this subject and make it very clear that several steps can be taken to help childhood trauma victims. Their advice is consistent with the following:

Safety and security is a priority – and where trauma has been identified (be that a recent trauma, or something of a historical nature that has come to light) we must ensure that the child is safe and secure, but moreover is reassured about the fact that they are in a safe place. In a later chapter we will address the role that partner agencies have to play in joined up efforts to ensure that this is true.

Routines and boundaries assist and support recovery. Things like sleep routines are important ways to mark the transition of the day. Being in school promotes a sense of this because schools work to timetables, bells, and schedules that repeat and reiterate the value of structure. Additionally, unacceptable behaviours are more likely to be challenged on a consistent basis, there is a prevalent code of conduct – and while upholding such at home around the clock can be exhausting for one or two parents – the shared benefit of multiple teachers can make this more manageable and provide objective insight from a broader spectrum of professionals.

Reassurance and talking are highly important parts of the approach. Reassurance can include telling the child or young person that their reaction, response or emotions are understandable – that you empathise – that you might feel the same way under the circumstances. Validating someone at a critical moment by telling them "There is nothing wrong with liking…" might seem trivial – but can actually prove very substantial. One to one time – even just at one point in the week – can make an enormous difference to the outlook of a child or young person – providing them with an outlet and something to look forward to. We have already discussed the fact that it is important to acknowledge and appreciate the things that are valuable to that young person and to allow them time to have 'their area' and lead in any conversation.

Talking about the traumatic experience may come in time – but clearly shouldn't come under duress or pressure. If we get the other factors right, that conversation is likely to come in due course. Our patience is critically important. In my experience a child or young person can initiate that dialogue when you least expect it to happen.

A conversation with a significantly obese girl who was showing all the signs and symptoms of depression – which included low mood over a very prolonged period, health worries, and strong feelings of disempowerment and lack of control – was typical of this. We circled the issues of her body weight and image, talking about a number of secondary problems that appeared to link back to the key area – but it was so sensitive as a topic that it proved almost impossible to verbalise or put on the table. This continued for many weeks and months, before – quite unexpectedly – it just broke in a cascade of tears and anxiety. While I wouldn't suggest that the obesity issue was itself a point of trauma (some would disagree – poor diet, nutrition and exercise are forms of neglect) – her size and some of the situations that arose from it, certainly were traumatic for her. The inescapable situation dominated her thoughts and feelings and this might be an example of the type trauma that some people wouldn't recognise or might fundamentally underestimate.

We should try to encourage the young person to engage in things they love and enjoy – and get back to the things that perhaps they have pushed to one side since the traumatic event happened. This is a really healthy step – which, if made as part of a gradual process of trauma informed recovery is clearly a sign of better things beginning to happen.

As a professional dealing with trauma you may yourself become susceptible to a type of 'vicarious trauma'. This is the type of trauma that you experience by witnessing and listening to children dealing with and struggling under their own pain – or where you feel that you somehow aren't doing enough. This is something that can be quite damaging and that you need to be watchful of. It is important that you have trusted professional colleagues that you can talk to about these situations.

Additionally, children and young people working to resolve trauma often don't know exactly what they want – often they struggle to verbalise it – and they do lash out occasionally. I don't mean that necessarily in a physical context – but I have seen teenagers who have been almost trained in delivering the most lacerating and apparently vindictive comments. Years of living in an environment or within a particular emotional dynamic where such is common would be likely to build up that ability to deliver quite the piercing blow. I have seen a fifteen year old girl turn on a forty-year old woman – *an amazingly supportive person* – and cut into her with a staggeringly inappropriate, but very pointed expression of anger. I'm not talking about a broad insult that someone is 'fat' or 'unattractive' or 'a bitch' – I think most professionals and grown-ups are ready and able to cope with that. A remark that cuts across the fact that – for example – if the child or young person has discovered that the teacher has a disabled child, and attributes that disability to her failing as a parent. Wow. In a moment – in one verbal explosion – that teacher has just received two-hundred and forty volts of trauma ungrounded. It is very hard to withstand something like that and not be hurt.

In another way, and in a very different light, receiving a disclosure, and having a conversation around a traumatic event – and then sending that child home to that same household, parents and family members (sometimes without being able to offer substantially more support, and rarely any immediate increase in such urgently needed welfare) induces guilt, anxiety, feelings of powerlessness, anger and other damaging emotional consequences.

It is therefore incredibly important to remain in a supportive professional framework – to speak to trusted colleagues – and when it is necessary, be honest enough to step back or step down from a particular case in a carefully managed way. *It is easy to stay plugged into a particular relationship that is mutually harmful, and finding the awareness, humility and modesty to know when to step down is not easy. Sometimes the best thing you can do objectively is to identify a person who fits their needs more exactly – and it takes courage to admit this to yourself if you find yourself getting too drawn in – or, in some way the whole situation is becoming harmful.*

Another source of personal trauma for the professional can be having too many children or young people on a workload. It is hard to say 'no' to someone in need of help – but if your skills become too diluted, you end up feeling exhausted and the net effect of your contribution will be reduced significantly. You give little help to anyone and only harm yourself.

'Trauma Informed' working practices take both time and money. There's no doing things on the cheap – it takes undivided focus and professional skills. These working practises demand that young people are given a certain amount of undivided attention from appropriate professionals. Of course, ten years of social, political and financial austerity has stripped away the ability for schools, GP surgeries, social care teams, early help teams, neighbourhood policing and so on to deliver against such goals in the way that they once could. Working in over-stretched departments and trying to hold rapidly shrinking services together – managing expectations of a demanding society – is massively fatiguing. It results in disillusionment and exhaustion – and both of these issues, scarce resources and low morale – have been identified by The Centre for Mental Health, in a paper entitled 'Engaging with Complexity'[45] as a genuine threat to trauma informed practises.

In a section headed 'The challenges of adopting a trauma informed approach' point four states clearly:

> *"Public sector services in the UK are subject to frequent cuts with many staff working long hours for low wages."*

They identify the lack of time available to train the relevant techniques, and the dilution of trauma informed supervision as key issues.

---

[45]
https://www.centreformentalhealth.org.uk/sites/default/files/2019-05/CentreforMH_EngagingWithComplexity.pdf

"To some extent, this is a systemic problem that requires a top-down solution. As the value of trauma-informed care is more widely recognised by commissioners and its tenets come to be enshrined in policy, it is likely that more funding and training opportunities will follow."

Perhaps this last remark is more optimistic than some professionals genuinely feel about the impact of austerity and government policy on service delivery.

There is a pervasive myth about 'front line services' and 'backroom staff'. There is repeated reference to 'red tape and bureaucracy'. The latest iteration of this has come in the form of promises for a 'bonfire of red tape' – a phrase attributed to the 'Policy Exchange' 'think-tank' and a political policy advisor name Jack Airey based in that unit. In this context the stated 'bonfire' was set to target planning regulations and development rules in towns and cities.

The truth – in my experience of having worked in the public sector and the voluntary sector all of my professional life – is that this distinction and dichotomy does not genuinely exist.

There aren't rooms full of people shuffling papers in our charities, our Constabularies and our social care teams – and I don't think there ever was. The double checking, triple checking and rubber stamping – the committees and the endless circular backroom environments that people have been persuaded to believe in *are not there*. In truth – a job will need doing and if nobody is available to do that job someone will have to drop their supposedly 'front line' role to get it done.

In the context of policing this means more time spent by skilled and specialist officers preparing case files that someone else could do, preventing the said officer from using their specialist skills in the real context of supposedly 'front line service'.

The 'front line' myth encourages a form of words that make people believe that cuts can be made without harm being brought to people in need. There is no reality behind this – it is verbal confectionary designed to make austerity more palatable. What these cuts actually result in is a hollowing out of services, a reduction in long term work, and an increasing reliance on 'fire fighting' and remedial measures – the antithesis of trauma informed best practice. This is contrary to the long term relationship building that is necessary for a genuine trauma informed approach. To enable trauma informed policies and structures, we have to acknowledge the fact that government has to invest to achieve those things – or at the very least, somebody does.

Likewise we ought to acknowledge how we shoot ourselves in the foot by not doing so. The UCL report referenced earlier ('The impact of adverse experiences in the home on the health of children and young people') addresses the costs of neglecting long term prevention strategies:

> "The cost of child maltreatment alone has been estimated to total £735m a year and reducing the health impacts of ACE could decrease pressure on the NHS and other local support services. In 2009 the costs of domestic violence in the UK were estimated at £1.9bn in terms of lost economic output, £10bn in human and emotional costs and approximately £3.1bn to government funded services."

The danger of the 'front line services' and 'no front line cuts' myth is a false perception of what is there – so it *appears* to exist, until you need to turn to it or ask for support or access.

A powerful personal experience that I had as a police officer in uniform underlined this absolutely. I visited a school for a scheduled meeting – but the meeting was interrupted when a breathless teacher entered the Principal's office and said the name of a particularly vulnerable student and words to the effect of "She has cut herself again, and she has run out of school".

Checking my police radio I was made aware by the control room that support in the local area was not immediately available – even in such acute circumstances. I went, with a teacher who knew this student, and we followed the route we believed she was likely to take.

I was informed that the girl had previously been talked down from a bridge over a nearby dual carriageway, and she seemed to be running in the same direction again.

It was winter, there was snow on the ground and it was exceptionally cold.

We caught up with the girl, and the teacher approached her initially. She was in a heightened emotional state and she broke a branch from a tree immediately by and she used it to attack and hit the teacher.

When I approached the girl – who was about 15 years old – I had to restrain her on the ground to prevent her continuing to run. She begged me not to detain her under the Mental Health Act and she was in floods of tears. It was incredibly distressing for everyone involved.

I spoke into my radio and I was told that still, and despite the circumstances, there was no immediate available resources. My relief was palpable when a tactical firearms vehicle moving through the county heard what was taking place and responded to me.

Detaining a heightened person – who is running on adrenaline – is a physically exhausting thing to do. People are used to seeing elaborate films where heroes villains fight with each other for half hour segments, inflicting injuries on each other throughout. In truth the most physically honed athletes only compete for three minutes at a time in boxing, before they sit down on a stool and try to recuperate.

Seeing the marked BMW X5 come round the corner and approach was a huge relief – the guys jumped out and we took it in turns to keep this young lady safe because she was in an acute and manic state. I tentatively got to see her injury and it was as bad as anything self-inflicted that I had ever seen. Her sleeve was saturated in her own blood, her arm had been carved in a one inch wide strip to a significant depth, deep into her wrist and the flesh hung in a gory way, opening and closing as the blood came out.

I later learned that this young lady had a history of being sexually abused, and was in and out of mental health provision on a regular basis. Her sister was detained on a psychiatric ward for her own safety.

I was told that an ambulance could be with me in *three hours* because she was conscious and breathing and in the presence of professionals. The injury wasn't deemed to be life threatening.

Through a process of haggling and phone calls to the ambulance control room we secured an ambulance in *one hour*. That is, we were at the road side with a suicidal juvenile, with a serious self inflicted injury, bleeding heavily, in need of treatment, in sub-zero temperatures, for an hour.

The Ambulance Service and the people who work within it are wonderful people. I have seen real heroism from the ambulance service, and for that matter from the Fire and Rescue Service too. I will always remain proud of the time I spent as a police officer – and that is largely because of so many of the people I worked with and came to know as friends and colleagues. Selling the message of 'front line service' was not intended to benefit or recognise any of these people – it has actually hurt our emergency services and affected service provision to communities that rely upon their skills and their efforts. It is an act of genuine political double speak.

We did as much as we possibly could from a trauma informed perspective (there and then). We treated that young lady not as an offender – but as an injured party. We gradually talked her down, we helped her to come out of that situation emotionally, we stopped her from reaching that dual carriage way. Tragically I was notified several months later that she lost her own personal battle against mental illness when she took her own life. I wish I could say that I was surprised, but I wasn't. The volume of juvenile suicides that I encountered in the second half of my police career massively outweighed the number that I encountered in the first half of my service. In reference to *professional trauma*, I do still think about that young lady from time to time – and that incident specifically will always remain with me. It is difficult not to think that we (collectively) failed her and that I was part of that. She did not get the help she needed.

Being more informed about trauma should make it very clear that any child who is attracted into County Lines drug dealing (or Child Criminal Exploitation more broadly) is more likely than not a person who has suffered multiple early life traumas. The paper published by the Institute of Health Equity (UCL) states that 59% of heroin and crack abuse cases and 38% of unintended/unplanned pregnancies could be attributed to victims of adverse childhood events (ACEs).

Attacking County Lines at the *front end* can easily overlap with mounting an attack on child trauma victims – that statement will make a number of people feel uncomfortable – but it is true. These are the human shields that protect and insulate the machinery and organisation that is behind County Lines. So robust is this mechanism that actually even most of the sitters that can be identified are juveniles or young adults themselves – and in actuality these people are not making significant lifestyle profits from their role either – they are partially employed through the same measures of criminal coercion, violence and (of course) trauma. No County Lines 'Top Boy' is going to give their sitter sufficient money to either create competition against them or to walk away and find a different lifestyle.

I am not disagreeing with the need for enforcement action against the supply of controlled drugs – but on a local level, in terms of actions taken outside of cross border agencies such as ROCUs and the National Crime Agency – I question the value of enforcement and prosecution in most cases. I have seen years of activity that have made little difference to the market and during that time County Lines has refined and polished its own presentation, evolving genetically to carry on evading the police. No matter what, the drugs still get through. Working in drugs enforcement is exhilarating and exciting – but it's a short term and repetitive cycle – and on a local level this usually also involves the police being preoccupied with the same small network of people, users and dealers time and time again.

What people think happens in such cases – versus what *actually happens* is probably very disconnected – and later in this book we will talk about what that looks like. I want to ask the question as to whether we are simply playing into the hands of County Lines by confirming most, if not all, of what young exploited people are told to expect from society and from law enforcement. We spend a huge amount of time and money trying to be on the front foot gathering information to mount individual prosecutions on low level to slightly above low level suppliers of controlled drugs. We take action through Misuse of Drugs Act warrants – recovering a cache of cannabis, cocaine or heroin – sometimes an amount of money, but rarely in such quantities that makes a break-through impact on a market across even an entire town – and definitely not for any substantial or meaningful period of time in terms of that disruption. If you need evidence of that, look no further than the consistent availability of drugs across the UK. Stable, reliable, undisturbed, and if it was a stock market price – you'd be comparing it to something undynamic, blue chip, dependable and unexciting.

DrugWise published their research in 2017[46] - they cited 'unprecedented street purity levels for heroin, crack, powder cocaine and ecstasy'. They state that their research was conducted between October and November 2016 involving thirteen police areas (counties). They looked across our largest inner city areas including London, Liverpool, Manchester, Birmingham, Nottingham, Glasgow but they also addressed their work to more remote and rural regions such as Devon and Cornwall, Somerset and East Anglia.

Crack, if taken as an example of their research, is stated to vary in purity between 40% (at £30-£40 per gram) and 70% (costing £80 a gram). The purity fluctuation and street value is self-regulated and reasonably consistent on that basis – worryingly consistent in fact. You might expect that supply chains, logistics, regional initiatives, independent efforts by Constabularies, and other enforcement activities might make these markets

---

[46] https://www.drugwise.org.uk/wp-content/uploads/Highwaysandbyways.pdf

volatile or unreliable. This does not appear to be the case at all according to the formalised academic research.

Discounting then, the apparent lack of impact or traction that localised tactics have had in dismantling drugs markets over many, many years (and now generations of cops trying) – we return to our original point: *The people being arrested and confronted on the street are inevitably going to be (usually) victims of multiple childhood traumatic events or ACEs.* They have been primed to anticipate a lack of help, support and understanding from a system that has been haemorrhaging resources since the international financial catastrophe of 2007 - 2009.

I am not criticising the police here. After all – I am actually very prone to a degree of bias towards my former colleagues, my friends and the world in which I worked for seventeen years. As austerity has bitten the country very hard indeed it is sometimes difficult to recollect the world as we knew it prior to the cuts. The contrast is severe – and 'tough choices' – as successive politicians have parroted, have had to be made. The consistent decisions have fallen in such a way that have deprioritised trauma informed structures and have promoted and prioritised apparently more immediate needs and concerns.

As services shrink to provide what budgets can afford, and central government support and responsibility has dwindled, it has not been politically expedient to announce a major change in drug strategy from enforcement to counselling, youth engagement, or long term prevention.

As a police officer I was told repeatedly that we were painted into a corner – and the argument went as follows (I paraphrase and attribute to no one individually):

'As a police service we have to respond to emergencies. Our response rate is measurable and tangible and we cannot afford to slip in that area. There must be an emergency response and people must be reassured about that. We must investigate crime – particularly serious criminality – which includes serious sexual offences, domestic abuse and child abuse. Burglary and serious acquisitive crime must be investigated and we have to have results. Everything else is intangible and up for debate.'

So consequently anything as nuanced as a multiagency provision on the subject of trauma informed youth engagement and harm reduction was clearly going to meet the scalpel. Things have been divided between 'nice to do' areas and 'essential areas' – neighbourhood policing itself fell into the 'nice to do' category and has broadly been hollowed out – often with officers being targeted from those teams to supplement response capacity.

Alex Homer, writing for the BBC in February 2018[47] said "one in seven officers axed were beat bobbies". Looking at eleven thousand police officers lost, and more than four thousand PCSO roles, he turned to Andy Higgins at The Police Foundation[48] who confirmed:

> "It's not the most acute emergency at the urgent end and therefore resources will be always get sucked elsewhere".

These exact potential consequences were highlighted ahead of time to Theresa May – then Home Secretary and, of course, subsequently Prime Minister, but her response to the Police Federation in May 2015 was shocking: "Scaremongering does nobody any good". In words that echoed across the entire service in England and Wales she said:

> "So please – for your sake and for the thousands of police officers who work so hard every day – this crying wolf has to stop."

Inexplicably, when interviewed in November 2018 on LBC radio, the Prime Minister then denied the use of the phrase (despite the incendiary words being recorded by numerous news outlets and broadcasted nationally)

> "...I'm not sure I used exactly that phrase Nick."

---

[47] https://www.bbc.co.uk/news/uk-42403590
[48] http://www.police-foundation.org.uk/

The emergence of Trauma Informed approaches – across public sector partners – began to take shape in 1998 and a succession of scholarly articles followed in the next ten years. As the Oxford University Press online 'Encyclopedia of Social Work'[49] concludes – "Trauma Informed is not so much a new model of service delivery as it is an approach to service delivery" – which, by my interpretation means 'it's not what you do, it's how you do it'.

The coincidence of improving how we do things for victims of trauma – and particularly children and adolescents – with the most severe programme of national public sector cut backs administered by any post world war government – was not, and is not, a happy combination. Although successive governments have announced the end of austerity (2016, 2018 and 2019 all saw proud political declarations that coincided with one election or another) nobody is really sure that austerity isn't simply the new 'business as usual'.

A discussion paper authored by Dr Ian Cummins[50] of the University of Salford, in June 2018, made his findings clear:

49

https://oxfordre.com/socialwork/view/10.1093/acrefore/978
0199975839.001.0001/acrefore-9780199975839-e-
1063?rskey=KYbKKK&result=13

[50] https://www.ncbi.nlm.nih.gov/pmc/articles/PMC6025145/

"These policies [austerity] had a disproportionate impact on people living in poverty. People with health problems including mental health problems are overrepresented in this group. At the same time, welfare and community services are under increasing financial pressures having to respond to increased demand within a context of reduced budgets. There is increasing recognition of the role that social factors and adverse childhood experiences have in the development and trajectory of mental health problems... More unequal societies create greater levels of distress."

We *know* that austerity is a counter force to an increase in Trauma Informed approaches. It is important to underline that it is a *deadly* counter force that serves to support County Lines organised criminal groups, promotes childhood suicide, and increases the likelihood of child criminal exploitation in every region of the country. In the meanwhile we continue to invest what money remains in political expediency – because the government cannot be seen to back down on 'the war on drugs', or take anything other than 'a tough stand'.

A 'tough stand' does not appear to be hand in hand with 'Trauma Informed' – *which is a bit too liberal and 'wishy-washy'*. As things stand we have a Home Secretary who is seeking to use the Royal Navy to intercept migrant dinghy boats off the south coast. While the Independent[51] reports that the Ministry of Defence consider the idea "inappropriate and disproportionate" and an unnamed source commented that the idea was "completely potty" and "beyond absurd". While this might appear to be an abstract issue – look at this political tone and then ask yourself the question – what chance that any of the funding not carved away by austerity will be deployed in a meaningful way towards long term youth engagement, counselling, mentoring, parenting skills or alleviating poverty as a significant cause of ACEs and household adversity?

As Priti Patel herself said – when unveiling her '£20 million pound solution' *"We're coming after you… We stand for the forces of right, and against the forces of evil."* I am sure that most professionals will agree that this does not appear to be a well researched, logical and scientific approach to take in the immediate social and economic context.

---

[51] https://www.independent.co.uk/news/uk/politics/priti-patel-migrants-channel-royal-navy-record-a9659346.html

Chapter Six: Why the PRU/AP System Doesn't Work

Perhaps it would be advantageous for us to consider the world from the perspective of a County Lines 'organised crime group' (OCG)?

Adopting the position at the head of an OCG you need to expand your drug supply chains so that you can generate enough revenue to perpetuate your control over your personal gang/organisation – keep people paid and to ensure that you sustain the lifestyle and appetites that you have developed over a period of time.

County Lines has been great news for you and great news for your industry overall – it's an effective delivery mechanism, you get paid fairly reliably, and you can keep your head down to ensure that the cops and other law enforcement teams stay preoccupied with front end runners and sitters. You stay fairly insulated from the law.

Recruitment is a key issue though – if you don't find and recruit enough kids who are susceptible to the messages and the ensnarement of what you have to offer, your business model won't succeed. Heroin addiction is reliable – but sadly also fatal – and the heroin market is an aging and dying demographic. Crack remains a decent cash cow product of course – and you're not worried about profitability on either of those things. Weed is selling easily and even parents are becoming more liberalised to the idea of cannabis just being a fairly soft recreational experience that young people pass through, or dabble in from time to time. So that's all good – *more or less*.

The recruitment thing is still a nagging issue though – I mean, it's not a problem at the moment per-se, but it's a risk to the business if people get their shit together and look after these kids because that would definitely be a huge bottle neck.

As it stands, as an ambitious gang leader, you've got a few rural communities under your belt – you have to do some unfortunate enforcement work, but that is pretty much the cost of doing business – but really what you need is maybe one or two reliable kids in each main secondary school. One of each – a girl and a boy would be ideal. Preferably an attractive girl (who you might make money from in other ways) and a popular boy – but there's some flexibility in that of course. If there are a thousand kids in every school the odds are forever in your favour!

What would make that recruitment strategy easier though?

First of all – if you could sit down with each Principal, on a one to one basis, and get them to highlight the more susceptible kids?

You could give them a list of the things that you're looking for: You want the kids who have dysfunctional relationships with their parents. Kids in care. Behaviourally problematic cases. Rebellious ones. The angry, the abusive, the violent, the antisocial types. Maybe one or two with SEND requirements that result in symptoms that are unsustainable in mainstream education. I mean, if you could highlight the ones already dabbling in drugs, drink and tobacco – that would also be ideal.

That in and of itself would be enormously advantageous - of course it would. But why would we stop there?

Maybe we could actually build or create a separate space where we could isolate and – what's the best word here? 'Radicalise' them a bit? If we could isolate them, make them resent their local communities, and get them to see themselves as a problem to society, a burden? Lower their expectations? We could really make it clear to them that education is not a viable way out for them – that they are not going to be the kids graduating from apprenticeships, with degrees, getting good jobs and professional lifestyles? If we could make them more angry and resentful, give them a sense of being rejected and on the outside – that would *really* help. We could even make that environment resemble a prison community as such to normalise the cycle of going in and out of places of restricted movement and institutionalised control. A precursor to what it would feel like in the police cells, magistrates' courts, young offenders' institutions, and possibly prison (frankly who cares by then?). All this with a 'no snitching' honour code, *of course*.

If we could persuade our schools to do this – and to pay for it out of *their* school budget to support and underpin *our* development – like a form of sponsorship, now we're really talking. This type of development doesn't come cheap – plus we could then make those kids legally obliged to be in a certain place at a certain time (which is great for recruitment and accessibility).

Getting all these kids together would give us the advantage of creating a really aggressive environment – so we'll know, law of the jungle, who the top dogs are. We can identify who the kids are who will carry a knife, and more importantly, who we can get to use it. All the qualities that we'd need would be brought to the surface, and then our new recruits can go back into their local areas, with the contacts that they still have in those schools, and they can get to work.

Plus – if all the kids are fairly desperate – it keeps the cost of business down and in our favour. They won't want to see us giving favours to the other kids, it keeps them hungry, competitive and that means lower costs for us. Instead of having to buy expensive trainers – we can get away with bunging them a bit of the lower grade weed instead (the stuff that probably wouldn't have sold anyway).

While we have these kids in the same place we can get to work on teaching them the street skills they need – like how to swallow drugs without the cops seeing, what to do when you get stop and searched, how to carry, how to palm off, where to hide things on your person so that the cops and the teachers cannot find it.

Pro tip: girls, use that bra, and get that stuff in your knickers – no teacher in a classroom is gonna want to get challenged for going there, and the cops are too over stretched to come out and take you into the nick for a full search, and you're a child, so there's no Police Inspector that's gonna put their name to that in custody anyway. And if they get too close to where you've got it, you scream that you've been touched and that the teacher is a pervert. Boys - stay close to the girls, get the girls to help you out, but remember, you can always swallow a small baggy and see it out later on, or just stick it in your pants. Don't wear boxer shorts because that shit will drop down the leg of your tracksuit bottoms. If you do though, make sure you wear those cool trackies that are tight round the ankles, or for fuck's sake tuck them into your socks...

So if you could do all this you'd be more than a step ahead and you'd be great.

But let's get serious – which Principal is going to back this as a concept? Which Minister for Education would allow that? Which Home Secretary? Which Prime Minister? After all I understand that the Home Secretary is calling you 'evil' and has said that she's out to get you. There's no way you'd even get this system on the green light in the worst and most corrupt area of the country – never mind somewhere like South Cambridgeshire, or in Devon and Cornwall, or in rural Derbyshire – or nationally. *What a shame...*

Actually County Lines OCGs won't need to approach Principals, Head Teachers, Academy Chief Execs. They don't need to petition government or write to their MPs. They don't need to bribe anyone for that access.

The Pupil Referral Unit or 'Alternative Provision' is exactly what they've been looking for – and it already exists.

A child enters mainstream education and immediately they become problematic to their peer group and cohort because they arrive weighed down with a huge number of adverse childhood experiences. They struggle massively and act out in all kinds of ways – disrupting lessons, fighting, setting off fire alarms, being confrontational and non-compliant with staff. All of the things that really make it possible for one child to ruin the whole day for the other twenty-nine kids in the immediate vicinity (maybe the whole school); The teacher is preoccupied with that stress, the other kids fall behind. Performance levels in the school drop.

Defunded educational environments have far fewer teaching assistants and much less capacity for one to one care, support and expertise. There is less availability for mental health support, cognitive behavioural therapy or talking one to one and mentoring time. Waiting lists for local support services are longer, and thresholds are much higher than they have ever been. Where is the additional support at home or the bridge between home and school? An over-reliance on charitable third sector contributions is starting to become a very recognisable thing.

Neglect is not really enough to tick the boxes any more – and abuse has to be deliberate and persistent to really get taken seriously. It's not that the boxes won't get ticked – because believe you me, the school will do everything they possibly can, but who is reading the referral? How long will it take for the referral to be evaluated? How much dialogue is going on?

The Pupil Referral Unit is the free market solution to this problem. That child is managed through a series of monitoring processes where efforts are made to make it clear to the child what the expectations and requirements are. If the process is not successful, we can look towards a managed move that transitions them out of that school for a fresh start at a neighbouring school instead (if the school is slightly less than ethical about it, they can undersell the problems and over emphasise the potential for success).

The child can start from scratch over a series of months – managing an inevitable repetition of the same behavioural cycles – but confronted with remarkably similar resourcing constraints this is always going to be a very steep uphill challenge.

After a couple of managed moves someone has to bite the bullet on this case – the behaviour is likely to escalate. A PRU/AP placement is expensive – maybe £13,000 per child per year outside of London, *more inside I would suggest*. The child is sent to the PRU, is kept 'on roll' at the school making the referral, and the school carries the cost of the referral in one way or another. Most PRUs need schools to buy places up front – or might sell a guaranteed number of places in advance to a group of schools together in a local area.

By highlighting a child in this way we are effectively nominating the perfect candidate for criminal exploitation.

The Unit will, of course, be located in one place – and all the troubled and damaged young people from a very broad local radius – will go there. We are talking 'the worse of the worst' cases – because, again, I'll ask you to believe me, in my experience, schools will bend over backwards to keep a child in mainstream.

I have sat with Principals who have talked to me about the extreme feelings of guilt, and the huge personal reluctance that they have in pushing the button and sending a young person away to a PRU. Having a child or young person rejected, not just by one, but several educational establishments, before getting sent to a quasi-young offenders' institution to be surrounded by a cohort of very unique and problematic cases – that in and of itself absolutely fits the bill of an 'ACEs' consequence.

Remember – two or more Adverse Childhood Experiences increases the substantial likelihood of a negative life outcome. Just two equates to an 80% increase in likelihood of death before 50 for the girls, and four means that the likelihood of crack or heroin use is eleven times more likely. I ask you to accept here that getting removed from mainstream education is not going to be the first ACE that child has had to absorb – but sadly I don't have the available statistical research to show how many ACEs most children carry before they are removed from mainstream education.

No wonder then, that Principals look long and hard at the PRU option and exercise it only with the greatest degree of reluctance. This is not a financial decision – although the costs of sending one or more children to a PRU is scary (three pupils for £39,000 p/a out of your shrinking budget). We are talking about life long professional, vocational educators who believe in saving these children and turning them around.

I have spoken with several Principals who have discussed their misgiving about this whole system with me. When I talk, not only with them, but the senior managers and teachers in schools, everyone seems to feel the same. The common anecdotal thread is that when students get high grades it is wonderful to see and a cause for celebration – but when a child comes from adverse circumstances and overcomes the barriers of outright disadvantage to achieve even a modest education – *that* is the real thrill of teaching.

It is heart-breaking for many professionals to see the limitations of their resources and options exhausted. I see safeguarding briefings given to teachers that warn about getting too close, about professional boundaries, and time and again teachers are sorely tempted to put a hand in their own pocket where school budgets are unable to afford support for basic items.

No child is ever packed off to a PRU in happy circumstances.

I am aware of one school who took it so much to heart that they opened up a safe facility of their own to manage the toughest cases, and evolved this concept to become a leading example of how this can be done. The whole facility was established in the first instance to manage just one child.

Many schools now are looking to try to make their budgets stretch by having more robust and reliable isolation and separation areas. These facilities de-circulate the most antisocial behaviours while they insulate the rest of the community. The high risk case is then managed, supported and reintegrated. This is becoming a more sophisticated process – and teachers are rapidly having to transition skills from becoming people who communicate and educate on curriculum topics, to people who can forensically assess and respond to safeguarding needs.

Notwithstanding these tireless and broadly unseen efforts – which most of society is rarely aware of – the PRU system is still on its feet, up and running.

To County Lines OCGs this is really excellent news and very good for business.

We have considered what type of a blue print the OCG leader would like to have in place in a local area to help his recruitment and distribution strategy – and the PRU system isn't just on a Venn diagram with what the OCG leader wants – *they inhabit the same circle*.

This isn't to disparage the professionals who work in the PRU/Alternative Provision environments. First of all these people are remarkable in many ways – but understandably turnover is high in this field, and in Cambridgeshire the Cambridge City PRU went quite publicly through a series of head teachers/principals, and for a period of time couldn't fill the vacancy at the top of this particular unit.

For the teachers and teaching assistants, these places can be violent, high risk environments where knives and controlled drugs are smuggled, and a light and careful touch has to be applied with much higher degrees of tolerance towards standard behavioural infractions.

We considered William when we were looking at what County Lines actually is. Will told me himself that he passed through a PRU and was eventually rejected even from there after assaulting a teacher and threatening his life. He told me directly *"There are bad boys in there that will eat you alive – and they get you convinced that you have to be the same – that's what the world is like"*.

There is evidence of the PRU system encouraging appeasement over reward. Appeasement is different to reward – and we need to be very clear and distinct about what that means.

Appeasement – as I'm sure most parents and teachers are aware – involves giving in to a pressure or an overt demand 'to keep the peace'. There can be an implicit understanding in the person making the demand that if they behave badly in a certain way that they will provoke a certain reward. Balancing up the disproportionate effect that a child can have on the education of others – a large class size – derailing a whole lesson plan and so on, appeasement can seem like a tempting offer.

"While everyone else gets on with their work – you can… [enter the appeasement] watch a YouTube video."

If appeasement were appropriate you'd let that child or young person sit and watch YouTube, listen to Spotify, play with their DMs on social media and so on.

I've spoken first-hand to young people brought back into mainstream following a spell at a PRU and they were deeply unhappy because their demands for fast-food (McDonalds) were not being met.

Appeasement – as we all know and recognise – is a desperately short term option. It doesn't care about the long term wellbeing of the child, it is literally 'anything for an easier life'. It is predicated by the needs of someone else – the teacher, the supervisor, the parent and so on. More than anything else it can only incentivise negative and disruptive behaviours.

When people get into appeasement cycles you often hear – particularly from parents – *"I can't do x, y or z – he'll just kick off"*.

What they've done is set themselves up in an appeasement predicament. The young person knows what they can get – and they are dictating and pushing a subjective boundary to get more all the time.

History is littered with examples of how appeasement fails – Viking raiding parties in the 6th Century were appeased by Anglo-Saxon settlements with gold. The raiders would leave, and return the next year demanding higher and higher volumes of gold consequently.

This is how appeasement functions. Taking a child back out of an appeasement environment is telling – because they feel that operating to the levels of expectation in mainstream are now both laughably unrealistic and unfair. They want to be appeased.

Commonly, establishing a pattern of appeasement will begin with something small (the thin end of the wedge, so to speak) and an escalating pressure follows for larger concessions.

It probably doesn't need to be highlighted – but this sets up the young person in all the wrong ways. We want young people to develop resilience and work ethic – an understanding that if they strive they receive a reward. We don't want them to learn that if they counter-strive, disrupt or harm, that they can ransom.

We all see that high levels of youth employment and the NEET (not in education, employment or training) situation is a serious problem for society. Young people who find themselves as NEET are clearly very worrying. The ONS (Office of National Statistics) shows that no fewer than 792,000 young people aged between 16 and 24 are recorded as NEET as at March 2019. This figure rose by 14,000 from the April to June 2018 data measure[52].

The statistics continue – 11.5% of all young people in the UK are NEET – a figure that is gradually increasing, not falling.

The NEET category is a prime target for people who want to offer 'get rich quick' dreams and easy money. Like County Lines drug dealers and organised criminal gangs.

---

[52] ONS Data

Children and young people who are primed with expectations of being appeased for negative behaviours are not equipped with emotional or psychological resilience – but they *are* often characterised by a stubbornness and a refusal to cooperate. For many professionals this results in the opinion that 'it's too late now' – while I might not agree with that opinion, it is definitely an uphill battle that has to be coordinated very carefully (and in many cases the evaluation is correct). We have made a figurative rod for our own backs.

When a child or young person is effectively recalibrated to understand that the world does not exist to appease you (and that employers won't be offering this) – it's only going to work if every key influencer is on message and holds the same line consistency. If any single agency gives way, that child or young person will take the path of least resistance.

Allow me to introduce 'Craig'. 'Craig' was a 15 year old boy recovered from the Pupil Referral Unit and brought back into mainstream. While objectively speaking this was a massive last chance for the young man – he didn't see it or accept it in that way.

Craig exhibited what you might consider to be a 'demand avoidance profile'. Any type of pressure or demand provoked an emotional outburst and a run and hide pattern of behaviour. He wasn't particularly confrontational as much as he retreated – his fight, flight or freeze responses definitely showed favour towards flight.

Demand avoidance can be tricky to understand. If I explain that he ran away from work, homework, going to class, having to wear school uniform – you would see that as obvious. It was deeper for Craig. If he showed any good behaviour, any positive work, any glimpse of talent or potential he would run if you *praised it*. He felt pressure from even being appreciated.

For Craig setting up a situation where he was good at something, created a situation where he was expected to deliver on something. If you told him that he was good at art and that a painting he had done was really superb – that would be the end of painting pictures. Looking down the road he saw nothing but pressure coming from that – and he would literally run away.

He was emotionally complicated. He had a deep interest in rap music – particularly 'grime' – and he wrote and produced 'beats'. 'Beats' are rhythm tracks with melodies that rappers can verse over – they contain tricky hooks to entertain the listener and make them catchy. It takes musical talent to put good beats together and people like Dr. Dre and Kanye West have made staggering fortunes from having distinctive styles in the way that they do this.

In addition, this young man filmed videos to accompany his beats, and enlisted local rappers to verse bars over the top – he wove and edited the whole thing together on very, very limited technology and zero budgets.

I was very genuinely, deeply impressed by this.

He had *never* shown any of this work to his teachers at school. His videos on YouTube were taking off and there was no denying his talent. As I praised him profusely and honestly, I didn't realise at that time how he was recoiling inside from every word. I thought I was building him up.

After a short while he actually ran off from me – but in his own peculiar way. He could easily out pace me – he knew the school building much better than I did – he is much younger and spends all day riding around on his bike. He is a fit young guy. He sprinted off – but didn't go out of sight. I caught him waiting, and looking over his shoulder, to see if I would follow him.

Initially I did go after him – asking him to come back. I was confused – why would this young man sprint off like this when I'd just been praising him. He was clearly not happy – and not knowing Craig particularly well at that stage I just couldn't understand why.

I followed him a short distance but recognised his 'cat and mouse' game. Not being interested in following him around the building – and trying to lay down a firm precedent that, if you want me, you can come to me (i.e. mutual respect). I didn't get drawn into this game. He came back towards me (advance and retreat, quite literally, once again).

Our session was over – he needed to understand – if you get up and leave, you end the session. Next time, you must respect the session and you must respect me.

On a subsequent day I was scheduled to sit down with Craig. I was told that he wasn't at school – he had been given a fixed term exclusion for misbehaviours. I went out to see him at home. As far as I was concerned, he was excluded for a period, but we still had a very important meeting. So I spoke to his Dad and I shifted the venue. I went round to his house – his Dad explained that Craig didn't know I was coming – if he knew he'd probably climb out of a window and make off on his bicycle.

I sat down with Mum and Dad first. They explained to me that they weren't happy that Craig had been brought back into mainstream and they blame school for his current issues. When I asked why, their responses shocked me.

Craig had been appeased while he was at the PRU – they gave him what he asked for – it kept him quiet, and they as parents didn't get calls from school to deal with; it was as simple as that. As far as they were concerned – they wanted a quiet life, and it was easier to avoid points of conflict, appease and marginalise the problems. "We just don't want the hassle".

They told me how Craig would be taken out bowling, bought McDonalds fast-food and only had to do a minimal amount of work. They (the PRU) kept the pressure off and for the parents it was a really nice period where nobody rocked the boat.

When I asked about Craig's movements – his schedule – his pattern – I was told that it was a mystery to them. If there is an argument – he leaves on his bike. He comes and goes as he pleases – at all hours. They don't ask because he won't tell. If he doesn't tell, they don't have to worry about it. They don't inspect the content of his mobile phone – he won't allow them to. *They don't really want to know*.

When I invited Will to come into school, cut hair and talk to boys, Craig was there – on time – looking forward to it. He had an immediate rapport with Will and they talked in a semi-opaque street lingo that reassured Craig that Will was for real.

Craig admitted to Will that he was 'shotting' – which means dealing. This involves him basically keeping a minor volume of drugs, and riding them around on demand in return for cash. This made Craig a dealer, a supplier, a target for rivals and liable to stop and search, prosecution and so on. Craig was rewarded with short term money – and pitifully small amounts. He was also given small amounts of weed to sustain his own use – and he was very open about the fact that he smoked. Craig found it ridiculous to even criticise cannabis, it was harmless and there was no way he was going to stop smoking it.

I watched Will try very directly to persuade Craig that this was crazy – that cannabis was bad for his mental health, his mood, and his long term future. He talked him through the trouble he (Will) had got into – and he implored him to stop.

Craig said "Yeah, I'm gonna stop, I don't want to be doing this long" – I was unconvinced. Craig had no long term plans and short of anything else, the dealing was likely to continue.

Both Will and Craig had been PRU kids and they talked about it. Will talked about how damaging it was, how it was a hostile environment, and how he failed to come away with anything positive. Craig talked about how they gave in to him.

I tried to work with Craig and shift him from an 'away from' motivation (running away from everything) into a 'towards' motivation type. I tried to suggest that we could get him work experience in a recording studio environment, or a radio or broadcast environment. I offered to find him support for his creative work – to link him up with local creative and artistic groups. I discussed reaching out to his favourite icons in rap and in grime to see what might happen – to have some excitement about that.

Craig ran from everything.

It is necessary to address the points that I'm making with Craig though:

I don't believe that he had a pathologically demand avoidant profile – that is, one that was born in him and developed as some part of the way that his brain functions (of course I could be wrong). From visiting him at home there was too much environmental evidence that he had been coached and conditioned to think that way and operate in that way to get what he wanted.

I see Craig very much as a product of his environment – and when he entered mainstream school his expectations of how to operate were not matched by the responses from his teachers. It is necessary for schools to apply some pressure to students – and for them to know what it is like to work under demands and deadlines. That is a life lesson. As I write this book I have a timeline that I am writing it to. We all work to schedules, we all deliver to people who depend on us. If the bills don't get paid, the lights go off and you lose your home.

When Craig did go out to the PRU he found an artificial environment that was willing to match his dysfunctional expectation of the world. He could plant his heels, and refuse, and run away – and the environment would appease and supplicate such behaviour. Indeed, he reaped the benefits, and because he was non-violent, and not disruptive, on such a level he was comparably successful and was looked at as such while there (parents even received positive feedback).

His parents saw this as a great thing – they were getting what they wanted – and everyone was happy. In fact this was 'confirmed' for them when he returned to mainstream, because when mainstream started to deal with the issues, they started to get negative reports – so the school was held to blame. In reality this PRU was merely a holding pen for Craig, and as an artificial environment the clock was ticking on how long he would be held there until he became NEET.

By his own admissions, Craig was already running drugs for someone. He was delivering and smoking cannabis – it fit into his world view, and nothing was challenging that. I believe until he sat down with Will, he didn't listen or pay attention to anything in school.

Craig was then offered the ultimate opportunity to 'run away' again. He was deeply uncomfortable with someone paying attention to him in the way I was, and when his family were offered a housing opportunity to relocate to a more remote part of the county (and to leave the mainstream school that was beginning to take those key issues strongly in hand) – he jumped at the idea and practically celebrated. Knowing the futility of this timescale – he threw it at anyone who approached him – and used it as a pass card, practically telling teachers and mentors to save their breath.

This is how I lost contact with Craig. The probability of him becoming a NEET statistic is verging on the inevitable, and the likelihood of him meeting a very negative outcome as a consequence of the County Lines structure is also severe and unacceptable. Am I confident that any specialist team would pick up on the information that was forwarded around this case with his move to his next school? No. I am not. Not at all. Practically speaking – despite promises from the Home Office to the contrary – these resources do not exist (they might exist somewhere on paper – but there is no evidence or reality behind such things).

In addition to this rather bleak picture of what a Pupil Referral Unit represents – both at their best, and at their worst – several news agencies, including the BBC and broadsheet newspapers such as the Independent – have paid attention to the additional problems of Pupil Referral Units.

In October 2018 Eleanor Busby at the Independent published her article[53] supported by evidence from the children's charity Bernardo's.

Ms Busby offered stark warnings about 'postcode lotteries' on the availability and type of provision, and high rates of centres being regarded by Ofsted as 'inadequate' or 'requiring improvement'.

---

[53]

https://www.independent.co.uk/news/education/education-news/school-exclusions-pupils-knife-crime-violence-pupil-referral-units-education-barnardos-a8609046.html

The Member of Parliament for Croydon Central is quoted within this piece as saying:

> *"This is heartbreaking. Schools need resources to support pupils through difficult periods. Too many children are being socially excluded and marked as failures, with tragic consequences."*

An unnamed government spokesperson – always for me a sign that nobody wants to put their name and career reputation prominently to the bad news (and let's face it, if this was good news the rush to take credit would be very evident) – offers the typical hand wringing of 'this is terrible and our heart is in this' (tick box), combined with 'we have to make difficult decisions' (tick box), obfuscation 'it is not clear what role exclusions play in crime' (tick box) and a small offer 'our £4 million innovation fund has created nine new projects around the country' (tick box). Please read the article that Eleanor Busby wrote – it is more than troubling.

In the words of Theresa May (perhaps her biggest cliché) 'I want to be very clear' – there is a plethora of evidence linking school exclusions to crime and other negative life outcomes (much of which we have addressed in this book contemplating the effects of Adverse Childhood Experiences). To suggest otherwise is gaslighting of the worst kind. Furthermore, to suggest that £4 million is evidence of a concerted effort to address this national priority is to also suggest that we are all very stupid indeed. There is no way that £4 million invested in just nine projects is going to address this topic on a strategic level.

Allow me to angrily contextualise what £4 million means to the national budget. In 2019 it was revealed that Boris Johnson spent £53 million of public money on a garden bridge that was never built[54]. This was largely regarded as a vanity project and not a planning necessity. In June 2020 the Financial Times reported that a pest control company worth £19,000 with 16 employees was awarded a contract to supply £108 million worth of personal protective equipment to the NHS.

The numbers – *in national budgetary terms* – make £4 million look like a very insulting and negligent attempt to grasp towards any available evidence of doing something to address these concerns. It is the fiscal equivalent of the money found down the back of the sofa.

The government are well aware of this, and it is for this reason alone that an anonymous 'government spokesperson' can only be attributed with such a feeble response.

I applaud Eleanor Busby for her robust and determined work – and many other journalists who have attacked the issue with similar conviction (both in print and on screen).

---

[54] https://www.bbc.co.uk/news/uk-england-london-47228698

In parliament a report was printed on this crisis on the 18th July 2018.

The House of Commons Education Committee has made available 'Forgotten children: alternative provision and the scandal of ever increasing exclusions'.[55]

The Education Committee is a cross party body with a membership of eleven serving MPs from the Labour Party, the Conservative Party and the Scottish Nationalist Party. The group is chaired by the Rt Hon Robert Halfon MP. It exists to provide scrutiny and oversight for the Department of Education (DfE) on the basis of expenditure, administration and policy.

The conclusions and recommendations in this report strongly backed the need to make it achievable for young people to stay in mainstream education and out of Pupil Referral Units. The committee blamed 'an unfortunate and unintended consequence' of Government focus on school standards leading to disadvantaged children being disproportionately excluded. At point 11 of the 33 recommendations the notes clearly state that "...at the moment too many pupils are falling through the net."

> "The Government should encourage [does this mean fund?] the creation of more specialist alternative providers that are able to meet the

---

[55]

https://publications.parliament.uk/pa/cm201719/cmselect/cmeduc/342/342.pdf

diverse needs of pupils with medical needs, including mental health needs." (recommendation 13)

At recommendation point 16 – however – a cosmetic point was raised around Pupil Referral Units specifically:

"Pupil Referral Units, and other forms of alternative provision, should be renamed to remove the stigma and stop parents being reluctant to send their children there."

Nonetheless, this worrying suggestion is followed up by a complaint that generally – at the time that report was published – there was a general lack of oversight, accountability, and requirement for registration in PRUs and AP (alternative provision) facilities. *I don't feel it is argumentative to suggest that the 'name' and the 'branding' of the PRU system is not the source of concern to responsible parents.* There is – as I have underlined – a far greater threat to our children within the PRU system than branding and until that is tackled comprehensively, no amount of rebranding will get the job done.

In February 2019 a report published in Schools Week[56] referenced how the TBAP Multi-Academy Trust – which exclusively operates 11 AP centres or academies

---

[56] https://schoolsweek.co.uk/systematic-failure-lifts-academy-trusts-deficit-to-2-4m/

"unknowingly racked up a £2.4 million deficit because of a "systematic" failure in its financial systems"

Claims were laid initially that the Trust was operating a £758,000 deficit for 2016-2017 – but interrogation of such reports revealed a far higher financial cost. The Chief Executive, Seamus Oates, blamed his staff and his systems – expressing a "level of incompetence" among trust staff.

Freddie Whittaker – of Schools Week - is unflinching in his evaluation of the situation. He highlighted that Oates – who himself admitted to growing the alternative provision business too fast and 'with too much ambition' – was on a financial package worth between £220,000 and £230,000.

The TBAP group were highlighted in March 2019 by the BBC as part of a Panorama Investigation. A headteacher spoke of bills being unpaid by the Trust and her school site being visited by debt collectors.

It was around this time that the Cambridge AP Academy, operated by TBAP, was subject to local authority intervention and it was discovered that inadequate safeguarding provision was being made for vulnerable children and young people. It was promptly prohibited from accepting new referrals until significant requirements were met. This intervention is referenced in a letter/report to the Cambridge AP Academy on the 10th October 2019 (addressed to Mr Nick Morley).

In October 2019 a further report by the tenacious Freddie Whittaker – announced that TBAP would be 'dropping' two centres, one in Harlow and another in Warrington – to help consolidate and focus their operational responsibilities. Evidently the Trust did not feel that it could meet the needs of the communities in Essex and Cheshire, whilst operating on a financial even keel.

Ofsted continue to rate the TBAP Cambridge AP Academy as 'requires improvement' and specific regard to the subject of safeguarding, Ofsted wrote to the academy:

> *"You were able to demonstrate that record-keeping has improved in underpinning pupils' safety, but some information is not as accessible and detailed as it could be."*

They reiterated the need to improve the systems for maintaining safeguarding and that recording needed to improve – the detail being recorded needed to be 'meticulous' and that it needed to sit in a more retrievable and accessible way to relevant staff.

What we know – and what we can deduce from all this – is that Cambridge AP, a source of concern in its own right, with genuine safeguarding issues and shortcomings, requiring a 'rapid action plan' to promote scrutiny and focus. Whatever those shortcomings and liabilities are – they are not to be compared, it would seem, to whatever was happening in Harlow (with the arrival of debt collectors) and Warrington – which like gangrenous limbs, were carved off and discarded as lost. A macro example, if ever there was one, of what happens to the children in such centres.

In the very best of circumstances, operating a Pupil Referral Unit is a very high risk proposition. You are placing all your eggs in one basket. All of the most severe cases of trauma affected and socially disaffected young people, herded together in a pretty vast social experiment.

I would conjecture that the biggest benefit of the PRU/AP system is not for the individual or the family referred into alternative provision (no matter what 'Craig's' parents might have thought or said). Instead, the benefits are to the schools who no longer have to cope with the pressure of such children and young people when relationships breakdown and the resources don't exist to safety net them in mainstream education anymore. This is about protecting *the majority* of children and young people in the mainstream environment from a spectrum of harms that range from lesson time and learning disruption, to violence and seriously antisocial behaviour. It is as if someone at the DfE has said *"Schools could cope if it wasn't for all these damn kids"*.

To refocus on the children and young people placed in alternative provision though, they have been rejected by society once again. They have suffered *another* recognised ACE and they have been placed on a conveyor belt. The message to, as an individual on a deeply personal level – is that they are a problem to the people around them. Their surroundings begin to resemble an offenders' institution. The security around them is beginning to offer more vigilance and intrusion. There is less trust. A self-fulfilling prophecy is starting to take shape and they can see where the conveyor belt leads. They are surrounded by people with a range of problems and issues – it's hard to find positive companionship when you are marked as an AP or a PRU kid. Which parent is going to welcome you into their child's life as a best friend? All your immediate peers end up marked in exactly the same way and it shapes your social expectation of what is 'normal'.

Speaking and working with Sabina Grey – a lady who I have previously referenced in this book – she has been through a series of adverse childhood experiences and did go down the route of juvenile drug abuse, leading to crack cocaine and heroin addiction. She offers a remorseful recollection of her time at school – but a vivid memory of the day that she was expelled. Sabina doesn't blame anyone for the mistakes that she made – or for the fact that she was excluded – she sees it as part of the inevitable road that she was on at that time in her life. She did graduate to burgling houses to fund and feed that class A drug dependency problem, she did become the heroin addict that she thought she'd never be. *Nevertheless* she also reflects ruefully on the network of minor contributions that took her down that path – and how things weren't defused in time for her – and everything she lost as a consequence. Talking to Sabina you are absolutely left in no doubt that exclusion is an adverse childhood experience – it marked her and it shaped her sense of self and her identity. We as a society remain responsible for every child who is marked by a system of being removed from the mainstream and shoved into a AP/PRU facility. Please remember that the Education Selection Committee recommended no fewer than 33 points of necessary reform to this system (presumably to make it adequate), and explicitly stated that it is unfairly biased against disadvantaged children on a disproportionate basis.

One of the key consequences of all this is very much in the favour of the County Lines business model.

All of these high risk young people are their platinum tier recruitment candidates – and we have created the ultimate selection and recruitment process for them.

An exceptionally well run AP/PRU environment *could be* a potentially safe and supportive environment – but given the vast challenges, the costs, and the careful balance between creating a security compound and offering trust/empowerment – this is an almost impossible task. Combine that task with a background of falling investment – not only in your local PRU/AP facility – but in the associated multiagency partners, including social care, police, probation, health (particularly mental health provision), housing and others, it would be miraculous to see this blueprint succeed.

In reality extremely well run AP/PRU facilities are not common. Instead we see an Academy Trust – like TBAP – whose eyes are bigger than its belly, who admits to having employed people not fit for task, running with top heavy corporate costs and aspirations. They carry endemic problems in the detailed work of recording, managing and accessing meticulous safeguarding data.

If the PRU/AP system was going to succeed you would need – logically speaking – the best of the best in those centres. The market based system is not going to provide that. As much as we might look to Seamus Oates at TBAP earning £175,000 – to £225,000 p/a and accuse him of being overpaid – in actuality, if TBAP thrived, I would have no issue with such rewards whatsoever (and more). *Perhaps this is a small price to pay for society to have a solution to this particular problem?* I think that is probably true. With no disrespect to Mr Oates at all though – his role as a CEO of an eleven centre Trust – pitches him against some people in private industry who receive rewards and share options and pensions and other bonuses that dwarf his recompense. As Mayor of London, our now Prime Minister was challenged for receiving £250k per year for his second job writing for a newspaper. His response was to refer to the salary as "chicken feed"[57]. I don't doubt that what Johnson said would infuriate most people working exceptionally hard on a full time basis for less than 10% of that amount – *but nevertheless* – at the top end of the salaries pyramid, a £225k package is not going to land you the 'best of the best' in terms of your new Chief Executive Officer. What it will get you is into the recruitment conversation for an average and possibly competent individual (at that grade), who you are about to throw into the toughest job they'll ever face – a high risk make or break moment for their personal C.V. It is a huge gamble for them, and a bigger gamble for the children.

In the context of running an AP/PRU – if you don't get the right people you do not succeed by any measure. On every pragmatic level – from rising numbers of NEET young people, to the increasing power and control of County Lines drug dealers, to rising levels of childhood suicide, self-harm and mental health problems – alternative provision and PRUs are not the answer. We cannot blame all of these problems on the PRU system, but are they a stakeholder? Absolutely.

What I am concerned with – *above all* – is the contribution that is made through this system to supporting an endemic model of distributing controlled

[57] https://www.theguardian.com/politics/2009/jul/13/boris-johnson-second-salary-chickenfeed

drugs specifically through the exploitation of children and young people.

We have to hold ourselves to account – as educators, as professionals and as parents, when political and societal expediency leads to perverse outcomes that support child criminal exploitation. What point does rhetoric about 'attacking evil' serve, if we cannot ensure that our own processes and social structures do not counter and head off the threat of County Lines?

You might be forgiven for thinking that I have launched a deeply personal attack on Seamus Oates as the CEO of TBAP in highlighting him and his organisation. My intention was never to do so. I do not believe that he wants to support County Lines and I am not accusing him of intentionally or deliberately doing as much. I have heard Mr Oates speak on the issue of Cambridge TBAP, and he himself has protested that many of the children received into TBAP are already well on the road before they went into that facility, and were not made dysfunctional by the facility itself. I am not accusing TBAP of such. *What I am accusing them of is not being the safety net we need under the prevailing circumstances.*

The truth is stark – our systems and business models have to run contrary to what County Lines gangs need and require. We design our defences according to the threat that is posed. We raise our aspirations – not to manage children day to day or to appease them and keep them quiet, but to recover and rehabilitate the worst and most damaged cases, and to help *all* of our children thrive and succeed in the utmost safety, irrespective of their past adverse experiences. We have to listen to the Principals of our mainstream schools, we have to listen to the voice of their consciences, and we have to trust their professionalism and expertise. This means providing them with greater resources to cope at a mainstream level on a more inclusive basis that prohibits additional trauma and promotes the chance of long term gains and outcomes.

County Lines as a business model is all about the short term – burning children and young people through fast lifestyles, minor rewards, false promises and day to day pressures and coercive tactics. *We cannot compete there.* Instead – we have to operate in a way that reaches long term aspirations and invigorates a sense of perspective about the future, and helps them to feel like they belong. AP and PRU environments manage from crisis to crisis, day to day appeasement and through high walls and fences. We have already lost our children when they arrive there.

Chapter Seven: Key Partners in Our Approach

Tackling County Lines is a classic example of a multiagency responsibility. By this we mean that the ownership of the key tasks and services that are needed to deal with this problem sit across a wide variety of participants in statutory and non-statutory teams.

I want to look at the main participants – keeping in mind that regionally there are some variations – and that perhaps a lack of national consistency is also part of the problem.

Across this chapter we are going to look at the following individuals, groups and agencies:

- Parents
- Health – both physical and mental services
- Social care & early help teams
- Housing Association/Authority
- Education
- Charities and voluntary sector (third sector) groups

For many people – when you talk about County Lines they think about law enforcement, and they talk about it being a problem of managing crime. They might stretch to thinking about the National Crime Agency or Regional Organised Crime Units (ROCUs), they *might* even think about the Probation Service. We will look towards law enforcement agencies in a later chapter.

Defeating County Lines is about shared responsibility at every level of society, and laterally across every sphere of public service provision. It is a subject area that every professional should be briefed to understand, and that every responsible adult can identify clearly. This is a huge ambition – *but no, I am definitely not offering hyperbole on this*. If we are determined to turn this situation around, this is the standard that we have to achieve.

In this chapter I am going to look at the key partners, and the type of contribution that they make. This will not be exhaustive – there is a whole book that could written on this subject alone. The aim of this chapter is not to critique, but to open up some thinking and awareness. As a professional you might recognise yourself to be clearly under one of these headings – I hope that you read this and give thought and reflection to the topic. I assure you I am appreciative of the pressures you are working under as I write this.

Before we look at each partner group – something really does need to be acknowledged: The shrinkage in service provision across the UK in all of these groups has been severe in the last ten years. An article in The New York Times, published in February 2019, written by Benjamin Mueller explained UK austerity to a bemused US audience.

This report cites the United Nations saying that the cuts brought in through austerity were *"entrenching high levels of poverty and inflicting unnecessary misery in one of the richest countries in the world"*.

The New York Times prices the total cuts introduced through austerity to be £30 billion[58] – attributed to welfare payments, housing, social services, the police and others. They have cited evidence of foodbank growth (nearly doubling between 2013-2017 alone). A subsection of the article references the impact on children: 600,000 children have fallen into 'relative poverty' since 2012 – irrespective of whether their parents are employed or unemployed (in fact two thirds are regarded to be part of the 'working poor'). Again The New York Times points to the Trussell Trust and the tripling of their foodbank provision since the start of austerity.

Not for political axe grinding, not for the purposes of posturing or for showing favour to any political party – we simply must be truthful and honest about what austerity has done to our collective ability to respond to the threat of County Lines. We cannot be delusional. We cannot be dishonest. Such behaviour will (and does) cost and ruin lives – and those lives will be vulnerable young people. It's an emotive topic – but it is also a logical and ethical conclusion to draw.

---

[58]

https://www.nytimes.com/2019/02/24/world/europe/britain-austerity-may-budget.html

So to begin with we acknowledge a Venn diagram of service provision that should overlap wholeheartedly on the subject of preventing, disrupting and reducing the threat of County Lines.

In the last ten years the circles of service provision have shrunk – there is no debate about this and there are no exceptions to this. Where services fail to overlap consistently – that is where we find the cracks that young people fall down. These cracks are not so much minor cosmetic blemishes as growing divides pulled further apart by the irresistible movement of political tectonic plates.

As services have shrunk their ability to overlap has reduced significantly – agencies can feel pitted against each other. Education might feel that if Social Care thresholds were lower, they'd receive more support and intervention. Police might claim that they are now doing more work than ever on mental health provision – and point to expertise in other services that ought to be doing the heavy lifting. Ambulance crews might feel that if police were more robust with vexatious callers, there would be less time wasted on bogus reports. The circles of opposition can be endless, and professionals in every agency have at some time felt let down by colleagues in an adjacent agency. The likelihood of such friction is increasing, and leaders of services are only likely to become more protective of whatever budgets remain – always knowing and anticipating that no matter how bad it is now, future cuts are always likely. Political leaders have tried to quell and quash such disagreements by creating new leadership roles at more senior but more localised levels to control and distribute budgets – Police and Crime Commissioners (some of whom are now taking control of Fire and Rescue services) and Regional Mayors being two such examples.

Thankfully most professionals are adult enough to look at things from each other's perspective – at least to some extent – and understand what must be going on in the other office to mean that certain cases don't meet a given threshold of intervention or support.

When I was left at the roadside with a suicidal and severely injured juvenile (as referenced previously) I knew for a fact that my colleagues in the ambulance control room were *mortified* by the lack of provision. They were hugely apologetic. In fact apologetic doesn't adequately cover this – between 11th and 21st November 2019, three staff at the East of England Ambulance Service Trust (EEAST) died suddenly and a suicide helpline was setup – I know that the experience I had was far from isolated and a number of critical cases were bearing down impossibly on the mental health of people in that service. The Eastern Daily Press reported on the situation on 25th November 2019 in an article that makes for incredibly difficult reading[59].

---

[59] https://www.edp24.co.uk/news/health/east-of-england-ambulance-service-staff-deaths-whistleblower-warning-1-6392546

[I remind everyone that people who join public service providers and the emergency services – as educators, as therapists, as counsellors, as police officers, nurses and more – do so with their heart and souls in vocational positions that don't expect to be richly rewarded on a financial level. One of the greatest privileges of my professional life is meeting and working with such people – and I admit without shame to being incredibly on their side (where I think we all should be).]

We must be pragmatic about one thing at this juncture – addressing County Lines will not come without additional provision. What that provision looks like – in my estimate – would be somewhere in the region of sustained billions of pounds of investment across a range of different services nationally, with a commitment for years to come. I underline and reiterate my skepticism and disbelief that anyone can trumpet any £20 million commitment as meaningful – or worse still the October 2018 '£4 million/nine projects' apology. I appreciate that we cannot simply pluck uncosted and irresponsible figures from the sky – but we also have to reshape our perceptions of what we *can* afford to do, and what we cannot afford to allow. There is a fashion for framing any national crisis and emergency into a challenge comparative to going to war. We have seen this rhetoric applied regularly to both Brexit and to COVID-19 – allow me to compare then, if we must, the UK military operation in Iraq which cost £8.4 billion.

There is nothing to be achieved without substantial backing or support on a financial level and at the highest levels of government. Good will and doorstep clapping will not get this done. County Lines is a huge and commercially successful operation with staggering levels of profitability backed by violence. We cannot overturn this with bake sales, crowd funding and good will. The sensational levels of profitability correlate only to the incredible levels of harm caused to children. Local partners need to be funded and equipped to respond.

When we cast our consideration towards an estimated £200 billion commitment to atomic weapons in the UK, or even the frankly staggering and questionable cost of HS2 high speed rail – *at an estimated £88.7 billion* – we surely must contextualise this national crisis (County Lines) as one that needs a genuine and determined source of investment on a central government level (AutoExpress.co.uk published an estimate that HS2 will cost £403 million *per mile* before it is functional and operational to save *half an hour* of journey time between London and Manchester).

While austerity has changed the way that people in the UK perceive the wealth of government (generally now convinced that there is no money for anything) – it might come as a shattering surprise to know that the UK is still a member of the G8. This means that we are still one of the eight richest countries on the planet and our economy was worth £2.1 trillion in 2018. I reference, once again, the bemused tone of The New York Times that such a wealthy country could engage in quite so much deliberate self-harm:

"...the British leadership is in a "state of denial" about the devastation its policies have wrought."

I challenge the reader to accept that there *is* money to invest in a meaningful, determined and heavyweight solution to the County Lines issue – we also have the skills and professionalism needed to dismantle this problem.

Everything that I will offer you subsequently about the various agencies who have a vested interest in confronting County Lines, and who play a role in bringing it down, is viewed through the prism of austerity (how can it not be?), and an understanding that these professionals have been doing some remarkable work to keep going through exceptionally difficult and hostile times, with very little political sympathy or financial support at a central government level.

Parents

"I blame the parents" is a cliché that I think we're all familiar with. We have been fed a diet of imagery that consists of poorly educated single parent environments where money is spent on flat screen TVs, cigarettes, booze, and mobile phones. We are asked to accept that mothers are out there having children irresponsibly in uncertain relationships that crumble and leave children without father figures (for some reason the mothers tend to take the worst of the stigma). We are persuaded that hit and run fatherhood is the norm now and that child support isn't being paid. The Daily Mail is a screaming, frothing mess of comments from people who blame the parents and paint these images while scrutinizing the numbers of people 'on benefits' – a new social stigma that appears to mark people as failures and as burdens.

In truth I have worked with – and work with – children on all parts of the social spectrum. Some from exceptionally affluent backgrounds. Public schools are being targeted by County Lines dealers too – affluent children have access to greater amounts of cash after all.

I work with young people at risk of exclusion and who are being drawn into County Lines, who have parents with doctorates (both parents, in one situation).

We need to change our thinking because this is not about a feral underclass of children being left to fend for themselves.

A sizeable proportion of the children that I work with cite, as best they can, a relationship problem at home with one or more parent. I do work with children who are being fostered, and children who are in care too. Fundamentally the bond between child and parents is an essential one – and the destabilising effect of having an insecurity in that relationship is incredibly hard to recover from or mitigate.

We cannot presume that parents – regardless of their affluence or their professional or academic success – possess all the parenting skills and all the support that they need. Even parents with very good parenting skills, and the benefit of a wider supportive family (grandparents, aunts and uncles) ask for help and assistance because they don't know how to respond to the signs and symptoms of drug misuse or County Lines involvement.

This is not about parents being tough and strict either. I previously referenced 'Zoe' ('All behaviour is communication') – the only consistency in her life *was* punishment. She was a broken child living a traumatic life. I have seen parents being both *incredibly* strict, and also being despairingly lenient and sometimes bemusingly inconsistent. Usually where the skills deficit exists is the decision making process, the communications style/method and the knowledge of signs and symptoms, combined with understanding the best way to respond.

Many parents don't know how to ask for help, who to ask for help, and they are worried that if they do ask for help – in this age of digital record keeping – that somebody somewhere will black list them permanently as bad parents, or that they might even end up losing a child, or that the state will enter their lives on a hideous, heavy handed and intrusive level (refusing to leave).

Well informed and supported parents are essential to resolving the crisis around County Lines. They are absolutely at the heart of the matter – working with parents, supporting them and giving them skills and knowledge is key, creating and helping to support happy and healthy family homes is a priority. When we reference the severe categories of chronic poverty we must understand that parents working more than one job, in low paid and unrewarding work, are not going to have the necessary time to support and engage with their families on an emotional level. The priority becomes paying the rent and keeping the lights on. In the short term this pays the bills, and the state can proudly boast that they are keeping the benefits bills down and employment up – but if further along the road we incur costs subsequently to deal with the problems resulting, this is nothing but a harmful false economy. I reference once again the research of the University College London, and their work on health inequality (referencing more than £700 million in costs of child maltreatment, and £1.9 billion in terms of lost economic output).

I have been involved in several 'child in need' (that is a child defined in law as needing local authority services intervention to achieve or maintain a reasonable standard of health or development) and 'child at risk' (a child who is experiencing or is at risk of abuse, neglect or other forms of harm) cases. These are upsetting things to be involved in. I am involved in many 'team around the child' or 'team around the family' situations where a multi-disciplined team of practitioners are brought together to support the family and the children in question. Thresholds are getting higher and harder to evidence. Professionals have less confidence in being able to reach these thresholds and very often several referrals need to be made before they are genuinely considered for help. It becomes more likely under these circumstances that appropriate referrals will not be made, and that children will suffer as a consequence. By only being able to deal with the very worst case situations – and by leaving others where early and more minor or moderate intervention would have worked – we amplify the harm caused, we increase the likelihood of a terrible outcome, and we increase the overall costs of support. Nobody wins.

The vast majority of parents that I work with, and have worked with, if approached with the right tone, have been grateful for some empathy and constructive support. They have been only too keen to engage and they want to do the right things. The number of parents that I meet who push back against guidance, support and advice are very much in the minority – and the problem of the selfish, ignorant, benefit sponging neglect monster is even less likely again. *Irrespective* – when people talk about parents who need help or support a very stodgy diet of irresponsible programmes such as 'Benefits Street' aired by Channel 4 or 'Saints and Scroungers' by BBC One, or 'Undercover Benefits Cheats' on Channel 5 (the list goes on and on) – has shaped expectations that people asking for help don't really need it, ought to pull themselves up on their own, and that at the heart of it is some measure of dishonesty or irresponsibility. This is lamentable – and parents who need early help or help in crisis or chronic difficulty should be able to access it without the fear of being vilified.

Where parents become isolated they are easily overwhelmed by County Lines. Speaking at a school in

Cambridge last year I was approached by Caroline – a very brave parent local to the area who is absolutely focused on the welfare and wellbeing of her son. As I went through the signs and symptoms of County Lines' involvement she worryingly ticked off most, if not all of them, one by one. Her son wasn't registered at the school I was speaking to – but Caroline learned that the talk was on – she asked that school if she could attend. She was worried and had an inkling that this was the issue.

Caroline spoke to me at the end of the presentation and I subsequently became involved in helping to support her through the immediate intervention around her child. She had found drugs in his bedroom, and his behaviours had become erratic, untrustworthy, and unmanageable. Caroline spoke to me tearfully about how isolated she felt, how much she had tried, and the fact that she needed help and support. She confounded any cliché around the type parent who has a child that is picked up by this phenomenon, and she was utterly honest and full of integrity.

We have had a very happy outcome over the last twelve months and I have stayed in touch with Caroline. Her son has been successfully extracted from the situation he was in and their relationship is getting stronger all the time. Very sadly such positive outcomes are not the most common ones. We don't have enough support groups or forums where expertise and parenting experiences can be moderated and shared.

In addition, for the parents of children who are not exhibiting overt signs of being drawn into County Lines, there should be preventative education. We need to thoroughly challenge complacency that exists around this and the first stage of that task sits with offering education and support to parents before this even becomes an issue. Parents need to know the signs to look for, how to manage their children on the internet, and how to monitor the whereabouts and behaviours of their kids in the least obtrusive but most thorough and effective manner. Most parents that I speak to are receptive to this and want to hear about it – but where it is rolled out, it goes out inconsistently and without the type of support or momentum to ensure that it reaches everyone. There shouldn't be a cost involved to parents in accessing this help and this knowledge, and the door should be open to everyone irrespective of their background and defining circumstances.

Health Services

This is a critical area of business in the fight back against County Lines. Many of the first disclosures of drug related and mental or emotional health issues are presented to local G.P.s and health care professionals.

The provision of help and support specifically for young people and children – as with everything else – has shrunk remarkably. It is increasingly difficult to get families in touch with the correct services and the appropriate expertise that they require.

Mental health crisis, chronic needs and drug dependency issues cross over. My professional experience is one of young people talking about self-medicating and finding a solution to their own problems. Adolescents who don't feel they can talk to Mum or Dad are far less likely to find medical expertise or seek out their family doctor. They get advice on the grapevine, through peers, and on the street.

The general practitioner service is over stretched, and as a consequence it feels inaccessible to young people who need advice and guidance, or feel that they have problems. Rigid appointment slots make it very hard to get into the details of a situation because young people need time and patience – rapport building. I empathise with G.P.s, the business model that they have to operate within does not allow for such time. It is incredibly difficult, even for the most personable and gifted doctors to project reassurance and friendliness to a withdrawn child inside the first two minutes of a ten minute appointment.

One young person in crisis that I dealt with did take the advice of going to see his doctor – but sadly he received the lecture on 'pulling himself together', 'getting over himself' and 'taking a bit of responsibility'. Unfortunately there is a broad inconsistency that needs to be tackled within the health service on how doctors approach teenagers experiencing mental health problems.

It is easy to see a vulnerable young person, who has possibly experimented with the early stages of self-harm (marked arms and so on) as attention seeking, navel gazing or over indulged.

Some doctors are quite amazing – and bring exactly the focus and awareness that you would hope for. Generally speaking – and without encouraging prejudice – younger doctors seems to find it easier to relate to younger patients in this category, but I personally (and without evidence admittedly) tend to think that the recent training and investment in learning is the key (not the age of the practitioner). I do know that young people find it easier to relate to younger people but in my experience you can follow the trend – 14 year olds pretending to be 16, 16 year olds pretend to be 18 and 18 less likely to pretend, but when they do, projecting into the golden age of the early 20s. A newly qualified doctor, still a little fresh faced and less exhausted, with a bright modern sense of humour is always at an advantage in this market.

Doctors are all individuals too – some with skills that are more adept to certain types of cases. We have a responsibility to ensure that all doctors are County Lines aware, know how to spot the signs of criminal exploitation, and know how to make all the relevant multiagency referrals to protect that child in a meaningful way. Doctors I have spoken to, in the process of their training, highlighted to me that the basis of their understanding on County Lines was delivered through self-read and slide based inputs within a broader number of other such pieces dealing with child protection. *This wasn't reassuring*.

Referral to specialist services is becoming harder - not easier. This is not because of the services themselves. The people who work within teams like CASUS (drugs/alcohol) and CAMHS (mental health) are tremendous individuals – in my experience. I've been lucky enough to meet the whole of my local CAMHS team and sit in on one of their meetings – I found that they were pragmatic, funny, passionate and very human. Their skills and qualifications ranged from mental health nursing and social care experience, through counselling and up to consultant child and adolescent psychiatry. There was no overt sense of hierarchy and everyone was valued and operated at a peer level towards the one single goal – the protection of children and the promotion of their health and wellbeing. The terrible shame is the limited availability of such teams across such broad geographical areas – the dilution of their skills – and not having as much time on the front foot to offer drop in services in schools and colleges.

Referral pathways are easy enough to understand – but thoroughly oversubscribed and it's not always easy to see the woods for the trees, and discriminate between cases that need immediate intervention, or represent lower levels of risk (such a process – no matter how robust and accurate, is also time consuming and an administrative burden).

Quite clearly – where adverse childhood experiences are concerned – and where a trauma informed approach is of paramount importance, our medical provision is absolutely at the forefront of our priorities. We cannot mount a successful counter measure against County Lines without addressing the needs of our children and young people in terms of their physical and mental health. When reclaiming children and young people from drug and alcohol abuse we absolutely must have professional drugs counselling.

One case that I have been working with for the past year admitted to a substantial dependency on cannabis that was increasing and causing him anxiety. His use was becoming more overt and drawing him closer to a criminal record. On one weekend he was subject to a stop and search and found himself handcuffed at the side of the road. He admitted that he smelt strongly of cannabis and had (in a rash moment) tried to run from the police officer. He was thankful that he had nothing on him – but by his own estimation, he was very lucky:

"Five minutes earlier and they'd have caught me literally smoking it there and then with my mates".

When it came to confronting the issues it was CASUS that really helped to turn that corner. He worked with a professional and they developed a plan that he could follow honestly that reduced his using cycle and gradually weened his dependency down. Verity Beehan of the Cambridgeshire CASUS service is an excellent practitioner and clinician – she is highly skilled and indispensable to the process of rehabilitation. She is highly qualified as both a team manager and a senior substance misuse nurse offering one to one treatment, cognitive behavioural therapy, sleep hygiene advice and relapse prevention measures. Despite her obvious professionalism and expertise she is incredibly personable and projects warmth and a caring rapport. As I continued to work with the young man in question, he told me that he was glad that he had engaged with CASUS and how much the advice and support that Verity was delivering meant to him.

To highlight – *without doing so in such a way to make him identifiable* – this young man has a background of ACEs that is as severe as anything I have ever seen in my professional history. His life is as chaotic and unpredictable, and his disadvantages are as acute as anything you might encounter. He would be in the top 1% of such situations. If I was to describe them here you would think he was a kid from the projects of New York – not a resident of leafy South Cambridgeshire.

The combined work of school (which we will come to), of CASUS, and external mentoring – this young man has gone from the verge of permanent exclusion to a strong likelihood of finishing his GCSEs and going on to college afterwards. I believe that he will.

When it comes to depriving the County Lines operators of their prime targets, the work that is done by the NHS and by medical professionals is absolutely instrumental and they must be regarded as pivotal to the collective plan to defeat the criminal exploitation of children.

Social Care and Early Help Teams

The social workers that I have engaged with have also been tremendous people – who like their counterparts in the area of mental and physical health – have been overstretched to an irresponsible extent.

The amount of exhaustion within social care teams is silently on the conscience of everyone – it seems to be overlooked. The trades' union UNISON published a paper 'A day in the life of social work'[60]. It is a tough read.

Key findings include 48% of respondents feeling that they are 'over the limit' with their caseloads and 60% felt that austerity had reduced their ability to make a positive difference. 80% expressed emotional distress as a consequence of their role, with 74% being unable to finish the day keeping up with vital paperwork and administration. 67% were going without lunch, 64% without breaks at all. *Please read this report for yourself* and appreciate that without social care professionals our ability to tackle County Lines dissolves absolutely. Make no mistake about it – County Lines trades' operators want to see social workers broken and overrun.

To tackle County Lines we need well trained, well supported and well resourced social workers. We need to listen to them attentively, and the information that they share with us needs to be at the forefront of what we do. These people get closest to the families and the children that we are concerned with – they help us to

---

[60] https://www.unison.org.uk/content/uploads/2017/03/CC-SocialWorkWatch_report_web.pdf

identify where the greatest risk and need is. Their continued engagement should be entrusted to them – but instead there is an increasing trend for them to be pressured to close cases and withdraw prematurely.

As with everything right now, Social Care thresholds are high – far higher than they were at the outset of the austerity crisis. They work tremendously hard to create dynamics in families where children can remain with their parents (the best place for any child to be) unless the significant evidence of abuse or neglect is in insurmountable and cannot be changed.

Early Help Teams do exactly what they suggest – they look for early evidence of need and try to intervene at such a stage that the requisite support and guidance is minimal. This is sensible, cost effective, and in the best interests of everyone.

Going through the spectrum, however, Social Care will be hands on with the worst cases of abuse and neglect – things that most people would quite understandably find traumatic and too stressful to contemplate.

As a police officer I had only the most peripheral involvement in a case where a family was living in such horrific conditions that they had taken to defecating in the bath. When the bath was full they started using other rooms. People in the UK would like to believe that such cases do not exist in this country – they do – and extracting children from such situations is largely in the hands of the social workers. Imagine the expectations of a child taken from such conditions, anticipate the vulnerability – and the huge amount of work required around that child. Susceptibility to criminal exploitation in that context is ridiculously high. If people perceive social works to be on the soft end of public service they are sorely misguided.

Social Care and Early Help Teams also promote good parenting skills. Parenting skills – I find – are like driving skills. You rarely encounter anyone who is willing to admit that they are not good behind the wheel of a car. People are sensitive and defensive on both topics in a way that they are not about anything else. This being said – at least people do start out with an understanding that driving lessons are a good idea. If you have a baby, a huge amount of expectation is placed on mothers to be 'good mums' by osmosis, or divine gift, via DNA or some other method of unspoken inheritance. A parental skills deficit can exist in families where parents are highly trained, intelligent and massively qualified in other ways. Such situations are not restricted to the cliché of the ignorant chain smoking television addict that we are confronted with in the tabloids and the online click-bait.

Giving Social Care the capacity to roll out more parenting skills sessions – making such sessions more socially acceptable, palatable and fun, is something that would make a very meaningful difference to our children and their happiness and wellbeing. County Lines' drug dealers would hate to see a fashion for parenting skills classes bringing parents together – mothers and fathers

– and support circles of non-judgemental parents who offer advice and help to each other.

I draw another comparison: in recent years the social attitude towards sex shops, erotic toys and liberated sexual attitudes has boomed. Jacqueline Gold is credited with taking the sex shop out of Soho and the neon lit backstreets of shame to create a high street chain that sells to everyone. What was once associated with dirty macs and dark glasses, no eye contact, and furtive, self-conscious activity is now mainstream. Gold is worth an estimated £500 million fortune as a consequence, and most towns and cities now have an Anne Summers' right next door to the shop that sells school shoes, mobiles phones or fast food. People welcome Anne Summers' into their houses for the equivalent of a sex toy 'Tupperware party'. My home town of Barnsley once protested the arrival of a sex shop so vociferously that it was refused a premises. Website 'Yelp' now offers a list of 'the best 10 adult stores in Barnsley'. Once such a cultural change has been achieved it looks inevitable – but it is important to appreciate that this has only come about in the last fifteen years – and the shift is remarkable.

While parenting skills are never going to become the new 'sex sells' mantra – so much is to be done on stigma of accepting parenting classes. Increasing the availability of early help, and in making it a positive thing to ask for would be such a cultural step forward.

The movement towards this should, quite rightly, be delivered through Social Care and Early Help. Resources, marketing, social media proliferation, and partnership with someone who clearly understands what Jacqueline Gold achieved is an opportunity for an important step forward. Celebrity example and endorsement is of prime value. Magazines like 'Hello' spend millions buying the photography rights to A list celebrities in attempts to make them look like perfect parents as they 'Introduce their new son Hector George Horatio' and so on. A new cooperative angle on this could explore candidly the sense of intimidation that most people honestly feel when they are becoming parents – and how parenting classes are helping.

Social Care and Early Help (particularly Early Help) are poised to lead this work forward – but in my experience – they are fighting fires, they are (again) over-stretched and under-appreciated, they are under-resourced but our expectations remain sky high.

Housing Authorities and Housing Associations

Housing Associations now manage a huge part of the rental housing sector. The market is now generally divided between privately owned homes, privately rented, or housing association stock. Government data tells us that 3.9 million households in England lived in social housing between 2016 and 2018 (17%).

Harriet Grant, writing in The Guardian in January 2020[61] focused on the way that housing associations do spot the signs and symptoms of exploitation at the earliest stages – particularly in cases of 'cuckooing'.

What I find particularly helpful about this article is the fact that rather than focusing on an area that would typically draw attention in this context – like a high unemployment area in the North East, South Yorkshire or elsewhere, Grant looks to York.

I know York very well. I grew up there, was educated there, moved away as a teenager, came back to University there, and then joined the police there. My first role in a uniform was in the City Centre and on the streets of the outlying areas that don't quite chime with the image of this medieval tourist attraction. Place likes Tanghall, Clifton and Chappelfields where there are plenty of disadvantaged children and young people that would be targeted by County Lines dealers.

As Grant underlines – York is an area that is prime for County Lines activity. It has excellent public transport links East to West, North to South – mainline trains can get you to London, Liverpool, Edinburgh, Birmingham – pretty much anywhere you like. If you're going into York – you just need somewhere to get your head down.

---

[61] https://www.theguardian.com/global-development/2020/jan/27/its-incredible-what-they-see-housing-associations-take-on-county-lines

Cuckooing a housing association premises should trigger awareness quite quickly. The same is true with the phenomenon of 'pop up brothels' – something that can be facilitated through the use of online apps to advertise temporary services. Drug dealing, drug availability and sex for sale can be setup quickly and temporarily, then closed down quickly. The movement is nimble and very much 'one step ahead'. When a flat or house is taken over for a substantial period though, the impact on the immediate surrounding neighbourhood is profoundly negative.

Housing associations know their housing stock – they have a good level of awareness of their residents (including their vulnerability) – and they have reason to go in and out of the addresses for essential repairs and maintenance. Knowing what to look for or being alert to the correct things is a massive advantage to the multiagency approach.

Increasingly law enforcement agencies are working hand in hand with Housing Associations, and through civil mechanisms (as opposed to the criminal courts) to evict and close down such addresses where they are misused. Disrupting these locations is just one part of the overall picture – but it is an important part. The people who are targeted through the phenomenon of cuckooing (taking over an address) are acutely vulnerable – borderline incapable of independent living – and may be suffering with a range of physical and mental health or cognitive disorder problems. They very rarely have the strength, the knowledge or ability to stand up for themselves to

312

seek help. They are incredibly scared – frightened – intimidated and they become another part of the chain of exploited human beings.

The first priority is always human life. Safeguarding always comes before any other consideration. Evicting such criminal exploiters and offenders from the housing stock that typically serves the most disadvantaged, the weakest and the most deprived is an essential priority. I've worked with Housing Associations very successfully and I have found them determined to protect their tenants, contribute to promoting harmonious living environments and very ready to play their part.

The powers that they have as the provider of the accommodation – to fine occupants in certain circumstances, and to initiate eviction if absolutely necessary – is very important. In my experience they attend local problem solving groups and stay on the front foot looking to identify and solve problems early and in a meaningful way.

For police officers swearing out, and executing Misuse of Drugs Act warrants, Housing Association contact is an absolute necessity – they will know the fine details of a property (What type of front door? What type of locks? How many children? Will there be animals? What is the layout of the property? Are there any vulnerable neighbours?) – they may even have keys that allow access so that damage and distress can be minimised for occupants and the surrounding area.

There is no question at all that Housing Associations play a critical role in assembling a live picture of information and intelligence – as well as taking a hugely pivotal part in the planning and execution stage. I have taken numerous housing officers to drugs warrants, and likewise, I have gone with housing officers to situations that they have flagged and reported from their own expertise and observations.

Education (Schools, Colleges, APUs)

Education – our network of schools – is actually a huge filter through which we pass all of our children and young people. A child who is attending school regularly, is seen by a professional who will evaluate them on the basis of their state of mind, their behaviour, their appearance, what they are talking about, how they are developing in comparison to their peers – even down to the basics of their weight, the state of their general health, do they look tired and so on.

Most schools now have meaningful organisational provision for pastoral care. Some schools opt for vertical structures that place people in houses and not by their peer group age. Some opt for horizontal arrangements by year group – with traditional year group heads and form systems that are led by more junior staff tasked with paying attention to welfare, behaviour and other needs.

Regular meetings are conducted to evaluate behavioural and academic performance – highlighting particularly the cases that cause significant concern. They also identify when such concerns exist in a sibling group or individually in contrast to the rest of the family.

The children become known intimately – changes are monitored and observed. Support measures and the need for intervention is often recognised at school first.

As agencies have shrunk through diminishing funding streams, it is education, more than any other service, that has been left with the responsibility for safeguarding. Everyone will repeat the mantra that the safeguarding of children is everyone's responsibility – but more often than not – it is the school that will carry that weight.

Fewer police officers and police community support officers are present in schools on a regular basis. Social Care thresholds are far higher. The availability of child and adolescent mental health services is greatly reduced. There are fewer young peoples' workers and there is a much greater dependency on voluntary sector staff, good will, and untrained contribution.

The consequence is very much that people who have a passion for teaching – for example English Literature, or Maths, or Physics – now also have to be trained safeguarding subject leaders too.

When a child is identified in a school setting and the signs and symptoms of abuse or neglect are spotted – it is much more likely today that a relevant referral to an appropriate multiagency body (such as the local Multi-Agency Service Hub or MASH, or via the LSCB) will be made *BUT* will that referral be processed without a backlog? Will it be dealt with in a timely way? Will it actually manage to attract attention above the other weight of concerns that have been raised about so many other children and young people?

I do not think that I am blowing any whistles by saying that shocking levels of neglect and mistreatment are not being engaged with on a reassuring level. I believe that a number of people from a variety of agencies struggle with stress, anxiety and sleeplessness because they know about this. Nobody is keeping this a secret from the government and it's not a concealed problem.

Schools are getting better at keeping decision making logs, at constructively and objectively risk assessing cases on an independent basis, and providing rationale around the actions that they take. For the last year I have worked in four schools – all of whom have found it difficult to 'stay in the loop' with law enforcement agencies or secure the full and undivided attention of professionals in key adjacent services.

What are the major tell-tale signs that a school will spot in a child falling into County Lines?

- Not coming into school and a deteriorating attendance record.
- Evidence of drug use, intoxication, or hangovers

- Expensive clothing, mobile phones and technology that are unexplained and out of character with their financial background
- Arriving and leaving with strangers or going AWOL on a frequent basis
- Increasingly levels of confrontational behaviours, violence and aggression
- Premature and overt sexualised behaviours
- Carrying knives, weapons or drugs
- Unexplained injuries
- Exhaustion and sleeping in class

Schools can and do join these dots very readily – and where they have been joined – a unified approach ought to be taken. Agencies ought to work on a consistent basis, to intervene together, both at a family level and on a personal level too.

A general lack of consistency and cooperation is a source of anxiety. Additionally – there is no button to push when a school says *"I reasonably believe that this child is being subjected to criminal coercive behaviour, County Lines, or child sexual exploitation"*. I do not doubt that schools would appreciate a clear and objective scoring matrix, and a trigger to alert and unify a collective multiagency approach focused on the specific issue of County Lines and/or criminal exploitation.

In truth – and I think as we have established – the teams who would be tasked to take the most intrusive response to find out what is happening at home are largely understaffed, over tasked, and their team generally carrying volumes of work that are over and above what could be reasonably seen as optimal or effective.

Of course, services such as 'MyConcern' have improved the process of registering and raising an alert across multiple parties – ensure that school safeguarding leads are notified promptly where a risk has been identified. All schools have safeguarding policies and dedicated safeguarding professionals to ensure that they are fulfilling their duty of care responsibilities. Getting a concern logged definitely helps the process – and the person who identified the concern will feel much better for ensuring that it is written down carefully – but if the back end of the process (i.e. the response that is received from police, social care, and/or others) is not immediate, is not reliable, appears inconsistent on any level, and doesn't communicate in both directions effectively – it generally doesn't invigorate confidence.

It is critically important to listen to the information being provided by teachers and school staff. There is a substantial disconnect between the information held by schools, their safeguarding leads, versus what is known even on a Neighbourhood Policing basis – and this should not be the case. It simply cannot be the case if we genuinely expect to dismantle the criminal exploitation of children, and quite specifically, the County Lines machinery.

Moving into a new rural area as a Neighbourhood Sergeant, I was confronted with a terrible offence in a small local town. A teenaged boy had been stabbed – in broad daylight – by another, slightly younger male.

I'm not going to identify the case specifically – I don't think it will assist the illustration or the community or the victim.

The offender was arrested very quickly – nearby the scene. There was little doubt about who was responsible and indeed he was later convicted of a Grievous Bodily Harm offence.

Starting to build a Community Impact Assessment around the event, I went to the school they had both attended. I wanted to know who the victim was, who the offender was – who their friends were – could we expect reprisals? How would this event be perceived? What was the general feeling about what motivated this event, specifically now and in this area?

I was told that the school were obviously shocked by the violence, but they *were not surprised* by the fact that this young man had done this.

"If anyone was going to stab someone – the indications were clear that it was him".

The school had been actively managing risk around this young man for a number of months – more than a year. He was identified as a significant risk to his peers. He was seen to be violent and unpredictable – even highly confrontational towards staff – and a policy of always having two staff in a room with him was in place. The boy was educated almost in isolation and specialist arrangements had to be made to find the space to do this. A huge operation had been organised and put in place to successfully mitigate risk posed to the community during school hours. This activity was both impressive and thorough – but the school was operating in a vacuum of support. Local police had no knowledge of it (even though school was sharing information in compliance with local arrangements). In comparison, the police evaluation of the risk around this young man was that he was broadly *unknown*. Very little of what had been communicated through the MASH, and via Social Care, and other concerned parties, was disseminated to a position where local resources could familiarise themselves with his circumstances.

This is a stark – but very real – and very genuine warning to be heeded. I would be genuinely surprised if such a story does not sound familiar to other regions too. Our schools must be listened to and we must have the ability to respond in a very quick and agile way when the signs and symptoms of risk appear. This incident occurred within two weeks of the local drug market being critically destabilised by the imprisonment of the recognised local supplier. None of the relevant agencies were sufficiently equipped, intelligence aware or ready to respond effectively to prevent this incident – in fact the offender clearly wasn't on the police radar at all, and hindsight isn't kind.

When budgets shrink, agencies retract – *away from each other* – when the gaps appear they present dangers of serious harm. I think we are all guilty of not listening or paying enough attention to our schools.

Charities and Voluntary Sector Groups

Reliance on the charitable and voluntary sector has increased significantly over the austerity period. Services such as the police (who employ a cohort of 'Police Service Volunteers' in Cambridgeshire and promote the concept of 'Active Citizenship') have come to rely more on the generosity of time given by members of the public to help manage and deliver an array of services.

Groups such as Romsey Mill – a Christian charity based in Cambridge – have become far more central and essential when it comes to diversionary activities with young people, the provision of young peoples' workers and helping schools and communities cope with the early signs of problematic behaviours. Such services are funded charitably and are made available free at the point of delivery where possible or with a mind towards cost effective delivery.

Schools, colleges, community initiatives and other essential services are more likely to be pushed to find innovative, creative and 'modern' ways to raise funds to support what they deliver. This can often include the crowdfunding activities available online, and match funding between agencies and donors that share similar or mutually beneficial objectives.

Dependable sources of income are more likely to be subject to budget reductions or 'rationalisations' – particularly streams that come directly from central government – but when central government funding to local authorities is reduced this is always likely to be passed along to local provision (schools, hospitals, libraries, day care centres, parent support groups, youth clubs and so on) in due course.

Many of the funds cuts by central government are being pushed in the direction of local officials to administer now – and central government is more likely to press someone such as a locally elected PCC to mitigate the cost by raising local council tax rates. As a political act this distances Westminster from any harm or risk, and places a burden of expectation on someone else – plus the tax payer is usually more concerned about the council tax rising, as opposed to the reduction in central government funding.

Council tax rises will never match or replace the funding cuts made by central government – they can only act to soften or mitigate the blow. As such any additional funds raised are usually targeted towards a specific priority or concern. Some members of the public are left confused then, when their local council tax goes up, but they see evidence of service provision in decline. Additionally, such policy making increases inequality – rich areas with high band residents have more ability to raise funds, are more insulated and they are less likely to be affected by social harms. Areas that really need help are already very much pushed to the brink and have shallow pockets.

Aside from putting up the council tax, or trying to fundraise for specific campaigns (which can be incredibly lucrative if something goes viral, but very ineffective if it gets ignored or fails to gain any support) – the alternative is to cut costs. This is why we look to the voluntary sector and encourage people to give of their time freely.

It is far easier to recruit volunteers in times of financial prosperity – but when businesses, services, and jobs are at risk, personal circumstances are likely to prioritise a focus on other things. In 2018 – despite the falling number of cops across the country, Surrey Police also experienced a 60% drop in Special Constabulary volunteers across a five year period (2013 – 2019). So getting people to volunteer may be a solution – *but it's not an easy solution*.

There is no question that the need for these teams, these groups, and these individual volunteers has been present and growing since the financial catastrophe of 2008 – but with more groups and causes relying on the same amount and shrinking amounts of funding and disposable income – it is a very difficult and competitive market to be in.

Immediate statistics from the Trussell Trust – the UK's largest food bank operator – showed that 1.9 million three day emergency food supply packages were distributed in the year 2019 – 2020. Their activity between 1st April 2019 and 31st March 2020 showed an 18% increase on supplies in comparison to data from only the previous year. In the last five years the Trussell Trust foodbank network has increased by 74%.

Writing on their own website, Emma Revie, the Chief Executive at the Trussell Trust has written:

> "This year has been an extraordinarily difficult one, with many more people across the country facing destitution as a result of the coronavirus pandemic… This constant rise in food bank use, year after year, cannot continue. More and more people are struggling to eat because they simply cannot afford food – and when we look to the year ahead, it's likely even more people will be forced into destitution."

This is a pretty chilling warning from one of the country's foremost indicators of prosperity or decline. It also gives an indication towards how much reliance can be placed on 'free' contribution, voluntary efforts and fund raising to solve social problems. This is another sector that is stretched – to say the least.

In 2020 the UK has been wrestling with COVID19 – and the public health risk competes against the damage it has caused to the economy. The economy was officially declared to be in recession following two quarters of successive decline. A 20% drop in GDP is doing more than ringing the fiscal alarm bells. At the time of writing Britain has the worst performing economy in Europe[62] in response to the global pandemic, as well as rivalling Spain for highest recorded death toll[63]. In a perfect storm of factors, the financial uncertainty is compounded by the impending impact of a huge change in international relationships with our closest geographic partners due to the result of the Brexit situation and an impending 'no deal' exit from the EU.

Given all of the above – and within the context of our social climate – it is still essential that efforts to tackle the County Lines emergency are founded in volunteer support and community engagement. It could not be more difficult to rally this support then right now and at this particular time.

Families and individuals who have been directly affected by County Lines and Criminal Coercive Behaviours will always be inclined to offer support of course – but we know that poverty (and absolute poverty) will also drive people to extreme behaviours, which may include turning to crime. County Lines offers a lucrative opportunity for young people to make money and few other people are competing to capture their attention in the same way. Parents who are preoccupied with paying the rent, living in unsustainable debts, or who have to

---

62

https://www.newstatesman.com/politics/economy/2020/08/uk-suffers-worst-recession-any-g7-country
[63] https://www.ft.com/content/6b4c784e-c259-4ca4-9a82-648ffde71bf0

queue at the foodbank, are far less able to give undivided attention to the vulnerability of their kids (and they are sorely tempted to look the other way when some much needed money appears unexpectedly).

On one hand community engagement and voluntary effort – the voices of victims and the views of the communities – must play a very important role in this solution. However, on the other hand I also reference Emma Revie again – *over-reliance is unsustainable and will not be the solution*. In looking at what will solve the issue of County Lines it is important to look at *what won't solve the problem too*. Armies of volunteers – with the best will in the world – are not the way forward, particularly if they are not backed by expertise, coordination and resources.

At the outset of the financial crisis in 2008, then Prime Minister David Cameron said that it was his ambition to end the "something for nothing culture"[64]. Seeking to highlight that an over dependency on benefits was "bad for our country". It is difficult to see how a country becoming over reliant on voluntary contribution, unpaid hours, and people working two jobs (one to pay the bills, the other to tackle social issues that they feel are important) is going to work in the long term either. Mr Cameron's speech was of course angled towards reducing benefits for people out of work, and towards

64

https://www.telegraph.co.uk/news/uknews/1574927/Tories-attack-something-for-nothing-culture.html

making people work in some way when in receipt of support.

I feel that the former Prime Minister has a valid point – things cannot be sustained 'for free', it is 'bad for the country' to mount an over reliance on charity, and finally when you are tackling a crisis issue (whether that is economic or social) it has to be costed and we must confront the need to fund it reliably, correctly and for the long term.

Chapter Eight: Police, Law Enforcement & Probation

Local Police Constabularies

In policing terms, austerity birthed a ubiquitous turn of phrase with forces and Constabularies up and down the country: 'threat, risk and harm'. Everything – *every decision that was made* – was passed through the filter of 'threat, risk and harm'. What this phrase meant was broadly misunderstood by many, but irrespective it was used as a catch all justification for all manner of decisions.

In actuality, the book definition of this term – as referenced by the College of Policing was as follows:

Threat was what the police were judged to have to deal with immediately and without exception.

Risk was what the police could manage and mitigate at a lower level – reducing the likelihood of the worst outcome and being willing to tolerate that reduced possibility of a negative outcome.

Harm was the category of events that the police could no longer afford to cover – what was left over when all the money was spent and there were no more officers to send. Prior to austerity the idea that the police service would knowingly acknowledge, allow and tolerate harm *was an absolutely unacceptable concept*.

As a consequence of austerity the overall number of police officers has fallen significantly. I sit here as one of 20,000 plus former officers who are no longer serving.

To contextualise what twenty-thousand officers actually means – *this is roughly 14 Cambridgeshire Constabularies worth of police officers*. Cambs is not the smallest police force in the country – Warwickshire is nearly half the size. In fact you can list thirteen smaller forces than Cambs. A loss of twenty thousand officers can account for the seventeen smallest forces in the country (including Cambs) *combined*.

These are fact that are difficult to absorb – but particularly so against a promise in 2012 from Prime Minister David Cameron that there would be 'no front line cuts'.

In an act that can be generously described as political gaslighting David Cameron claimed in Prime Ministers Questions (22nd February 2012):

> *"If you look at the figures from Her Majesty's Inspectorate of Constabulary, they believe there will be more police in visible policing roles this March than there were a year ago"*

This claim was swooped upon by the media, and Channel 4 News (Emma Thelwell)[65] for example, was quick to respond:

> *"It was misleading of Mr Cameron to say the HMIC expects more bobbies to be out on the beat by March. The HMIC does not expect this; last Summer it predicted a drop in numbers – and Home Office figures issued just two months later proved the HMIC's forecast to be ridiculously over-optimistic…"*

There is a robust argument to be made that the most severely hit aspect of police service provision – on a local constabulary level – is neighbourhood policing. Generally speaking this is the 'bobbies on the beat' department (a phrase that I personally don't like – but it is an enduring phrase).

To focus the mind on what the police do – 'response policing' is about what is happening right now, 'investigations' are made into what has happened, 'neighbourhood policing' is about what is going to happen and what we can prevent from happening.

Neighbourhood policing is particularly focused on harm reduction and crime prevention. The Peelian Principles[66] are the manifesto of policing – the stone tablets, the

---

[65] https://www.channel4.com/news/factcheck/factcheck-cameron-caught-out-on-frontline-police-cuts
[66] https://en.wikipedia.org/wiki/Peelian_principles

constitution. Sir Robert Peel set out what a local constabulary must strive towards in nine clear statements. The ninth is very clear – that the police must be held *"To recognize always that the test of police efficiency is the absence of crime and disorder, not the visible evidence of police action in dealing with them"*.

Despite this – over the last ten years – neighbourhood policing has shrunk[67]. Robert Merrick, writing for the Independent in August 2018 cited a loss of 7,000 neighbourhood police officers in a three year period. Merrick quotes Lord Stevens, a former Commissioner, who described the situation as "incredibly alarming".

Neighbourhood policing is about building multiagency relationships that tackle long term problems – 'designing out' crime by utilising many resources and skills across the full picture of service provision. Neighbourhood policing creates an intimate knowledge and relationship within communities – and promotes another of the key Peelian concepts:

> *"To maintain at all times a relationship with the public that gives reality to the historic tradition that the police are the public and the public are the police, the police being only members of the public who are paid to give full time attention to duties which are incumbent on every citizen in the interests of community welfare and existence."*

---

[67] Independent article August 2018

This is known as 'policing by consent' – and marks our brand of policing out distinctly versus other brands of 'law enforcement'. It is arguably the finest tradition of policing the United Kingdom.

Neighbourhood policing is not the 'sexy' branch of kicking in doors and chasing criminals down streets. It is the moderate environment of long term planning, reassurance, and creating dialogue. None of these qualities make for particularly compelling viewing, headline writing or twenty-four hour rolling news. In many ways they are incompatible with what the media want to see – and the absence of crime – as a clear objective, rather than 'locking people up' is not a very saleable product to the bystander.

Fully resourced Neighbourhood Policing Teams (NPTs) are a nightmare for County Lines dealers. They get to know children who are at risk on an intimate basis. They know every secluded area. They patrol the vulnerable people who are living alone. An effective Neighbourhood officer who works in a given area for a sustained period of time will know a new young person in a village or even a small town – and the qualities and behaviour of that individual will stand out a mile.

Gathering and feeding intelligence into the overall system is a daily and routine duty. They embrace and reassure all the other services in the task of dismantling County Lines. They cement the overall project together.

The more diluted our NPT resources become and the more they are diverted into response cover and to supplementing other policing disciplines – the more opportunity there is for a runner or a sitter to infiltrate and exploit a local community and to stay there untouched.

Moving in and out of schools on a regular basis I would give a message to convey to parents: *the police are not in school because there has been trouble, the police are in school because we work together closely and we have no complacency about protecting the children*.

Going back into schools as a Neighbourhood Sergeant in 2014 I was met by senior school leaders who said that police presence was becoming increasingly uncommon (even then). School communities – student bodies – felt that police presence was conspicuous when it arrived and that something must have gone wrong badly because we were there. Sadly – and despite any efforts I made to the contrary – the in-school presence that I wanted to provide actually declined from 2014, although I personally tried my best to buck that trend.

Increasingly Neighbourhood officers are doing more work managing Organised Crime Group activity in the form of investigation ownership, and prosecution responsibilities. The College of Policing[68] offers guidance

---

[68] https://www.college.police.uk/What-we-do/Standards/Guidelines/Neighbourhood-

and definitions of what neighbourhood policing should be – *and this isn't it.*

Enforcement activity conducted at a local level is less likely to be about a long term intelligence led investigation as such work is usually escalated to ROCU[69]s or (if it is of the utmost significance) to the National Crime Agency. A local police force might lead on the disruption of a string of cannabis factories (for example), or a misuse of drugs act warrant that unveils a reasonable value of cash and drugs – *but it is increasingly unlikely that this will be part of a tenacious on going, proactive investigation into a particular criminal entity.*

The National Crime Agency and ROCUs

The National Crime Agency was formed in 2013 to replace the Serious Organised Crime Agency, and it also 'absorbed' and took responsibility for CEOP – the Child Exploitation and Online Protection Centre. Comparisons are often drawn to the Federal Bureau of Investigations (FBI) in the United States – but the comparison is generally an over simplified one because there are such remarkable structural differences between the UK and the United States, and issues of jurisdiction that don't apply in *quite* the same way.

Policing/Pages/definition-of-neighbourhood-policing.aspx

[69] Regional Organised Crime Units

Nevertheless the NCA is a strategic group that works throughout the UK and reports directly to the Home Secretary. The Director-General is broadly a more powerful individual than the local Chief Constable of Police, and can actually require local resources to support their mandate when necessary.

The NCA has a huge interest in disrupting County Lines – which by their very nature move between police force areas and need a coordination of intelligence and disruption tactics to achieve any measure of successful enforcement.

The NCA is massively involved in tackling the sale, distribution and use of illegal firearms, human trafficking and Modern Day Slavery. The County Lines business model cuts across all of these issues. The NCA operates and controls a 'most wanted' list and a number of names and faces appear there who are directly involved in the illegal importation of cocaine and heroin – it gives you an idea of the level that we are speaking about.

One individual is listed highly due to his alleged involvement in a conspiracy to import 255 kilos of cocaine. We have talked about the highly lucrative and profitable market in cocaine supply. A kilo of cocaine in Columbia is bought for around £350. Sources report that a kilo of cocaine at street values in London can be £40,000 (so more than 100 times the original price) and suggestions are that values have *risen* as a consequence of the COVID-19 lockdown. The importation of 255 kilos of coke equates to more than a ten million pound sterling (£10m+) haul of drugs.

This is the level that the NCA sit at.

Another wanted person is alleged to have murdered a man in South Shields in May 2006. He is also wanted for offences of supplying controlled drugs – drawing the dotted line again, between the supply of drugs and extreme levels of violence.

Other wanted individuals face allegations of international criminal enterprise. In one case between the UK and the Netherlands where coordinated strikes in Britain and mainland Europe are believed to have disrupted a location used by cartels to negotiate, finance and traffick huge quantities of illegal substances. *It is important to understand that neither heroin nor cocaine are produced in the UK and disruption of these markets, and the value of both drugs in our country, are very much dependent on what gets through our borders.*

The NCA works with international enforcement agencies, sharing information securely across international borders to help promote global security.

ROCUs are *Regional* Organised Crime Units. An example of this would be ERSOU – the Eastern Region Serious Organised Crime Unit. This Unit is a collaboration of seven police forces in the Eastern Region – Bedfordshire Police are listed as the lead Constabulary.

A ROCU has two main priorities – regional organised crime and counter terrorism. With regard to regional organised crime County Lines is a sub-strand of this work – as is CSE (Child Sexual Exploitation), Modern Day Slavery, and gun crime. There are overlaps between all of these areas under the umbrella of serious and organised crime, and a County Lines operation is likely to be involved in economic crime, serious violence, modern day slavery and CSE.

There are ten ROCUs that operate across England and Wales – they provide specialist capability in investigating and disrupting such activity, undertaking a wide variety of tactics – which includes covert options. ERSOU – for example – also has an economic crime team to focus on the financial gains made by criminals. The Proceeds of Crime Act offers very substantial powers to seize cash and assets, and to keep them when a lawful source of income cannot be reasonably shown.

As with the National Crime Agency, a ROCU operates across broader geographical areas – and while the scope and focus on the work is not likely to be international, many regions have centres of import and export and through which people and contraband travel – such as Stansted Airport, or the port of Felixstowe. A ROCU will collect information, disseminate it as intelligence, and move seamlessly across county boundaries, initiating appropriate measures to identify, intercept, and convict.

There is a good deal of secrecy and confidentiality about the work undertaken by both the ROCUs and the NCA –

and the reason for this is quite obvious. The integrity of the work being done is of the highest value – and any breach of trust or intelligence (either by professional mishandling or through corrupt inducement) can cost lives and is worth substantial sums of money. Irrespective, the information collected and gathered by local Neighbourhood Policing Teams, and offered by the providers of local services is absolutely invaluable to these heavy-weight enforcement agencies who depend upon local insight to fill gaps and omissions that can critically sway a regional investigation.

It is uncommon that local service providers, *even local police or emergency services*, will find themselves working along-side the NCA or indeed their immediate ROCU on a local basis regularly – but it's important to acknowledge the role they play and the impact of their work on County Lines at the very top end of the picture.

The National Probation Service

I don't think there is a more misunderstood, under appreciated or overlooked branch of public service provision in the United Kingdom today than the National Probation Service. What they do is unglamorous, it is unassuming, and like being the goalkeeper on a football team, you only tend to hear about them when something has gone wrong (and let's be pragmatic – things do go wrong in every public service). If a mistake gets made at the National Probation Service – because they manage high risk category offenders – that stuff tends to be a big deal. As most people don't come into direct contact with the National Probation Service they probably don't see the work that goes on. *The work that goes on is huge*, it is complex, and it is happening every single day.

The role and responsibility of the Probation Service is managing (high risk) offenders in the community. Twenty-one privatised Community Rehabilitation Companies (CRCs) manage low and medium risk offenders across the country as a whole – this is a structure that has proven to be expensive and has been criticised for under performance. A reform package is currently in hand, as we will consider shortly. The National Probation Service – as it stands - is focused on the highest end of the scale.

The definitions about high, medium and low risk depend (broadly) on two key factors – the likelihood of a relapse in offending behaviour, and the scale of harm that is likely to result as a consequence of such.

My dealings with the Probation Service have included criminal court cases – where Probation prepare pre-sentence reports when people are found guilty of crimes. Additionally, when working as part of groups of professionals protecting children, and brought together to trace high risk missing persons, probation sometimes have a part to play in the sharing of key information. This might be to do with worrying individuals linked to the child, or who reside in the immediate area in which a child has gone missing.

Probation workers support offenders in the community to help them abide by the agreed terms of their release

– and when offenders on license breach their terms it is the Probation Service that notify the court with sufficient evidence and organise the process of recalling them to prison.

The National Probation Service also communicate with victims of serious sexual offences and violence offences where the offender has been imprisoned for 12 months or more. This is to prioritise the welfare and wellbeing of the victim.

As the National Probation Service website says for itself:

> **"Our priority is to protect the public by the effective rehabilitation of high risk offenders, by tackling the causes of offending and enabling offenders to turn their lives around."**

Where does this fit into the conversation on County Lines you ask?

It helps if you have some understanding of both MAPPA (Multi-Agency Public Protection Agreement) and ViSOR (Violent and Sex Offenders Register). These are multiagency tools used to facilitate the management of the most dangerous people in society. Commonly they are divided between violent offenders and sex offenders. We are talking about the people who, if left to their own devices, would harm the people around them in their immediate community, in their families, their partners and even complete strangers – physically, sexually or otherwise (but predominantly the threat is physical or sexual).

People who are listed on ViSOR (a database of offenders) are categorised by the severity of their crimes and potential harm, plus the likelihood of them offending/reoffending.

The categories are as follows:
- RVOs (violent offenders)
- RTOs (terrorists)
- Cat 1 (MAPPA & registered sex offender or RSOs – with required notification terms under the Sexual Offences Act 2003)
- Cat 2 (MAPPA offenders meeting certain standards as a consequence of sentence received, generally more than 12 months custodial and this can include mental health act cases[70])
- Cat 3 (MAPPA and other dangerous people posing risk to the public who are managed on a continual basis – this might include offences that *do not* appear under schedule 15 Criminal Justice Act 2003.)
- PDPs (potentially dangerous people who may or may not otherwise fall under MAPPA)

PDPs are generally not defined in law – but they are people that don't qualify under the three main MAPPA

---

[70]

https://www.legislation.gov.uk/ukpga/2003/44/schedule/15

categories. The general examples furnished include people charged multiple times, but not convicted, in specific circumstances that includes domestic abuse, terrorism, causing sexual harm to children, particularly dangerous mental health patients, and people convicted abroad but not under UK law. We are not talking about people who cause financial or property harm, we are talking about physical and sexual risk – which can of course include psychiatric harm.

It is generally police (including Special Branch and Counter Terrorism resources), the probation service and the prison service that do the heavy lifting around making this essential work happen. Such a person/suspect is either not yet in prison – but behaving in such a way that gives rise to reasonable grounds to list them, or they are being managed in prison and they may be subject to assessment prior to release, or they are post-conviction and they are being re-integrated into society.

Anyone listed under the terms of PDP are subject to continual review based on live intelligence and behavioural reports. This is to respect the human rights of the subject and to ensure that the process is fair, robust and subject to scrutinised accountability (preventing abuse of the system – or getting the system clogged up with unnecessary cases).

Please understand that managing MAPPA, ViSOR, and people with serious offending tendencies in the community and on license is an exhausting and relentless career choice. It exposes your work force to some of the most graphic and at times traumatic forms of contact and information that you might commonly imagine. *This is the type of work that prevents paedophiles from hanging around play parks but likewise could prohibit a drug dealer from targeting juveniles with criminal seduction.*

People who run organised criminal gangs – *or who depend upon such activity to fund their lavish lifestyles* - do not tend to put up their hands when caught. They rarely offer full and frank confessions, or offer early guilty pleas (unless the evidence against them is *completely* overwhelming). They will do everything they can to stay out of prison. I have sat in interviews with such people and gone through the motions of hearing them offer the most ridiculous and implausible stories, or simply 'no comment' (as is their right to) all the way through pertinent and reasonable questions that would help exonerate an innocent person with a reasonable opportunity.

> *"I kept the money (£7,000) behind the microwave because I was going to buy a car for my wife as a surprise birthday present"*

[By the way that is a genuine response I was offered when that sum was discovered as part of a Misuse of Drugs Act warrant some years ago at an address in Cambridge.]

When they are arrested – and even after being sent to prison – they will commonly look for a way to comply

344

with the terms of their sentence, to appear to cooperate or rehabilitate, but at the same time they don't just drop everything they have built and walk away (very few do). Many offenders will try to continue to run their operation, steer and guide their OCG, and will try to recover from any losses or seizures made by the authorities.

Probation Officers are usually the eyes and ears that monitor what is going on. Their ability to monitor with enough detail and focus is of paramount importance. As with every service, vulnerability arises when they are spread too thinly and – like social workers – if the case load becomes overwhelming the tell-tale details can be missed or overlooked. It places the offender at a huge advantage.

There are incredible examples, which are a massive credit to the National Probation Service, where their tireless efforts have successfully extracted someone from a criminal lifestyle and rehabilitated them. This is the number one goal for the service and they never stop trying to succeed in this way.

We can therefore clearly recognise how the contribution of the National Probation Service is more than influential as a partner in solving the County Lines threat. Despite this they are significantly compromised in their ability to contribute. The Financial Times ran a significant article in January 2020[71] and it pulled no punches:

> "Three out of five staff in the National Probation Service are overworked leaving it unable to fulfil its role of monitoring serious offenders, government inspectors have warned"

Nor did the FT have any hesitation in attributing why – blaming reforms introduced by government and specifically cabinet minister Chris Grayling MP in 2015.

Identifying that the National Probation Service monitors and manages 106,000 high risk offenders in England and Wales, the article (written by Robert Wright) also underlined that 60% of staff held caseloads beyond their theoretical maximum, and that a crisis in recruitment meant that the service was running with more than 15% of roles vacant at the time the article was published[72].

The NPS has been struck so badly by austerity that they have an immediate and urgent problem with building maintenance – and some of the buildings used by the service were identified as being infested with rats.

A twenty-four point plan for recommended improvements to the National Probation Service was published as a consequence - the full report that the

---

[71] https://www.ft.com/content/1f1c5c48-33d8-11ea-9703-eea0cae3f0de;

[72] Citing 653 vacancies in an organisation of 3,926 posts.

Financial Times article is based upon is in the public domain – which includes a list of all the recommendations[73].

It is shocking that when writing about some of the most incredible professionals in public service provision, and pointedly how to address the issues of County Lines, we have to make reference to the fact that they are having to work in conditions that are not fit for habitation. The report in detail reads:

> "We found a catalogue of problems, including faulty plumbing, broken lifts, vermin infestations... and some older premises that are unfit for purpose in a modern probation service."

This sounds like I might be describing a third world country, or a demilitarised or post war environment. To see this in Britain today is very difficult to understand or condone. I don't lay this at the door of the senior figures in the Probation Service – I lay it down as part of the crumbling infrastructure of austerity inflicted Britain. We have to ask ourselves how we can reasonably expect such services to defeat the determined efforts of an organised, highly effective and extremely profitable criminal network?

---

[73]

https://www.justiceinspectorates.gov.uk/hmiprobation/wp-content/uploads/sites/5/2020/01/NPS-central-functions-inspection-report-1.pdf

If we want to close down County Lines – and of course we do – we need a Probation Service running on all cylinders, fully staffed, and able to focus efforts on the people who are targeting children with physical harm, drug addiction, debt slavery and worse. People at the top end of the drug crime pyramid are the very high risk individuals who coordinate human trafficking, child sexual exploitation and make profits off the backs of inflicting harm and trauma on a daily basis. The intelligence function, the supportive role in managing and scrutinising such individuals is clearly with the Probation Service alongside other agencies that the general public are more familiar with.

The National Probation Service is, organisationally, in a position of flux – reverting back from the NPS/CRC structure – with a clear desire for the National Probation Service to regain management of offenders at all points of the risk spectrum.

An action plan to address the twenty-four point requirement was submitted in March 2020[74] - but perhaps somewhat startlingly point 22 (which addresses the physical conditions in which Probation Officers and staff have been/are working) was only *partly agreed* however:

74

https://assets.publishing.service.gov.uk/government/uploads/system/uploads/attachment_data/file/871302/Action_Plan_PDF.pdf

"This recommendation is partly agreed as whilst the below indicates an intention (and a degree of resource) to start to address the question of long-term under-investment, the full achievement of this will require the security of a long-term funding/resource solution (beyond the lifetime of the Probation Programme) which cannot be guaranteed at this point."

I think we can paraphrase that statement by saying "We don't really have the money and nobody is stepping up to pay the bill". I cannot say what the estimated cost of refurbishing and restructuring the National Probation Service is (in some ways I dread to think) – but the BBC estimated that reversal of the Grayling reforms would cost in the region of half a billion pounds[75]. No part of that article – published in May 2019, and predating the twenty-four point Inspectorate recommendations, and the subsequent action plan – actually suggests that part of that cost projection included the physical resources, computers, premises and infrastructure issues that are clearly compromising the effective role of the National Probation Service.

If you had a figure in mind for the overhaul of seven regional areas of provision across England and Wales – adding something like £500 million to that figure could be a sensible idea.

---

[75] https://www.bbc.co.uk/news/uk-48288433

Chapter Nine: Local & Central Government

Local Government & Problem Solving Groups

Local government is generally divided into three tiers:
- County Council
- District and City Councils (also borough councils fit here)
- Parish Councils

I include Parish Council where many would not (Parish Councillors are volunteers) because where they are well run and tightly organised, Parish Councils can make an incredible difference to a local area and a local community.

It is County that controls the commissioning and the provision of essential services like education, public safety and social care. Local Children's Safeguarding Boards operate at the County level and steer the strategic approach to the overall question of protection and the reduction of harm.

It is District that administrates the provision of housing and other more localised services.

Both County and District have an active role to play in helping to create environments which are not susceptible to crime – and this is also very true of dealing with County Lines.

The LSCB format (Local Safeguarding Childen's Board) is repeated County by County to provide oversight, expertise and to bring key agencies together for this purpose in a coordinated way. As previously discussed these agencies include police, health services, the probation service, social services and so on. The LSCB can also accommodate other groups and individuals who offer special interest, expertise and knowledge.

Each LSCB has to draw up plans that are specific to their region – but their remit is much broader than the issue of County Lines, and County Lines and Child Criminal Exploitation (including Child Sexual Exploitation) are topics that also sit alongside the protection of children in schools and colleges, sexual abuse of children within the family unit, honour based violence, missing children, neglect and more.

Each LSCB will provide a gateway to information and training for professionals and for parents and a great deal of emphasis is placed on information sharing between key partners to promote child protection.

For anyone looking to establish knowledge of specific resources aimed at advancing the welfare of children, or reducing harm to young people, they would do well to begin with their county LSCB who should have a clear oversight on what is present in that part of the country.

LSCBs, although branded in a similar way – *and clearly learning from national guidance* – are not carbon copies of each other. The first word in the title is 'Local' and the key aspect around that is an awareness of the local communities in a specific region, and the unique diversity of a given area. We know, for example that one particular region may have far fewer cases of honour based violence and female genital mutilation when compared to another. Other areas may have other significant child protection issues that incorporate the management of regional poverty and/or different forms of community cohesion challenges that impact in a negative way upon children. Likewise, the number of charities, local groups, the amount of expertise and engagement in every area is going to vary. The LSCB exists to help the region provide services in the interests of children overall that reflect the best use of available resources, helping to match such resources to identified and substantial needs.

Local Safeguarding Children's Boards are high end, strategic entities – they learn from and work through tactical service providers. They support others in the delivery of key provision. As with all public services at the time of writing, resources are strained and thresholds are high. There is an overall preoccupation with children and young people entrenched in the immediate issues of neglect or abuse – and as resources become more stretched is it more difficult to justify taking resources away from such cases to invest in cases of less immediate need with the aim of supporting long term prevention measures. As with policing services – where the prevention services provided through neighbourhood policing have been cut – it is this type of work on a strategic level that has suffered. It is also relevant and important to remind the reader that the LSCB is *not* purely focused on County Lines or even Child Criminal Exploitation – the remit is a vast landscape of issues that harm children and undermine their wellbeing on an emotional and physical and psychological level.

Local Problem Solving groups (or PSGs) generally operate at District Level and where matters are significant enough they are likely to report their work into Community Safety Partnerships – which tend to sit at the higher strategic or County level and bring a number of multiagency partners together.

A PSG, or the higher level CSP, both operate by invitation and are not open to the public. Both are likely to offer opportunities for members of the public to attend and witness proceedings – but both have to be careful about General Data Protection Regulations and the stringent control of information.

Such bodies will deal with a range of concerns – from a developing antisocial behaviour issue, to the dangerous use of vehicles or accident black spots, or crime (such a significant burglary pattern) – any of these matters might attract the involvement at either level depending on the gravity of the concern and the measure of community impact.

PSGs are a great place for a number of teams to provide each other with insight about a specific family subject to concern, a frequently missing child (for example) or other issues. Action plans will be drawn up and reviewed on a frequent basis – for example fortnightly, or monthly or quarterly – to assess whether problems are getting better or worse (and to respond accordingly).

Increasingly such groups are adopting an approach that incorporates the 'problem solving triangle' – this is the triangle that exists between the victim of the crime/problem, the offender or group of offenders (or cause), and the location where the offences are being committed.

By taking a logical and methodical approach to these three key areas, questions are asked that lead to certain hypothesis and conclusions on why that victim, why that location and why that offender in this situation?

Steps are then taken with regard to each giving consideration towards how the situation can be improved – how the location could become more resilient to crime, what could be done to disturb, disrupt, apprehend or deal with offenders, and of course what support and care could be implemented to help the victim.

A basic example of such work might include a (hypothetical) flare up of antisocial behaviour in a park in the middle of the town: the park is near residential and commercial premises. The offenders are generally young adults who appear to be taking over the park, drinking late at night and after dark, using controlled drugs, and subsequently leaving litter, graffiti and other evidence behind in the morning.

A simple problem solving triangle might help you to identify that the area is poorly lit. That the park is fairly secluded from view, and that it is usually empty by the time the incidents happen at 9pm... The offenders seem to be known local drug and alcohol dependent users who are largely reliant on local charities to house them temporarily or overnight in shelters. The victims are people in that local area who don't seem to have been 'targeted' – but they are complaining of lack of sleep, and business owners are left counting the costs of repairs. Local children don't like going into the park because broken bottles and needles have been found.

Running through such a basic and typical scenario you could see how identification of the group would be beneficial – so lighting and CCTV could be a good investment to reclaim the area. Lighting might also disrupt and disturb the offenders making it feel less secluded. Signage and civil Public Spaces Protection Orders (PSPOs) – that prohibit the drinking of alcohol or the playing of music for example – might be helpful. Police patrols could take names and stop and search individuals under the Misuse of Drugs Act where relevant. Liaison with the local housing/shelter charities could make provision of services dependent upon residents not going into or using drink/drugs in that area. Investment in the park – clearing it up, cutting back undergrowth, trees and bushes, and/or replacing old seating and so on could make the whole area feel much more cared for and a subject of focus. This is always less welcoming to criminal behaviours. The combination of different teams around the table can take away actions to implement immediate change and to achieve objectives within a specified time period. An overall plan holder should be designated from the lead agency that is generally going to monitor the progress that is being made.

Local PSG groups and CSPs pull together local funding and share budgets to achieve things identified collectively as a priority. The CSP is likely to identify and list a small number of key priorities relevant to a broad community – so for example an area where racial tension or segregation appears high, policies that promote community cohesion and integration would be encouraged. The PSG is the more 'hands on' and 'tactical' part – that operates at district level, takes action and feeds progress back into the higher and more strategic group.

These groups work well and I have had some really excellent experiences and observed successes at both levels. A key element to the PSG/CSP relationship is listening to the public, and feeding voices and concerns into the process so that action can be taken promptly and effectively on issues that matter.

PSGs particularly tend to steer away from the idea that we must hit every problem with a 'crack down' or a Criminal Justice based solution. Instead emphasis is placed on thinking around a problem and undermining causational factors in the longer term.

A well run, well organised PSG can achieve a great deal in terms of promoting the health and wellbeing of local residents and groups of people. Helping people to feel empowered and part of the process is critically important – and very often a PSG is an excellent way to do this.

PSGs are also very good at embracing the voluntary and charitable sector – helping to find and distribute funding for specific priorities and issues. They form a substantial communication network that helps to bridge gaps between services and service providers.

Highlighting extremely vulnerable families or young people to the local PSG can be an excellent way to open numerous doors toward diversionary activity and opportunities. Early help teams might step in with parenting support and education. Exhausted parents might receive opportunities for respite – particularly where one member of the family is disabled or suffers with permanent impairment which causes huge caring responsibilities and mounting levels of stress.

A real strength of the PSG format is the ability to look at things on a case by case basis (and not just thematically) – not take a broad brush approach – and to actually show the kind of intelligence and nuance that is required to unpick the relevant early life trauma or problem situation by steering and referring to the best and most experienced services available. Additionally they can apply broader measures to protect others from the lessons learned in that specific circumstance.

The weaknesses and problems associated with PSGs are usually in the availability of relevant services to attend however – because often persuading everyone to get round the table and invest the time is difficult when individual workloads are high (recall what we have said about the National Probation Service and Social Care specifically). For schools it can be difficult to free up senior leaders to go along for what might be a half day session and for some going without a specific problem to put on the table – and only to support the problems that others present – can be an unattractive prospect (particularly if they have more than enough problems of their own). There can also be issues with publishing the availability of meetings and sign posting people into the methods of getting issues onto the table for discussion. Someone has to work through and create the agenda, and there has to be a gravity scale/matrix that objectively decides what gains the time and focus of the group overall. This process needs to be transparent and consistent so that everyone is reassured by how fair it is, and pet projects aren't given predominance over more significant concerns.

Consequently PSGs can be a powerful tool used at a local level – and there can be some outstanding results – but they don't come without an investment of time, membership and quality leadership. Every PSG needs to be empowered with a source of funding too – and while such groups can engage in fundraising events – the nature of a dynamic problem solving environment is such that having to fundraise before you can effectively respond is a significant barrier to success. If people come to see the group as a 'talking shop' or simply an empathy circle, the membership will quickly fade. PSGs stand and fall by their outcomes and at the end of every year there should be a catalogue of issues that have been tackled, remedied and improved significantly. In the best case this portfolio will sell the group – in the worst case scenario an absence of progress and a mounting list of pending cases or forgotten about matters becomes its own indictment.

Being perfectly honest I have seen both variations – I've seen very successful groups doing fantastic things. Usually this is a reflection of a dynamic chairperson who holds people to account in a friendly and inclusive way, who lists very specific actions and expectations, and who is fearless about requiring updates. I've seen weaker groups that appear to waste time, have endless meetings, and circle back round on topics without really affecting any remedy at all. The worst types of groups try to take credit for things that members were doing anyway, or things that they weren't really involved in – or include members who take a sudden interest when they need to evidence things for PDRs, promotion processes or impending local elections.

The framework of the PSG and CSP concept is fundamentally sound – however – like all teams it depends on the work rate, commitments, talents and abilities on the roster. A good, strong leader and a collective passion for local improvement can lead to remarkable things. As far as County Lines is concerned, operating within a district that has a well empowered

Problem Solving Group is much harder, and is likely to be far less successful than compared to an area with a weak one, or where one hasn't been setup.

Central Government

I don't apologise for reiterating the effect of austerity on the problem of County Lines and child exploitation. I can only say that I have arrived at my position as a consequence of genuine consideration, professional experience and numerous conversations with trusted professional colleagues. I am not the member of any political party, and my commentary on the responsibility held at central government does not reflect an axe that I have to grind due to political colours or ambitions.

My personal views on politics to one side, it would seem that the vast majority of available data underlines that 'austerity' (a huge central government responsibility) has not been a particularly successful venture.

Notwithstanding the crisis around COVID19 (which has taken a huge impact on the economy recently) or Brexit (which appears, at the time of writing, to be poised for 'no deal' exit and consequent supply chain issues) – *austerity has not successfully reduced the burden of public debt.* Ten years later on we seem to have few tangible dividends to show for our collective sacrifices.

On the 21st August 2020 most news outlets were leading with the fact that British debt had risen above the £2 trillion threshold for the first time. Andreas Wittam Smith wrote in the Independent on 30th June 2018 that Austerity had *eliminated* the budget deficit (this is to say – we were operating a balanced or surplus budget so that repayments to overall national debt could be made in addition to servicing what had been structured) *"...but at what cost?"* read the headline.

The article, broadly speaking, then examined exactly what the costs have been in terms of public services – including increases in crime and violent crime types, fewer police, youth crime up, special educational needs provision decreased, homelessness up and a deepening of the housing crisis, a reduction in health spending and an increased dependency on charity and foodbank welfare. We have discussed and considered many of these problems and how they harm the communities most vulnerable and susceptible to organised crime.

Andreas Wittam Smith goes further and accuses George Osborne – the Chancellor (who invoked austerity originally along with Prime Minister David Cameron and coalition partner Deputy Prime Minister Nick Clegg) of taking political advantage of an opportunity to inflict ideological changes when other options existed.

What we do know now – with the benefit of hindsight of course – was that the fable of 'no front line cuts' was deeply misleading, and proved to be false in every regard. In fact, when the COVID-19 crisis hit us we were incredibly unprepared – with a panic process for PPU purchases and a request to any manufacturers who *could* make ventilators to start making them under a promise from Health Secretary Matt Hancock that the government would certainly buy them. Such was the anxiety that an emergency line was setup for people to call if they could help to source or provide such equipment.

Companies like Dyson (vacuum cleaners) and JCB (heavy building equipment) were enlisted at short notice to step in. Even the Aston Martin Red Bull motor racing team were cited in a Guardian article dated 4th May 2020[76].

This, of course, is the cost of running beneath the standard of public provision required in *average* circumstances. The UK was already reduced to the ends of any possible means – street lighting was turned off after midnight in many areas (a gift to drug dealers) – every consideration was given to reduced expenditure. In the Guardian article, written by Rob Davies, Prof Carl Heneghan – Director for the Centre of Evidence based Medicine at Oxford University has been quoted:

> *"We've really cut to the bone in this country far too much."*

76
https://www.theguardian.com/business/2020/may/04/the-inside-story-of-the-uks-nhs-coronavirus-ventilator-challenge

No matter what the colour of government (red, blue, yellow, or green) it is the responsibility of government to walk the line between fiscal responsibility and provision. Significant threats to the public have to be considered, evaluated, and provision has to be made. There is an ongoing debate about how much central government should be involved in delivery – and whether delivery is a question for local government once provision of financial and other resources has been made.

Government intrusion on delivery in all aspects of public sector provision has been very strong and very evident over the last fifteen years: Michael Gove and the 'Govian' reforms to education provision. Chris Graying and his ill-fated venture into the National Probation Service. There has been varying degrees of privatisation – from rail networks, to NHS provision, to sections of the police and public security.

Whether you feel that it is private industry or government that should control certain essential functions I would ask you to acknowledge that a now endemic problem like County Lines cannot be defeated without a reliable and heavy weight commitment from Westminster. If that commitment does not arrive with a package of considerable resources, funds, expertise, and legislation – any commitment is not really worth the paper it is written on.

Politicians of all persuasions do lie. I admire politicians of past and present on both sides of the House of Commons – and there are good people in politics. Unfortunately there are also some very disreputable individuals who clearly don't worry about making commitments that they know they cannot honour. *Nick Clegg's infamous 'sorry' video was not received with a great deal of sympathy when he admitted to as much via 'YouTube'.*

Seeing a Home Secretary or a senior minister, Prime Minister or other leader come forward to make a commitment on ending or significantly compromising County Lines with a £20 million investment is very poor – but it's also deliberately misleading.

I contend that if the UK government wanted to *end* County Lines it absolutely could. It has all the powers, levers and mechanisms – plus the access to resources, finance, and expertise that are required. I reiterate however – that it would be a huge commitment and a long term project. It would also involve having a political figurehead courageous enough to put their career on the line by making such a commitment.

Foreign wars and military interventions are staggeringly expensive – David Cameron's actions against Libya in 2011 cost £234 million for a relatively curtailed venture. The UK contribution to the NATO activities in Kosovo in June 1999 amounted to a £339 million commitment. The Labour led military interventions into Iraq (now infamous for misleading the nation on 'weapons of mass destruction') between 2003 and 2009 amounted to a breath-taking £8.4 billion.

Six years and £8.4 billion – so £1.4 billion per year – what difference could such determination at central government make to the safety of children under the threat of criminal exploitation?

The bills for our military interventions do not, however, conclude there – Afghanistan and actions against the Taliban are listed as being something like £25 billion over a 13 year period. This is a £1.9 billion investment, year after year, and for thirteen whole years. An unshakable commitment and, when it was initiated, a blank cheque was signed. Tony Blair was quoted in the Financial Times saying:

> *"I cannot disclose, obviously, how long this action will last... we will not let up or rest until our objectives are met in full."*

The FT itself believes that the quoted £25 billion commitment "may even be an underestimate because it excludes costs such as wear and tear on equipment, according to a report by the Commons Defence Select Committee"[77] (article by Jim Pickard).

If you want to put a political commitment into context look at the steely eyed determination with which austerity has been pursued. You can measure this not merely in pounds and pence – but in life and death terms.

---

[77] https://www.ft.com/content/4bf155c8-fc8e-338b-9f7c-e41b7f5e3ba4

A Patrick Butler article[78] in the Guardian on 1st March 2020 took this issue head on – addressing the 'incredible secrecy' surrounding the deaths of vulnerable benefits claimants denied support or subject to draconian financial sanctions.

This article cites the death of Errol Graham "a severely ill man who died of starvation after his benefits were cut off". The article also cites a number of cases where people had committed suicide – feeling that they had no other way out. In late February 2020 a list of no fewer than twenty-four names of deaths linked to immediate benefits cuts by the Department for Work and Pensions was read aloud in the House of Commons. Frances Ryan[79] and Tom Pollard[80] have also written moving and difficult to read pieces referencing the death of Mr Graham, and the broader issues that contributed to his passing.

Frances Ryan has written:

---

[78] https://www.theguardian.com/society/2020/mar/01/dwp-criticised-for-incredible-secrecy-over-deaths-of-benefit-claimants
[79] https://www.theguardian.com/commentisfree/2020/feb/04/errol-graham-welfare-uk-benefit-cuts-disability-deaths
[80] https://www.theguardian.com/commentisfree/2020/jan/30/death-errol-graham-dwp-benefits-ill-disabled

"Graham is not so much an aberration of the benefits system but the latest in a long line of its victims. They are Britain's déjà vu deaths, where a bare cupboard or unpaid electric metre [sic] are the warning signs of institutional neglect."

While the contrast between the unearthly commitment to funding war, and the cost of defunding support for the most vulnerable is, in itself impossible to ignore – my actual point is this: it requires a particular degree of genuine passion, determination and unwavering commitment to drive home such policies that result in such outcomes. It is an act of zealous fixation and focus.

A fierce commitment to austerity has reduced the DWP budget by more than 40% in a ten year period. The budget for housing and communities has suffered likewise[81].

Government has talked about many things – and with all things political, some are red herrings or dead cats designed only to win votes and convince or distract voters. Irrespective, there has been a clear demonstration of what real, long term commitment looks like, when you witness the implementation of austerity. Our national unwavering dedication to austerity has been one example of how – even in the face of many terrible and negative consequences – policy can

---

81

https://www.instituteforgovernment.org.uk/explainers/departmental-budgets

be seen through to the bitter end. On the other hand, our general acceptance of wars and international military interventions has made the fabled 'magic money tree' appear to be a magic money forest, *when we really want it to be*.

Pockets of investment, and small scale localised projects, are not the signs of a government that wishes to eradicate County Lines and Child Exploitation. If we really went after such criminals with the vigour and enthusiasm that we adopted against the Taliban, Osama bin Laden or Sadam Hussein (or dare I suggest it, the DWP benefit claimant) – believe me, we *could* eradicate this problem.

What I find to be quite scary is that part of the solution is actually self-funding – and later in this book we will look at how a reformed approach to controlled drug regulation could actually pay for a concerted move against exploitative drug dealers, compromise their profit margins significantly, and help to fund more support for young people and families recovering from adverse childhood experiences or problems with misuse and addiction issues.

It's important to note that not only does the government hold the purse strings – a majority government can change legislation significantly. The Misuse of Drugs Act 1971 is the main piece of legislation that dictates the offences around possessing, sharing, distributing, importing and cultivating controlled drugs.

This legislation is something that is urgently in need of overhaul. *You might ask why?*

The purpose of the legislation is to control drugs on the basis of two key factors: the harm and risk that is posed to society in general, and the immediate risk that is posed to the user of the drug. On this basis drugs are classified under categories A, B or C. A is the most severe or serious category to be convicted under – this group of drugs, predictably, includes crack cocaine, cocaine and heroin. Category B is for less damaging substances – considered to be too dangerous to legalise – and this group includes cannabis, codeine, amphetamines and ketamine. Category C briefly included cannabis (for a period of time) before it was re-listed under advice to category B, but was confusingly downgraded in other regards towards less meaningful criminal disposal options. Class C tends to include prescription drugs when they are not held by the person to whom they are prescribed and without lawful reason or excuse (for example being collected by someone for a housebound patient is a lawful reason).

This system of tackling drugs and enforcing drug regulation is enshrined in the 1971 Act – and this legislation empowers officers to stop and search people on the street, or swear out search warrants to search their homes. It has not made any significant, material or successful inroads into drug culture in the UK over the last 39 years.

Much as with alcohol prohibition in the United States (1920 – 1933) a market exists and people want to profit from that. Moonshine and poorly made and unregulated beverages and spirits probably caused more harm than legalised, standardised and regulated products would have during that time. Vast amounts of money were spent on enforcement and face saving exercises from government agencies – and in the end, the determined consumption of alcohol prevailed.

I am not advocating carte blanche legalisation of drugs – which I feel would be irresponsible and deeply harmful – but a shift away from criminal justice solutions to health based solutions has already been the subject of extensive research. Seeing people with addiction problems as patients rather than determined criminals, would be a step forward.

There is no question that the supply of the most dangerous drugs and substances must continue to be prohibited – but taking cannabis as a prime example: shatter or spice should never be considered on the same level or simply 'the same' as cannabis. Cannabis *within itself* at different THC and CBD combinations becomes a varied experience and poses completely different risks and threats. The current situation of very rarely being able to know what someone is taking, is in and of itself part of the collective risk. A cannabis product with 5% THC and 5% CBD is a world of difference to a cannabis strain that is delivering 20% THC and 2% CBD or less.

Such is the importance of engagement at central government level. A determined approach to drug legislation could very rapidly assess whether the existing regulations and policies around controlled drugs actually makes it more profitable and more lucrative to be involved in the County Lines business – and whether simply rebooting and clarifying the legislation to cope with modern circumstances could be a much better idea.

In 2003 a brand new Sexual Offences Act was brought onto the statute books. It replaced and repealed previous legislation under the 1956 Act. As a young officer I was briefly taught under the 1956 laws, I was then retrained under the newer more modern legislation.

The 2003 Sexual Offences Act is one of the clearest and best defined pieces of legislation on the books today. It is a fantastic piece of modern law making (not perfect but regardless it is outstanding). It is clearly worded, easy to understand and comprehend, and brought into the modern era legislation that mirrored attitudes of the 21st Century. It is well overdue that we replicate this process with misuse of drugs legislation and responsibility for that urgent task sits with central government.

Chapter Ten: Are we the baddies?

'Are we the Baddies?' is one of my favourite internet memes. Taken from a Mitchell and Webb sketch between two German second world war SS officers where one turns to the other and admits that he's having a crisis – *and when he adds it all up* – it might just be that he's on the *wrong side*...

We're not just laughing at the realisation dawning on this stormtrooper – *you might realise that we're laughing at ourselves*, and our lack of self-awareness. Aside from it being a very funny piece of comedy writing, it also unearths a very uneasy truth for a great many people (probably all people actually): we are so wedded to our opinions and our perceptions of ourselves that we cannot entertain that things might be our fault, and that we could be wrong about literally *everything* that matters. We can always apparently justify a state of affairs – we rarely stop to think about our accountability for that state of affairs.

We are living in an age that is post-centre ground politics – when everyone seemed to be in consensus and agreed upon most things from approximately 1997 until at least December 2005. The governments of Tony Blair left successive shadow cabinets of the Conservative party bereft of argument, because largely, they *kind of* agreed on a lot of things. The whole situation seemed very awkward. The fight was to prove who owned the middle ground and led that consensus. Even after the election of a coalition (apparently consensus based) government – *when the pendulum of political preference did swing* – the initial result was remarkably in sync with what had been offered before.

The brilliant Armando Iannucci broadcast the frankly alarming but mesmerising video "Changes" (August 2006) in episode one of his satirical comedy series "Time Trumpet". This video is a musical montage constructed upon the classic David Bowie track 'Changes' which shows how seamlessly the political baton was passed between Blair and Cameron (via Gordon Brown) and how Cameron must have studied and replicated the presentation and style of his predecessor in some amount of detail with very few apparent differences. [This video is still available on YouTube[82]]. Between the issues of Brexit and more recently the coronavirus, times *have* changed – and sadly we appear to be collectively no more self-aware or reflecting as a consequence, only a great deal more confrontational and oppositional.

Today we seem to have a flaming bin fire of completely juxtaposed parties and individuals – COVID19, Brexit, the climate crisis and every minor issue in between – only seems to pit people against each other in a blood feud that paints one side as the 'goodies' and one side as the 'baddies' and both sides are incapable of seeing

---

[82] https://www.youtube.com/watch?v=3yEi72XfNbA

themselves as anything less than virtuous, sensible and wise. Even political parties are tearing themselves apart from within. *This is equally true on both sides – the Conservatives fighting for their identity between the ERG and Mark Francois and Jacob Rees-Mogg, and the more moderate and traditional approach of Michael Heseltine and Kenneth Clarke. In the Labour Party we see a group of people shredding each other publicly – Momentum (the pro-Jeremy Corbyn support group) versus Blairite and New Labour – both claim the moral high ground, and seem to oppose each other with a vicious and irreconcilable fervour. The whole scenario in both camps resembles estranged couples in marriages at breaking point – and particularly with Labour – the worst kind of impending divorce where neither party will concede on who gets to live in the marital home or keep the dog.*

An important part of dealing with the threat of County Lines and Child Criminal Exploitation is that we have to actually take the time to sit and contemplate the fact (with adult objectivity) that we have a lot of blame to carry for the fact that County Lines exists at all. We have to *own* what we have allowed to happen and how we have structured our communities, our society and our country. I mean that on a deeply personal level and of course I include myself in that indictment.

Charles Darwin discovered an orchid which possessed a long hanging (foot long) nectar sack, that drapes down behind the flower head. The orchid – *'Angraecum sesquipedale'* – was so unusual that it was difficult to understand how any conventional insect could possibly pollinate it or recover the nectar that it held. Darwin – the father of evolutionary theory – drew a very logical hypothesis that was revolutionary for his age and profound in its simple genius:

> *"in Madagascar there must be moths with proboscis capable of extension to a length of between ten and eleven inches"*

It wasn't until 1992, *and 130 years after Charles Darwin made his pronouncement*, that actually the 'Xanthopan morganii praedicta' was found feeding on the orchid, thus completing Darwin's theory, and offering further support for the concept of co-evolution.

Allow us then to adopt this mentality – this scientific, this logical approach. If Charles Darwin was to look at the children of early twentieth century Britain – *as the long hanging nectar of our flowering society* – surely something out there has evolved to best effect to take benefit from that, whether we want it to or not. What we have created has co-created a predator suited to their vulnerabilities – *and we are aware of that.*

Unlike the Orchid – however – we are sentient – we control the evolution of our society, we direct and we structure and employ our resources based upon collective decision making (where we can manage to form consensus and agreement). We *maintain* a society that suits County Lines – where County Lines fits and is successful in its aims. As I write this book we are not deciding to do otherwise. This places culpability upon us – and in my opinion – we have a duty to review and make some very fundamental changes.

Child protection has become – in late twentieth century, and in early twenty-first century Britain – a far more developed topic, and a much greater priority for us all. We have come to accept our shared responsibility towards children and not merely our direct sons and daughters – but all children (quite rightly).

The nineteenth century and the industrial revolution was notorious for the exploitation of children for profit – from the image of the child chimney sweep, to the children used in mills and factories to unknot jammed machines with their tiny fingers. Criminal exploitation was also rife and Charles Dickens wrote the timeless image of the juvenile pickpocket in his classic Oliver Twist (which of course has now been adapted to both stage and screen). Child protection legislation didn't really begin until 1889 when the "children's charter" was passed – this was the first time that the government allowed the police to intervene in domestic relationships between parents and their children. Extensions to this legislation came in 1894, and The Children's Act of 1908 followed.

We can jump forward sixty-two years and Social Services departments began to evolve and take shape in 1970 under the Local Authority Social Services Act 1970. The death of Maria Cowell in 1973 – *a child murdered by her drunk and violent foster father following systematic physical abuse* – became a landmark case that shocked a nation into pushing the agenda forward once again. But it could be argued that the modern standards of child protection really began in 1989 with The Children Act (of that year) which in principle gave *every child* the right to protection from abuse and exploitation.

In terms of the security adopted around children – and centres of education – the horrific massacre at the Dunblane Primary School in 1996 did more than change firearms legislation. Sixteen children and a teacher were murdered in a previously unthinkable tragedy which emphasised the need for surveillance, visitor registration, and the closer scrutiny of how school sites were operated and controlled. Personally I grew up in a generation where people walked into insecure school buildings and took themselves straight to the classroom – for example – to collect a child, or drop off a forgotten lunch box or P.E. kit. *Unthinkable today*.

The Soham murders of 2002 were headline making because of the macabre and sinister way in which a school employee sexually abused and took the lives of two children (Holly Wells and Jessica Chapman). The offender – Ian Huntley – was a dangerous paedophile – and it was a failure in the sharing of information between Humberside Police and Cambridgeshire Constabulary that meant that he could clear any background checks unhindered and work at Soham Village College. Every parent in the country was shocked and deeply worried by this concept that a predator could walk among us and there was wide-spread fear about the worst abuses of a position of trust. When I transferred to Cambridgeshire Constabulary (in late 2005) the force was still feeling the impact of the killings and the criticisms of the Bishard Enquiry that followed (although the worst criticism was reserved for Humberside Police). When I was interviewed for my role as a transferee Police Constable a Superintendent actually took the time (in the middle of the interview) to reassure me that if I had read any adverse publicity, that close internal scrutiny had been applied to the organisation and that lessons had been learned. It was Soham and consequently Bishard that lead / led? to the Independent Safeguarding Authority and the establishment of CRB checks (now Data and Barring Services) nationally.

The Laming report into the death of Victoria Climbié followed in 2003. The Laming report identified no fewer than *twelve* opportunities that had been missed, by the combined efforts of health, law enforcement and social services, to save the life of this child. The Climbié case was perhaps as distressing as you might be able to imagine – an eight year old girl, subjected to torture, and eventually murdered by members of her own extended family. It was Climbié that led to 'Every Child Matters' – published in September 2003. This paper was authorised by Paul Boateng and was the forerunner to new legislation in 2004. Lord Boateng (as he is today) wrote about the importance of consultation with practitioners, academics and of course children and young people, to shape the guidance in his findings.

The 'Every Child Matters' report and agenda made a clear and important statement, that every child under the age of 19 (or 24 if coping with disability) shall be:

- Safe
- Healthy
- Able to enjoy and achieve
- Integrated in the community and able to make a positive contribution
- Protected from economic disadvantage

Commitment to the 'Every Child Matters' agenda has frankly fluctuated over the years – and approaches and interpretations of the recommendations have changed in the years that followed (with sides arguing over how best to achieve such aims – but nobody willing to publicly disagree with the aims and objectives).

Much of this evolution of child protection – and admittedly that is a very brief and general over view of it – is focused on the aspects of child protection that surround exploitation in the work place (early legislation) and sexual and physical abuses inflicted on children by the people who surround them in positions of trust (family, friends, school teachers and so on).

The Modern Day Slavery Act 2015 is a significant step forward when addressing the concerns around *anyone* who seeks to exploit children and young people for criminal purposes. This legislation states:

> *'A person commits an offence if the person arranges or facilitates the travel of another person with a view to them being exploited.'*

This legislation covers children and young people being trafficked within the UK and out of the country too. It *doesn't matter* if they verbally consent or believed that they consented to the trafficking, and it is also irrelevant whether the offender travels with them.

A highly informative and well written guide was published by the Youth Justice Legal Centre in 2018[83] and the targeting of vulnerable children is described as followed:

> *"Gangs specifically target vulnerable children and those who do not have support networks... The gangs seek to fill that emotional gap for the child and become 'their family'*
>
> *Male Children are most commonly exploited but female children are also used and exploited by gangs. It is thought that 15-16 years is the most common age for children to be exploited by these*

[83] https://yjlc.uk/wp-content/uploads/2018/02/Modern-Slavery-Guide-2018.pdf

gangs but there are reports of children below the age of 11 years being used."

In the evolution of our complete understanding of how children are victimised and mistreated – for a host of reasons and in numerous ways – be that physical, sexual, emotional, psychological or for financial profit – we are only beginning to acknowledge the need to address criminal grooming, coercion and radicalisation as a specific and pressing category of its own.

Let's be honest with ourselves – we have constructed a society that is hospitable to County Lines, our learning about child protection is incomplete, and along the way a lot of mistakes have been made (with tragic consequences). The mistakes and tragedies that I have cited are the ones that made the headlines – but I prompt you to understand, that right now, there is a child living in fear, subject to physical harm, who will be murdered in circumstances of County Lines abuses. I can predict this with as much certainty as Charles Darwin could predict the existence of the *'Xanthopan morganii praedicta'*. Very sadly many already have. We are already in possession of statistics that suggest that we are aware of 46,000 children involved in gang activities in England alone, and 4,000 teenagers in London being exploited as part of County Lines[84].

---

[84] https://anyoneschild.org/get-the-facts/

While building legislation around the misuse and supply of drugs (remember we are reliant upon legislation passed in the early 1970s at the moment) it should be, and deserves to be, a whole different offence to supply drugs through the criminal seduction and misguidance of a child.

I think we know that we haven't got this right yet – County Lines continues to grow and prosper 'on our watch'. The native environment is susceptible to and encourages continued growth. The bottom line of that concern is not with drugs and drug related harm – it is with child protection. It is perhaps our fear of drug related harm that stops us from focusing on the child victims of coercive violence and physical abuse. *There is a strong argument to be made that our moral responsibility is with the children first, and the social effects of drug proliferation second.*

A fairly rigid adherence to the same traditional enforcement tactics and approaches – warnings of tough punishments and an 'us versus them' attitude which alienates child victims – results in both the same predictable outcomes and lack of genuine progress against drugs. It also gives Organised Crime Groups (OCGs) a static opponent that is easier to out manoeuvre.

A welcome element of the Modern Day Slavery Act 2015 is the acknowledgement that a child victim of trafficking has a statutory defence to any crimes committed by organised gangs who exploit them:

A person is not guilty of an offence if:

  a) *The person is under the age of 18 when the person does the act which constitutes the offence,*

  b) *The person does that act as a direct consequence of the person being, or having been, a victim of slavery or a victim of relevant exploitation, and*

  c) *A reasonable person in the same situation as the person and having the person's relevant characteristics would do that act (s.45 Modern Slavery Act 2015)*

We are beginning to change our approach – *gradually* – and we are starting to redefine who we target consequently with law enforcement measures.

As we have already discussed – however – law enforcement is only one part of this overall jigsaw. The picture is made up of many pieces, and law enforcement generally only comes into play when the offence is being committed or has been committed. Neighbourhood policing is the avenue of prevention and reduction – and is a world that is and should be integrated with partners and not acting independently or alone.

We know – from speaking to children and young people rescued from exploitation – that they are commonly told and advised by their exploiters that they cannot disclose, they cannot hand themselves into the police, and that they cannot trust the authorities. All of the main services that we have considered – from Social Care, to Schools, to the police – are painted as the enemy.

In huge example of 'gaslighting' combined with gift giving and other seductive actions – young people are taught who to listen to, and who to be angry at.

> *"They did this to you"*

> *"They don't understand you like I do"*

> *"You don't owe them a fucking thing"*

> *"They just want you to shut up and be a good little boy/girl"*

> *"I look after you better than anyone – who got you those trainers?"*

> *"All they want to do is blame you"*

> *"You don't want to end up like him, right?"*

A constant 'drip, drip' feed of messaging is designed to reassure the child that they are being shrewd, listening to the right people, that they are cared for, and that they don't want to be one of the 'sheep' that has to turn up to school every day and play by the rules.

I have spoken to a teacher who was actually ridiculed by an exploited child who had clearly been radicalised to the criminal life style with the *"I make more in a day than you can make in a month"* mantra. *"I don't want to turn out a loser like you did"*.

All of the values within this seduction are built upon commercialism, consumerism, and a shallow drive for financial benefit. *"Get that money"* is the simple three word belief system that goes along to justify anything that has to be done in the course of these criminal behaviours. All virtues are steered towards the ability to do that – determination, tenacity, bravery, loyalty - everything.

The 'no snitching' ("snitches get stitches") code is present in every single school – and even the most successful, focused, and criminally disengaged children are aware of it. *Of all the behaviours in a school or social environment the one that appears to be despised and collectively agreed upon is that of 'the snitch'.*

To have "You're a snitch" attached to your name and reputation is social poison and immediate isolation (at best). At worst it results in violence and discrimination, bullying and harassment (both on and offline) that follows you everywhere. Even people who can see through the 'no snitching' synthetic – and respect the courage that it takes to speak out, are hesitant to admit it or associate with people who do pass forms of information on to figures of authority. The danger is that they'll attract the fatal sobriquet too. I've genuinely lost count of the number of times that a nervous child has said to me *"I don't want to look like a snitch"*.

What is behind all this? It is an adversarial construct in which professionals, teachers, the police, social care and others have been successfully marketed as 'the baddies' – and even if the child subject to exploitation has experienced mistreatment or abuse, even if they are selling drugs, they don't see *the gang* as being in the wrong, or blame the people who actually abuse them. We are the adversary.

This is a pretty massive fail for all of us. Even if we don't see ourselves as being on the wrong side of this – losing the war of perception with the people that we are seeking to protect or save from criminal exploitation – is a huge piece of ground to lose. It is a wall – a huge wall – and we have to come to terms with it and break it down.

Having already made a case within this chapter for why we should all look towards ourselves to take some accountability for County Lines – I want you to understand how the most vulnerable children and young people can become convinced that we are their enemies.

Allow me to help you to understand exactly how this works – because it operates in two very clear and fundamental ways that I have witnessed personally and on a first-hand basis:

First of all, let's consider someone in a school setting who has done something wrong. It doesn't really matter too much what it is or where it sits on the gravity scale. It could be worthy of a fixed term exclusion, it might be something that is commonly dealt with by way of an after school or even lunch time detention.

This behaviour could be ranging from verbally abusing a teacher, using violence against another student down to common littering, causing minor damage to the estate or even not handing in homework.

I am willing to absolutely guarantee that child or young person is going to *expect* a particular type of treatment when they are being dealt with – and this is specifically the case if the matter is being dealt with by *certain teachers*. I am not singling out teachers here – they are simply the figure of authority in this context, and the same is definitely true with police officers as I have witnessed it.

If you get onto a certain level of trust and rapport with a child or young person they will tell you exactly who their favourite teacher is and why. They will also have a list of teachers that they don't like – and they'll probably tell you who those people are and the reasons behind it. Life is not a popularity contest and we shouldn't run our institutions and organisations as such – but there is a nuance to this that I will try to explain.

At that moment in time – the heat of the moment of wrong doing – they've been apprehended doing something and usually nothing in the world is likely to stop them in their tracks and make them reflect, and accept that they are guilty of wrong doing. Most young people will have a sense of exceptionalism and will already be priming themselves with their excuses, denials or the case for mitigation. Taking whole hearted responsibility without any of the above is not unheard of but to say the least – *it is uncommon*. At this moment in time they are sorry – sorry they have been caught.

Their preoccupation is with whatever made them do it, and right then and there the fact that "Crap, I'm in trouble".

We've all had the *"Sorry I got caught"* type of apology that comes as part and parcel of the hamster wheel process of getting that situation dealt with. We are familiar with seeing it from our celebrities, our politicians, our sports personalities and our other prominent people.

We are all familiar with the 'whataboutism' that commonly accompanies such a situation *"…but what about David Smith – he does far worse and you never do anything about that"*.

We are all familiar with the 'ad hominem' response – *"It's just Miss Smith, she hates me/she's a bitch etc."*

We ought to be familiar with the strawman argument – *"Yeah I did it, but the school is wrong – I should be allowed to because…"* (insert misrepresentation of the school policy here).

One or two young people are just *so* stubborn or intransigent that they won't cooperate with the process – and refuse to mouth even fake apologies to help get themselves out of bother. They don't feel sorry, and their anger and pride forbid them from offering any flexibility. This can be infuriating.

A large number *will* offer a forced apology under duress if it gets them out of bother or gets it all over with. From a process perspective getting them to 'say' sorry, or write down an apology, ticks a box, but does little to change any behaviours or get in behind what the behaviour is significantly communicating or sign posting. Specifically so, when their heart is not in it and their mind is elsewhere.

Being presented with a 'good hard bollocking' at the moment of their acute vulnerability is exactly what they're expecting – and for those who are most deeply entrenched – it is what they are taught to anticipate. There are young people who look at the stern disciplinarian figure (there's usually at least one really strong disciplinarian in every school – and don't get me wrong – there is a place for that) and they're really thinking *"God he/she really loves this. He just gets off on being a bully."*

When we vent our anger at a child by raising our voices, and by using other methods of demonstrating that we are emotionally connected to what happened, or respond to provocation emotionally, we are (whether we actually accept it to ourselves or not) trying to intimidate them. We are not trying to win hearts and minds. It's about control and power. On reflection we have to ask ourselves "To whose benefit are we driving this?" Our own (in terms of ego)? The school (in terms of broad measures of control and boundary reinforcement)? The peer group (to make an example of someone)? Or to the child or young person themselves? I am not saying that assertive behaviour is wrong or inappropriate – if it is correctly done, if it is well considered, if it is proportionate and necessary. *It doesn't come without a cost though* – and I want to explore that.

In conversation with one particularly troubled girl, I was told that it was her view that actually her teachers *hated* her, she couldn't trust anyone, and that the Principal wanted to take the first opportunity to kick her out of the school. I'm going to use the name of Maddison to represent this girl and protect her identity.

It was very moving to hear her disclose that fundamentally she really, genuinely believed that her identity and her presence in the school was an affront to her teachers. She was in a hostile environment and that she was subject to constant scrutiny that only served the purposes of affording the opportunity to reprimand her, punish her, or eliminate her from the community.

No wonder that she was so guarded, that her own demeanour was so hostile, and that her first instinct was to take issue with anything.

It was probably more upsetting to know how wrong Maddison was. I had sat in countless meetings where her personal circumstances, her behaviour and in school performance was discussed – not out of a conspiracy to remove her – but to try to find any method to help and support her that she would accept.

We could never get beyond the wall of adversity for any meaningful amount of time. I got brief opportunities to get in behind it – but they didn't last long, and eventually she closed down to me completely too.

Maddison was not subject to what I would describe as a full criminal radicalisation – but she was so close to what was going on. She smoked weed daily – in the evenings – and told me that she couldn't sleep without it. She was suffering the early signs of cannabis induced psychosis but didn't trust anyone enough to access the help that she needed.

She associated with her weed dealer and his immediate circle of friends – she listened to those people – and her views of the world were very much shaped by allegiances formed there. Maddison had been in a substantial amount of trouble when she had been younger. Experimenting with drugs she had given an ecstasy tablet to a friend who had collapsed and been hospitalised. She carried that guilt with her and it was 'scratch the surface obvious' and never far away. She told me that she'd never venture away from cannabis now (towards other drugs) – although she was a bit scared by how strong the street supply of weed actually was. She recognised that she had been hearing and seeing things that weren't real when she was high.

Maddison still got into lots of trouble at school – mostly through a very confrontational and angry attitude that wasn't helped by being on the downswing from her cannabis misuse cycle.

At times Maddison was verbally abusive to staff and to teachers – hot-headed and massively wilful. Sometimes she would work in a very engaged way – but could turn in a moment on someone who had done an enormous amount to support her. Although she never apologised, I sense that she did reflect on such things – she repressed her guilt – and she couldn't find her own way to show her genuine remorse. Maddison really demonstrated a fear of displaying any weaknesses.

The day I lost my access to and rapport with Maddison was the day I sat down with her to reflect on a particularly horrible confrontation that had occurred between herself and a teacher (which she was entirely responsible for). Walking back through it got too much – and even using 'advance and retreat' tactics the emotions overwhelmed her. She got up and walked out of the room – she slammed the door in anger and she never opened that door up to me again. In hindsight I think I pushed too hard.

The fragility of Maddison was a stark contrast to her tough outer appearance. What she cultivated was an appearance that she could take anyone on – and that she would stare anyone down. She might seem like the young person who needed 'putting in her place', but that was exactly what she didn't need. It was a gradual and tentative approach with Maddison – and she had been taught (and self-taught) on a hair trigger basis, to expect hostility and negative judgement from figures of authority. There appeared to be nobody in her life offering her unconditional positive regard. Her confrontational attitude meant that she was likely to escalate conflict quickly – flash with rage, scream, run out of rooms, slam doors. It is so easy to get drawn into a personality conflict with Maddison – to take it as a personal affront, as disrespect and a loss of face.

Every time we give into that emotional impulse to react – which is natural, instinctive and defensive – we confirm for a 'Maddison' (in her eyes) that we hate her, that we are her enemies, and that she was right all along.

Coaxing a Maddison from that view is a nearly impossible job, doing it once in a handful of cases would be an exceptional achievement. We have to acknowledge what is happening. *It is very possible to misinterpret her and to believe that she is just a particularly horrible young person (some young people are regarded in this way)* – but actually, in that moment of acute vulnerability, when her emotional state is escalated – *that is when she expects the worst.* She is in her fight or flight condition. *That's* the moment to challenge the paradigm that she lives inside – by ironically not being confrontational with her.

Derren Brown is an illusionist who utilises the power of people's subconscious thoughts to create bizarre and difficult to believe outcomes.

He recommends that when confronted with a mugger/street robber – as he claims he once was at 3am[85] - the best form of self-defence is not karate, jujitsu, judo or kung-fu – it's just a lack of 'logical' responses.

When a demand was made for his wallet he said *"The wall outside my house isn't 4ft high"* – as if the assailant had asserted to the contrary.

The situation of being held at knife point or under the threat of violence, is pre-programmed to make you comply with certain social options and boundaries. Comply and give your wallet, refuse and fight back, run away – these are all of the most common options the offender is prepared for. Challenging the fundamental of the entire paradigm is rarely considered or discussed.

---

[85] https://www.independent.co.uk/news/people/derren-brown-explains-how-to-reduce-a-mugger-to-tears-using-nothing-but-words-9859017.html

"He started breaking down in tears because all of that adrenaline and aggression had to go somewhere. So he did the adrenaline dump. They use it in martial arts where they get people to relax before you hit them to make the blow more powerful."

It's actually really difficult to come up with something completely random in that type of situation so Brown recommends that you think of a song lyric – the more random and off centre the better.

Going back to Maddison – who is by now probably in the girls toilet (another part of paradigm – safe place – half the adult staff can't go in there) or the place where she likes to smoke on school premises, but in any regard a place that she associates with comfort and safety – the typical responses are available:

a) Speak in a disapproving and lecturing tone. Continue the argument – tell her off – "I don't know who you think you are but that behaviour is not acceptable, I am about to phone your mother, and you will be removed from this school site – you might as well come with me and stop making this situation worse for yourself" (etc etc) OR

b) Try to calm and sooth her. Empathise. Be non-judgmental and offer personal warmth. "Maddie, it's ok – you didn't mean it – we're not angry, we just want to understand. Can we talk about it? I know you feel upset, I just want to make sure you're ok, why don't you come out"

[Generally if you're going to do B I'd send someone that she has some rapport with, and not the person she just blew up at]

A third method is akin to the 'Derren Brown' – *it's a little bit Derren Brown, and it's a little bit Monty Roberts/horse whisperer*. I'm not recommending that you go into the girls' toilets and freak Maddie out with abstract song lyrics but going in and talking about something *completely different* is an option. And just be incredibly patient. Particularly if it appears that the member of staff has no idea why she is in there.

"Hiya Maddie. I like your trainers. I need to get some new trainers but I have no idea what to get. I'll be honest I do like Air Max but I think I'm too old for them. Do you think I'm too old for them?"

You'll get a lot of silence before, eventually, she will either say "Why are you trying to talk to me?" or "I know what you're trying to do and it won't work" or she'll say something that latches onto the trail of the conversation – quite unexpectedly – *"...I think you'd have to be careful about what Air Max you get because some of them are definitely too young for you... (implied insult of course) [sniff]"*

It doesn't matter. She's calming down. You haven't fulfilled the paradigm of attacking her – you haven't

397

prolonged the source of the pain by needing to talk about it there and then – you've helped her own coping mechanism of trying to supress it. You haven't drawn attention to the fact that she's just run crying into the girls' toilets slamming doors (which, believe it or not, has caused her acute embarrassment).

Even if she only gives back "I know what you're trying to do and it won't work" – it's an acknowledgement from her that she can see that you're trying to be nice.

When she's been talked down, and she's had her own adrenaline dump, you'll find her much more cooperative. You can explain to her "Look Maddie – we all have ups and down – I don't get to overlook what just happened, but let's do what we can to set it right and move on. It'll all be ok."

You don't need to over do it – you can be tough but fair with her – but she won't forget the fact that right there and then you were 'alright'.

Most importantly though – you have challenged a preconceived idea, not by words but by actions and behaviour, in the heat of the moment, when she needed it the most. You have begun our 'drip drip' that counters the narrative that everybody hates her – and it will take time for that to accumulate and work. It's about reversing the impression that *we are the baddies*.

In this situation it's not about letting her get away with it. Actually it's really important that we do impose the sanction consistently – but it's her seeing that regardless of the sanction the person who dealt with her liked her, empathised with her, built some rapport through it – and did it in a way that was fair.

She is far more likely, in a quiet moment, to herself, to reflect and criticise herself for getting it wrong. *Personally* I'm a supporter of optional apologies. I know that when people do things wrong – they should apologise. But false apologies are spotted a mile away – they are offensive, they only inflict more hurt, and they persuade the person giving the fake apology that there is some merit in telling a lie.

I'd rather spend time talking about why a genuine apology has merit and what it should include. *"If you feel self-conscious, perhaps you'd rather write it out? That way you can say whatever you really feel"*.

This is the value of restorative justice – delivering a sanction that doesn't simply alienate the young person and make them feel like they are 'on the wrong side'.

Many young people literally don't know what an apology consists of (and we can't presume that they do). In fact it wasn't until I was a police officer and in my late twenties doing restorative justice courses that I really learned how to structure an effective apology and how powerful an absolute apology could be.

I was taught the five point apology – and I try to explain this to young people:

1. Say your sorry without saying 'but' or offering any excuses.
2. Explain what you are sorry for and why you are sorry. Include the word 'because'.
3. Acknowledge that what you did wasn't ok. Empathise with why it was hurtful.
4. Tell them that you are not perfect, but you will try to ensure that you don't do that again to them, or to other people – that you've learned something.
5. (This is always the most difficult part) Ask for forgiveness.

It is exceptionally difficult to *fake* a five point apology. Anyone can say 'sorry' and snatch at a limp handshake with no eye contact. Writing out or saying a five point apology actually requires some thought and consideration. It doesn't allow a lot of 'wriggle room'.

Receiving a five point apology is a powerful and emotional thing – and I've seen people cry when they give them, and I've seen people cry when they receive them. The forgiveness is almost inevitable for all but the most hard hearted of individuals. *You tend to surrender your forgiveness in the most unexpected way.*

I'll take you back to the girl who sat shocked in front of the teenaged boy who had really made her life a painful thing for the last number of months, when he broke down and cried and apologised.

"I just want to give him hug and tell him it's alright"

Because of Covid-19 she couldn't. It was an almost painful form of restraint.

This is – allow me to take liberty with the statistics – one-hundred times more powerful than 'a good bollocking' ever could be. Most importantly we circumvent the 'win/lose' situation and scenario – we actually do something more meaningful than see who comes out on top. We deny the situation the opportunity to create us as the 'baddies'.

It can be very hard to bring a teenager into a situation like this – to this form of acknowledgment. It is an admission to self, as much as to anyone else, that they have done wrong. *I think we've all had glimpses of it though* – it all comes tumbling out. Once the catharsis hits – the relief is overwhelming. It's like putting down a burden. That's when the dam tends to break.

There are always opportunities to undermine and to diminish the effective paradigms and constructs that these alienated young people live within – but some are easier to recognise than others. Some are genuinely 'level 10, master grade' challenges that combine patience and the ability to recognise the opportunity – but in other circumstances they are just right there, and in fact, that child or young person might even be waving them at you.

The first person I ever came into contact with that resembled someone who had been reduced into County Lines was a young man from Highbury in London. The case that I worked on regarding this young man resulted in my first *meaningful* police commendation.

Believe me, in the police there seems to be little rhyme or reason to the way in which commendations work. *Right place right time it would seem* – but generally you'll get formally commended for something which you might be frankly embarrassed to accept – while another piece of invaluable contribution that should have been recognised, goes unrewarded.

In this case I did feel that this commendation was meaningful. The young man was a drug dealer from the Highbury area of North London. He was 18, and he had been picked up and reduced into the lifestyle from the age of about 14.

It was December 2006 – and many years before the term 'County Lines' had been coined. By any stretch of the imagination this young man was a prototype and a forerunner to what we now know to be such.

Living in the shadow of the old Highbury football ground he and his brother were picked up and used by a gang. His rewards were always in material forms – rarely in cash – so he received computer games consoles, games, trainers (lots of trainers) clothes and numerous mobile phones (mainly needed for the dealing of drugs).

Just before the schools and colleges broke up for the Christmas holiday, a young man studying his A levels began asking around in a pub if anyone knew how to get hold of some cocaine. The young man wasn't eighteen and he was frighteningly naïve. Eventually he pestered enough people until someone gave him a telephone number and told him to go away. His friends didn't want anything to do with experimenting with coke – and they melted away from him. Undeterred he made a phone call.

The voice on the other end of the line made an arrangement to meet him somewhere secluded – Mill Road Cemetery, it was approaching midnight and the young A level student was alone. He went to meet the dealer with a small amount of cash – enough to experiment with.

He was met by three north London males slightly older than himself – who finding him completely alone – decided not to sell him drugs at all. They robbed him instead. Stripped of his possessions and of his clothing – which included an iPhone, his wallet and anything else of value – one of the offenders dragged him alone and naked, deeper into the cemetery and subjected him to a traumatic sexual assault.

He was orally raped. The offender was identified by the DNA swabs that were taken less than an hour later from the face of the victim.

The offenders made off from the scene, no doubt back to London – but ultimately we did identify the one offender who had committed the sex crime.

As a detective sergeant, I was the deputy lead officer in the investigation, and when the identification was made I led an away team of officers to arrest him from his home address in London.

At the address we found him in possession of a handgun, ammunition, a house brick sized quantity of heroin, approximately £20,000 in cash, several mobile phones that were utilised as buying lines, and an array of other items including crack cocaine, c.s. incapacitant sprays, and more. Thankfully for us, when we entered the address, he panicked, threw the gun out of his bedroom window into the garden, and urinated himself on his bed.

His initial presumption was that we were from the Metropolitan Police and that we were there to arrest him for drug dealing. He blanched an incredible pale colour when we told him that we were from Cambridgeshire, and that in fact, he was being arrested for rape.

It took the best part of twenty hours to search the house from top to bottom and ensure that we left with everything illegal that was inside. The house was littered with pieces of paper and he'd written out rap lyrics on them – some were recognisable from popular music – some seemed to have been written by himself. His whole bedroom was covered in posters of rap icons.

As far as this offender was concerned, I would challenge you to find anyone who could be looked upon as more deeply entrenched in the criminal lifestyle. He was absolutely radicalised to it. He was taken back to Parkside police station by two officers while the rest of the eight-person team and I remained behind to search the address.

This young man – legally an adult – was little more than a very broken teenager. His crimes were horrific – and who was to know if this was his first offence, if some previous victim had felt too humiliated to come forward? In person, however, he was a broken child. He resembled a waif like fifteen year old, he just seemed utterly broken and dysfunctional. His paradigm seemed to include the belief that when he got back to Parkside he was going to be beaten up. *He was terrified*.

I got to talk to him – briefly. I stood in a holding cell with him the next day. He was wary. I threw out a deliberate hook for him. I've enjoyed many types of rap music and I was a big fan of the New York rapper Jay-Z – who was particularly huge and popular at that time. I had many albums and I'd seen him perform live in London.

Apparently 'unaware' of him being there, and of course not to him deliberately, but in an undemonstrative way, I rapped to myself to pass the time:

"The year's 94 and my trunk is raw

In the rear view mirror there's the mother
f*cking law
I've got two choices y'all,
Pull over the car or,
Bounce on the devil put the pedal to the
floor…"

It's no different to humming a song to yourself or, running over the lines of a chart hit that has got stuck in your mind – but to him, this was incomprehensible. Just for a moment it was like he wasn't in a holding cell. He looked at me bemused and said something to the effect of *"You like Jay-Z bro?"* – his tone was quite surprised. I reassured him that

"Oh yeah, I really like him – did you see him a couple of months ago when he came to Wembley?"
"No I didn't get tickets"
"Oh it was amazing" (I enthused) "He brought Nas out, Beyoncé was there, Memphis Bleak…"
"You know who Memphis Bleak is?"
"Oh yeah definitely"

This was absolutely playing with his preconceptions and his paradigms in that one short conversation. It absolutely attacked what he believed to be true. It just deliberately over-turned one simple thing. Coppers don't like black rap musicians.

When he went into interview – with his solicitor- he made full and frank confessions to everything. He completely broke down. I'm not saying that by some Derren Brownesque mind trick I prompted that confession – but I'm sure that he had a moment that got in behind his programming. He was a young man trapped in a violent reality, he couldn't escape from it, he was terrified of the people that were running him, and worst of all, *he was ashamed that he was gay*. If they ever found out he was gay he was a dead man. He had to pretend to be heterosexual, and the only way that he could express any form of emotional or sexual connection was through violence.

He *could* stand up in court and have his 'boys' see him get convicted of possession with intent to supply, of supply, of possession of a hand-gun, of money laundering offences, of robbery – but he was presented with a psychological crisis that he had been suppressing for years. He was gay, and he raped a man.

He told a story of criminal coercion and fear – as tragic as it was brutal – with the most horrific outcome:

> *"I was given the gun to make me look serious and hard. I used to have to ride in his [criminal boss'] car – and wave it at people to scare them. I was scared to death. I had to do whatever I was told whenever the phone rang – no matter what time it was."*

He went to court and he was convicted of all of the many serious offences he was charged with. He pleaded guilty immediately to everything. Despite entitlement to a thirty-percent sentence reduction on the basis of an early guilty plea he was judged to be such a risk to the public, and such a danger to society – that he was given an indeterminate sentence – with no fixed release date. It was difficult to argue that he wasn't incredibly dangerous. There is no doubt that he was an exploited teenager, that through his life he had been trafficked and coerced to do criminal acts – but aside from actually killing someone – his offences were about as terrible as you could contemplate. The rape – no doubt born from his traumatic inability to cope with a sexuality that was entirely incompatible with his lifestyle, his gang code, and his surroundings – that was completely on him and there is nothing to condone that expression of his trauma.

I've thought about him a lot down the years – what if some form of early intervention had gotten to him sooner? *What if?*

I have a great deal of faith that a properly resourced Probation Service could actually work with that young man – who will now be in his early thirties and probably still in prison.

I have every reason to believe that he came to realise, all too very late, that the police, and other authority figures he had been taught to hate and show enmity towards – were not the 'baddies' at all. We didn't want to beat him up and brutalise him. He had to sit there many, many nights and contemplate that maybe he was on the wrong side of things – but I can't help but contemplate that if we collectively had more in help for people like our young man from Highbury, this might never had happened at all. *So maybe we are the baddies too?*

Chapter Eleven: How do we win?

There is genuinely good news at the end of this terrible and admittedly rather bleak journey through the phenomenon of 'County Lines'. County Lines is not – as much as it might be depicted as such – a disease or a war. We might imagine ourselves fighting it as such – but actually it isn't. I actually find it unhelpful to constantly conflate the challenges that we confront with wars – with 'front line' rhetoric and worst still references towards the Second World War, to Dunkirk and so on. For one thing, I truly believe that such language only leads to greater entrenchment, resentment and fear.

If you are a child or young person who has realigned their world view towards a future that is built around criminal affiliations and drug dealing – how are you going to feel when you hear the Home Secretary saying that your choices are 'evil' and that the forces of 'good' are coming after you?

It is very well to suggest that this is a 'strawman' argument – *"No, no, no, the Home Secretary said that we are going after the gangs, the people that target our children, not the children..."* – how do you think that is perceived by the child who has made the choice to join the gang? Do you think that the child hears that rhetoric and thinks "Oh good, they're going to rescue me"? The fact is that such children and young people don't believe that they need to be rescued – and when someone announces that they are attacking the 'evil' that they (the child or young person) have chosen – that child or young person is expecting to be attacked by the weight of the authorities.

County Lines is a social and economic phenomenon – with social and economic causational factors that underpin it, and social and economic consequences.

Instead of wasting time on grandstand speeches to an already appreciative choir of party faithful – we need to make material choices that are going to fundamentally address the social and economic circumstances that allow this particular criminal business model to thrive and succeed. We can choose – on a local and national level – to adopt several significant changes that will eliminate or significantly minimise County Lines as an overall threat to our children. Some of it is to do with enforcement – but, perhaps surprisingly, in my eyes, only a small piece of the remedy is actually to be found in the basket of law enforcement.

We can win against this phenomenon – but we have to be ready for the fact that when we do win, organised and gang related crime will evolve again and adapt itself in a relatively short period of time to the new social circumstances we have created. That is just what it is. That is Darwinism. Nevertheless – we still must tackle this. We still have an absolute duty of care to all children – and all children and young people *do matter*.

What follows in this chapter are my clear recommendations for the steps that can be taken, locally and nationally, to achieve the collective aim that we all share. Some of these steps might appear to be controversial, for some they might be considered too 'soft' or too 'liberal' – one or two are possibly a whole book in their own right. I don't want to get bogged down in the debate – I want to stimulate conversation and consideration of their relative merits and independent consequences. That in and of itself is a step in the right direction. I personally advocate that we should adopt them collectively – we must either invest wholeheartedly in this – or we must acknowledge and accept the liability that is upon us for not doing all that we can.

I am not saying that my position is infallible – but it is a position that is merited by time and experience.

I will start with the issue of controlled drugs as they are currently defined.

Recommendation 1: A root and branch review and reform of outdated Misuse of Drugs legislation

The Misuse of Drugs act 1971 has been the framework by which we perceive and contextualise drugs in the UK over the forty-nine years it has been in existence. It has created false parallels between certain drugs and psychoactive substances. As particular substances have been promoted or demoted through the classes it has also caused confusion and misunderstanding.

Although very different substances – crack cocaine and heroin are graded together in the highest category of risk. While it is generally acceptable to continue to refer to crack and heroin as the 'most harmful' drugs overall, class B becomes more confusing and contains amphetamine, cannabis, codeine (a pharmaceutical opiate), as well as ketamine and other drugs.

Ketamine has been enjoying a surge in popularity – and sitting alongside cannabis in an overall grade of a broad and imprecise spectrum of harm reassures many juvenile experimenters that it can't be that bad.

Cannabis itself – as currently defined – appears to offer a spectrum all of its own. You really don't know what type of cannabis you might be consuming – and the risk is massively varied – but it's all considered to be 'cannabis' in law. Furthermore, government policy has confused people by oscillated between cannabis being a class B drug, a class C drug and then a class B drug once again, *within a relatively short period of time*. In truth purity is clearly very important with cannabis. It's not quite like heroin or cocaine in a simple argument about purity ('of course a 100% pure version of coke or heroin is going to be more dangerous') – cannabis is actually an *entirely different drug* with very different consequences depending on the THC/CBD ratio.

We can then briefly consider the sentencing powers around controlled drugs. The legislation threatens a maximum of *six months imprisonment* and a £5000 fine at Magistrates Court for *simple possession* (not possession with intent to supply) of a class A drug. At Crown Court this goes up to seven years and an unlimited fine. *I have never seen nor heard of such punishments being handed down of course – not ever.* I would be very surprised to see street dealers and adult runners handed seven years for *supply* (never mind possession). It isn't a reflection of the world in which we are living or the reality of the criminal justice system today. Offering such powers to judges and magistrates serves no purpose to anyone. In fact advertising such penalties to young people – *as is often part of the agenda for scaring them into avoiding drugs* – only creates a situation where the whole system becomes less trustworthy in their eyes. The first time one young person is caught in possession of an amount of cannabis, with clear implications that they were supplying (and keep in mind that young people will speak to each other and know who *is* supplying) and they only get dealt with for possession, and in doing so

415

they receive an out of court disposal – *we have critically undermined the integrity of the system in their eyes.*

When we contemplate what we *actually* want the legislation to achieve, we find that it is lacking. The statutory position on controlled drugs now needs to include specific provision for people who are found to be supplying through exploited children and young people. There is such a clear evidential overlap between the exploitation of children, modern day slavery and the supply of controlled drugs that particular consideration must be given to such circumstances. Where the use of children to carry or supply is an essential part of the criminal M.O. the offender ought to be charged under a separate offence. This would mirror the way in which sexual offences are charged separately where children are victimised. Rape is s.1 of Sexual Offences Act 2003, but a separate offence of 'Sexual Activity with a Child' is charged under s.9.

An option or alternative would be to also look across at racially and religiously aggravated crime. 'Hate Crime' attracts legislation under s.143 Criminal Justice Act 2003. Where specific offences are committed by targeting a victim due to race or religion (or perceived membership of such a group). The CPS policy on hate crime is not to accept pleas to lesser offences on 'Hate Crime' for the sake of expediency, and the sentencing provisions for 'Hate Crime' offences are increased and appropriately more robust.

My point is – tougher sentences for people who abuse and victimise children in the supply of controlled drugs – a more pragmatic and helpful attitude towards people who are common day to day users.

Considering the implications of controlled drug management and the regulation of public health is becoming a far more pressing concern and a more substantial cost to the UK. The best thing that can be said about the two dimensional so called 'war on drugs' is that it has been fought to an incredibly expensive standstill.

You might be able to persuade yourself of this 'standstill' *if you try* but the costs of enforcement are huge. These costs grow exponentially when you consider the broader costs to all of the associated partners who uphold existing drugs legislation.

Carefully considered reforms to drug legislation are showing benefits abroad. The Independent cited Portugal as an example where drug related deaths have fallen to three per million versus the UK which has forty deaths per million[86].

Writing on 9th September 2018, journalist Jonny Winship said:

---

[86] https://www.independent.co.uk/voices/uk-drugs-addiction-marijuana-crime-government-nhs-a8529731.html

"It is time to open an honest discussion around the harms of these drugs, accept that we have one of the worst drug problems in the world and take more progressive steps, or risk falling behind."

As things stand, the outmoded legislation that we adhere to is designed and intended to protect us from drug related harms. It is this legislation in fact that creates a huge and highly lucrative black market for organised criminal gangs to exploit. We are giving them a market and an opportunity, we are forcing users into their hands, and the harm that is resulting to our children and young people through the mechanisms and machinery of supply is clear and obvious. We are effectively saying that the harm we anticipate from reviewing and re-writing our statutory position on drugs is worse than the existing position that we have on Child Criminal Exploitation and County Lines. This is a staggering assessment and one that needs to be revisited urgently.

I write this not because I am a drug user or drug sympathiser (I'm not), nor do I advocate drug use or experimentation – but I adopt this position because the welfare and the protection of children is a greater priority to me than whether or not an adult can make their own choice on whether to smoke cannabis (for example).

Recommendation 2: The licensed and legalised supply and availability of cannabis under a specified THC percentage

The children and young people that I have spoken to who have admitted to experimenting with cannabis tend to have problems. Invariably there is a reason why they are smoking weed – and of the problems that they have – the cannabis is but one of the problems. It's actually an expression of the fact that they are struggling to cope with numerous other things in their life – and it's a temporary measure that they have adopted. As such – and as things stand – there are considerable risks around that which are not inherent to the drug as a pharmaceutical product, but because of social interactions and connections that are made around the drug and how they get their hands on it.

I don't consider it to be 'ok' for children and young people to use cannabis. It is a dangerous thing and the medical evidence is very much against THC being introduced to the developing brain because of the negative side effects and consequences.

As Dr Dicken Bevington of the Cambridgeshire CASUS explained to me when I spoke to him:

> *"There isn't necessarily evidence that it causes psychosis or makes something appear that wasn't there before – but if that person has an*

*underlying condition or susceptibility to it – it is
more likely to open the door to it."*

Several children and young people have talked to me
about the fear that they have of the strength of cannabis
on a street level. One specific girl who had been using for
less than a year – albeit fairly consistently in small
quantities – was upfront about the early signs of
psychosis that were beginning to cause her real concern.
She told me that she was genuinely worried and did have
fears about what the longer term consequences would
be – *she's not the only young person who has spoken to
me with this anxiety*.

The current position on cannabis specifically has led to a
spiralling level of THC product that is on the streets, and
a lack of informed choice for those who do use.

Legalisation and regulation can introduce the same levels
of control and quality assurance that we apply to more
everyday products – such as a chocolate. If you go to buy
chocolate you can decide exactly what level of cocoa you
like, and how dark or bitter that chocolate needs to be
for your tastes. Cannabis is becoming – and has become
– a race towards a hallucinogenic experience. More akin
to an LSD (or 'acid') trip. 'Shatter' is the most recent
incarnation of this brain bruising product. Synthetic
cannabinoids such as 'Spice' simply sever the user from
their reliable interpretation of the world around them –
creating a condition of unmanageable anger, aggression
and literal insanity.

Few – *a tiny minority* – of young people, and I would hazard to estimate adults also, are looking for this when they dip into cannabis. It's like comparing someone who would like a glass of wine in front of the television to someone who wants to go on an alcohol fuelled binge through the city centre on a Friday night.

A massive step that we can take to protect both young people and adults is to allow them to simply differentiate and make reasonable and informed choices. Looking into the market that now exists in Canada, for example, you can see that choices have been made to allow adults to legally buy super strength cannabis strains if they want to – but equally they can buy CBD dominant products where the THC levels are 3% or less, or even 0% if that is what they prefer. Likewise they have CBD/THC balanced products like 'Even Keel', available from the Ontario Cannabis Store for less than $6 per gram[87].

Importantly – *you don't have to smoke it either*. The legalisation of cannabis allows for other simple preparations and presentations – such as chocolate, vapes, oils and extracts to be sold in ready to consume forms. We know that one of the most harmful things about smoking cannabis is the fact that nicotine is one of the most addictive substances in the world. We know

---

[87]

https://ocs.ca/collections/balanced?product=4571297777484&sort_by=products_custom_pricing_desc

that smoking is a leading cause of cancer. We are aware of the statistics that surround smoking related deaths.

I don't think that the supply of cannabis should be 'free market' or unhindered – it needs to be regulated and monitored in exactly the same way that we do successfully with cigarettes and alcohol. I personally don't advocate for legal supply to people under the age of 21 – given the development of the human brain not reaching maturity until after that age generally. I do recognise that THC levels above 15% cause significantly different outcomes and experiences – so in my view drawing a line somewhere (and scientific research would be appropriate towards this) seems like a sensible and cautious idea. I pragmatically accept that this won't stop people under 21, and teenagers, from buying and using it (just as absolute prohibition doesn't today).

While all of the above promotes public health there are further profound and important reasons to address this recommendation.

First of all – we are talking about immediately taking this drug, as a key product, out of the hands of County Lines' drug dealers and organised criminal groups. In one simple move we are depriving them of a huge revenue stream and we are dealing a massive blow to the black market. Why would anyone choose to buy an inconsistent criminal product, when an approved, cheaper, regulated product is easily available from a pharmacy or dispensary? We know that cannabis is an entry level experience – I don't use the contentious term 'gateway drug' – but from speaking to children and young people regularly I know that there is a huge difference in the minds of most when considering experimenting with weed, versus experimenting with cocaine or heroin. By cutting the potential reasons for young people to actually go towards organised crime at all (if they are determined to experiment with or sample cannabis) we are immediately promoting their safety. The Institute of Economic Affairs published their report in 2018[88] that the illegal market for cannabis is believed to be worth £2.5 billion per year. That is – my honest opinion - £2.5 billion of revenue that I would simply prefer not to be controlled by organised crime.

Secondly – but of equal importance – is the potential value in taxation that could be gained by the government to fund the support of young people and reduction in child criminal exploitation. The IEA suggest that the tax income from legalisation could be above £1 billion per year "before considering savings to public services".

So contemplate a measure that would actually result in a funding injection of £1 billion per year – and one that would save other public resources in areas such as public prosecution, criminal justice, and policing.

---

[88] https://iea.org.uk/media/uks-illicit-cannabis-market-worth-2-5bn-a-year-finds-new-report/

Chris Snowdon is the Head of Lifestyle Economics at the IEA he is directly quoted in their article saying:

> *"It's high time for reform of cannabis policy in the UK. Canada and the USA are showing the way. Done properly, the legalisation of cannabis is a win-win-win: criminals lose a lucrative industry, consumers get a better, safer and cheaper product, and the burden on the general tax payer is reduced."*

The 'win-win-win' scenario that Snowdon cites only glances at the huge material effect that legalisation would have on the issue of County Lines drug supply – *which is clearly my first priority*. My second priority would be reinvesting every single penny of taxation into funding the essential services that are required to protect children and young people from criminal exploitation. Every single penny.

Recommendation 3: Drastically increase the resources that are available to protect young people from criminal exploitation

We have immediately identified a funding source that could create as much as £1 billion per year in additional resources to protect children and young people from organised crime. In previous chapters we have looked at the terrible effects of austerity and how genuinely our ability to respond to a phenomenon like County Lines has crumbled over the last ten years.

It is clear that the government has a responsibility not only to invest any monies gained from legalisation of cannabis into children and young people services – it ought to 'match fund' that figure as a priority issue – taking from other budgets where necessary. I'll remind once again of the blank cheque written for war in Afghanistan and Iraq – north of £20 billion. I'll remind again about the controversial HS2 high speed rail project costing more than £80 billion. I will highlight reports from the media – such as the Independent – where Jon Stone wrote in 2016 that the total cost of renewing our commitment to a nuclear arsenal and Trident will be "at least" £205 billion (The independent Trident Commission is quoted as saying it would be around £100 billion)[89]. This really is an 'at any cost' commitment.

There are huge and numerous arguments towards nuclear disarmament – but if anybody feels that our nuclear programme puts us in some position of parity with 'super-powers' such as a Russia or America – it's a falsehood. Armscontrol.org – a disarmament and non-proliferation interest group cites that we have 215 nuclear warheads (by estimate) whereas the US has

---

[89] https://www.independent.co.uk/news/uk/politics/trident-replacement-cost-nuclear-submarines-205-billion-independent-trident-commission-cnd-caroline-a7025956.html

5,800, and Russia has 6,375. We have 1.76% of their combined strength and just over 3% the strength of Russia alone. My main concern is with the colossal amount of money that is being wasted – and just a fraction of that money (approximately 0.5% per year) would match fund the revenue derived from taxing legalised cannabis.

All of a sudden, instead of talking about pocket projects, and £20 million initiatives – we would be talking about £2 billion plus super concepts and determined, joined up, national policy that can be compared to our approach to radicalisation, terror and the 'Prevent' agenda. We must not pretend to ourselves that we cannot afford this or that the money cannot be found. We can afford this investment – we choose not to make it and we live with the consequences.

Recommendation 4: Statutory framework, responsibility and accountability on a 'top to bottom' basis

It is clear that a specific framework for protecting children and young people from County Lines and Criminal Exploitation would be advantageous. Such a framework could sit specifically with the MAPPA (Multi Agency Public Protection Agreement) agenda and clearly there is relevance to managing offenders and suspects within a specified category through the ViSOR database.

Children being drawn into County Lines and Criminal Exploitation need to be subject to assessment in a similar way to the attempts that have been made previously to score and evaluate victims of Domestic Abuse (utilising the Domestic Abuse Stalking and Harassment question set).

Creating an evidence led system that objectively recognises the children at greatest risk of exploitation in specific local communities would be an enormous step in the right direction. We are talking about mapping a dynamic picture of risk over a period of time to monitor and improve the chances of such young people and their families.

Such a framework needs to be revisited by designated local authorities and accountability has to be ascribed to agencies who receive the financial support and other resources to help them to maintain this specific picture of risk.

The framework should be an integrated national picture – a digital database – which is something that is used in the same way by every local area. Cases of children in foster care who move between agencies should be equipped with digital passports that move with them and become open to local authorities as they arrive. When a missing child is located in an out of county location it is clear that a record of that movement should be created – and where possible the route and purpose of the event should be ascertained.

We are capable of creating digital tools that can hold such information securely, and which can be unlocked and consulted for proportionate and appropriate reasons compatible with the GDPR.

A senior figure in the local authority – be that the Chief Executive of the County Council, the Chief Constable, the Police and Crime Commissioner, the regional Mayor or otherwise – ought to be placed under statutory responsibility to ensure that such measures are introduced to ensure that these are in place by a specified date, and that from that date forward that such information is managed and updated through a regulated set number of meetings between the relevant partners.

Such meetings must create immediate actions that are designed to intervene on identified children in a way that it supportive, protective, and diverts them away from harm and exploitation. It is clear that this framework must be stitched into the work of the Local Safeguarding Children's Board.

In addition to this, such a framework must include a multiagency trigger which can be activated by any relevant partner that identifies a need for immediate intervention in the appropriate prevailing circumstances. This would include a school Principal being able to press the button where any specific child gives rise to the worst symptoms of exploitation and where their escalation into abuse has been rapid, unexpected or previously unidentified.

Activating such a trigger should place an immediate requirement on agencies to convene to discuss recommendations and actions on that specific case within a seventy-two hour period – resulting in the delivery of further material steps (i.e. delivery against an action plan, not the writing of an action plan) within a fourteen day period provoking a special case review within a month. Actions should be delivered by the agencies best equipped to deliver – *not the nearest agency with general availability*. For example – enforcement action handled by police, social care to work with family through the Early Help Team and so on. Failure to deliver to deadlines in trigger cases should have statutory consequences.

Recommendation 5: Increased investment and research in De-radicalisation and Criminal Seduction research

It is clear that a portion of the resources identified to eliminate County Lines should be invested in robust academic research that is tasked to deliver against fundamental gaps in knowledge. This is a specific knowledge area that needs to be advanced very clearly – academics commenting on both County Lines and the issues or radicalisation and de-radicalisation (both criminal and political/ideological) respect the fact that we simply do not know enough about either topic area and have not developed effective and objective, evidence led measures to carry ourselves forward.

I am reluctant to draw war based analogies, but in one specific circumstance I find it relevant and I will. The work of Sun Tzu – the timeless Chinese writer, philosopher, strategist and general of the 6th Century wrote:

> *"If you know the enemy and know yourself, you need not fear the result of a hundred battles. If you know yourself but not the enemy, for every victory gained you will also suffer a defeat. If you know neither the enemy nor yourself, you will succumb in every battle."*

Academics and researchers need to be given complete access to professional environments where they can engage first-hand with victims, families, offenders, professionals and all of the intermediate steps, mechanisms and structures that we currently utilise to tackle this issue. In creating a thorough, intellectual, and rigorous audit of what we currently do, what we have done in the past, what has worked (and in what circumstances), what has failed (and why) we will take the upper hand with organised criminal gangs who do not have access to such resources or facilities. There is no reason why our society should be out planned and out thought by such offenders – and yet we are. County Lines is growing and we are not 'winning'.

By creating clear and implementable plans we can bring consistency of approach at all levels of our action – whether that is from the earliest stages of prevention strategy, or working to extract the most severely entrenched victims and return them to comparative normality.

Additional investment in the management and treatment of adverse childhood experiences clearly has the potential to reduce many forms of harm – not merely the threat of County Lines or Child Criminal Exploitation.

At a time where tuition fees and the costs of education in the UK are higher than they have ever been we can logically expect to see fewer people going to university and higher barriers for people who do want to study. Young people are more inclined to stick to areas of study with high earnings potential because they realise that they have to repay student debts and that other cost of living pressures are rising.

A programme which takes a student through a long term process of investment in the specific research areas would provide long term dividends and could be incentivised with full tuition and living expense bursaries escalating in line with their qualifications. Further incentives could be offered to post doctoral research in the fields of criminology, law, sociology, psychology which would be highly relevant – and the funding of a collective research group that combines expertise from several fields for a collaborative purpose would be even better.

Recommendation 6: Training and Skills for professionals & partner agencies

Surprisingly there are still individuals in key roles who have poor levels of knowledge around the issue of County Lines. Additionally there are agencies and authorities who satisfy themselves that training can be delivered on a read through slide show basis completed in less than half an hour, or bundled along with generic approaches to child protection more broadly.

I would suggest that a lot of this is due to the costs involved in high quality training and development of staff – which can be very high – and the time it takes to deliver such. It is easy to satisfy requirements on a 'tick box' basis that training has been 'made available to all staff' through a self-read process.

Creating and delivering training courses that introduce – for examples – General Practitioners - to genuine survivors of County Lines and Child Criminal Exploitation in their older years is a win/win. It is a cathartic process for subjects willing to offer themselves, and it is utterly compelling and unforgettable for the person being trained.

Utilising convicted drug dealers who have operated within this model should be an aim and objective with the Probation remit for rehabilitating offenders and helping them to recognise and repay the debt that they owe to communities they have harmed.

Recommendation 7: Unified and coordinated communications strategy

Where possible and appropriate, very similar learning opportunities should be extended to schools through the PSHE agenda with appropriate rewards and expenses for the people (both those who speak out about being exploited, and convicted offenders) who take the time to do this.

For a long time such things have been badged under the category of 'nice to do' and not 'essential'. For many years 'nice to do' things simply do not get done.

Clear mechanisms should be developed to make high quality resources more available – and this could include utilising online services for eConferences, eSeminars and live stream broadcasts. Content, generally, on this subject is *not* strong and you have to work *very hard* to find good content.

Many schools are left asking police officers in the hope that they can get hold of one at a time and date that works, and that the officer they get hold of will make a compelling effort out of the time or opportunity they have been afforded. It is frankly quite hit and miss – and miss is doing the heavy lifting in this subject area.

We are still talking about leaflet format information services, and click through slides shows – living in a world of opportunity that surrounds interactive viral social media such as TikTok, Instagram, YouTube, Facebook, Twitter and Zoom.

Our approach needs to be graphical and eye catching, provocative and imaginative. In the UK we have some of the most incredible, vivid and popular artists in the world. What have we learned from them? How do we get them to focus on this agenda? It is time to commission our artists to come to our assistance.

I would suggest that our media offering on County Lines is staggeringly short of where it ought to be. We need to enlist the services of key YouTube and social media 'influencers' who have millions of young subscribers in an immediate information sharing task that should have been actioned yesterday (quite frankly).

Recommendation 8: Powers to require drug and alcohol testing in schools

There is an obvious correlation in risk between children and young people who are drinking and using drugs in their early teenage years, and those who will be subjected to criminal exploitation.

What I am not recommending is the mass screening of all students for drink or drugs – but where there are objective and reasonable grounds that can be corroborated, school principals should have a power in law to require a sample of breath, a saliva mouth swab or a urine test as appropriate to identify whether a child or young person has been using drink or drugs, or has been coming to school hung over or intoxicated.

This is not to say that the Principal should have the power to compel the child or young person to take the test or provide a sample – or that parents shouldn't be present or consulted. It is perfectly possible to allow for both parents or an appropriate adult to be present, and for the child to refuse without a use of force being made.

Children or young people who refuse should be treated like athletes who refuse – that a) the refusal or avoidance of a test itself is treated as a serious offence and that b) an adverse inference around their misuse of drugs and alcohol will apply formally and be placed on their record.

In doing so we begin to formulate a more robust evidence base around those people at risk – and there is little need for this to be carried out by another agency (for example the police).

To make the process more objective and considered, a short list of available professionals in other local services could be contacted through the LSCB (for example) and it could be a requirement of the process that more than one agency agrees that a necessity test has been met and that reasonable grounds to require the test have been satisfied.

Children and young people who do test positive should be referred as a matter of course to drug and alcohol counselling and support, and parents should be given the opportunity to engage with Early Help Teams with a view towards supporting them in the home through a time of crisis.

Recommendation 9: Increased investment in mental health services, drug, alcohol and treatment services, and holistic or 'wrap around' provision

It is very clear that children and young people tend to choose who they reach out to. It is not a simple process and you can't just expect children in crisis to accept the first person that comes along – particularly if they seem preoccupied with a heavy workload.

Mental health practitioners, and the drug and alcohol counselling process needs time and consistency. Many young people are dispirited because they go through a series of social workers, young persons' workers or family workers in an alarmingly short amount of time.

We need to create mechanisms of fully funded services that give experts the ability to decide when it is appropriate to withdraw – not merely because of pressures to see other clients, or because a set and arbitrary number of sessions have lapsed.

How can we expect our young people to develop rapport and trust in these circumstances? We need to fund specific youth workers, counsellors, and drugs workers who can reassure their young clients from the off that they are developing a long term relationship – with support that can be relied upon. The support itself needs to be available in a variety of settings to reassure that child or young person this isn't just about 'in school' or 'at home' – *this is a whole life change*.

So that professional needs to be able to come in and out of those settings with flexibility, and show continued commitment during school holidays.

This person should be the lead practitioner with the child and their family, and instead of creating multi-agency fatigue, all things should be funnelled through that point of contact once it is established that the child or young person and their family is really happy with that relationship.

It is enormously frustrating when working with a young person in crisis, when quite abruptly, one key partner announces that they have to withdraw because their own agency has an arbitrary limit of service which has been met.

Services are not designed from the perspective of the child, young person, or the family – they are designed from the perspective of the service provider and their budget.

In most circumstances this is deeply inappropriate and it needs to be challenged. Until we reach an objective position when the grading of risk around a young person is agreed – *and it has been demonstrated that a sufficient level of improvement has been made* - there should be no consideration of withdrawal. If the risk escalates, the response and engagement should shift accordingly. Very sadly there are cases where we are withdrawing from children and young people in cases where the rationale is based on organisational expediency and for no other reason.

Recommendation 10: The urgent removal/reduction of the PRU/AP system

An entire chapter of this book has been dedicated to the additional risks and the inherently problematic structures that the PRU/AP system presents. These environments are particularly unsuitable for children and young people at risk of criminal exploitation. They create precursory expectations of institutionalised containment and social rejection. They are a barrier to successful reintegration and create a degree of separation and isolation that cannot be maintained in the workplace or post educational environments.

Putting all of our eggs in one basket is a clear gift to the organised criminal gangs who seek to identify the most vulnerable children and young people to subject to criminal exploitation. We have to amend this urgently and significantly.

Many schools are stretching budgets to create spaces within mainstream learning environments that promote the ability to keep young people in mainstream, and help them to work through their problems without exposing them to such risks.

Trauma Informed policy inbuilt into the fabric of such centres – but most schools are incredibly over tasked trying to do this within existing budgets and with the existing number of teaching assistants and behavioural professionals.

Schools and Academy Trusts should receive significant support for creating such centres, they should be incentivised and resourced, and rewards should result that benefit the entire school as a consequence.

In short, everything ought to be done to create schools that can afford to keep difficult to manage and highly challenging students within their community in an appropriate setting that acknowledges and supports their needs.

Recommendation 11: Increased neighbourhood policing presence in schools

With few exceptional differences the relationship that exists between schools and the police has gotten more distant and less consistent as resources available to neighbourhood policing have been withdrawn. It is less likely that a school will be able to rely on a confirmed point of contact, and even less possible for officers and PCSOs to host regular workshops, drop in sessions or prevention surgeries in centres of education.

Neighbourhood policing really thrives when staff and officers can recognise the most vulnerable young people on sight. Being on first name terms with families, with mums, dads and young people is a simple preventative tool that mitigates and prevents harm.

If we first learn about a specific individual because they have stabbed someone, something is very wrong.

Having an officer who moves between a small number of schools, offering drop in support and community engagement, after school sessions, and who gets physically involved in the process of constructing diversionary activities, PSHE provision, and who might even go on school trips or over-night visits is the gold standard that we should all aim towards.

This role is about building rapport and trust between all young people and the police – about them growing up reassured by a police presence, and not feeling worried or intimidated by it.

As with social workers and mental health professionals and drugs' counsellors – it is important to put people into role for a minimum tenure. Moving and changing personalities really undermines that relationship building process, and ideally when people do change they should taper out with an appropriate handover and clear communication to all partners.

Being able to do something as simple – and frankly unimaginative – as this would be a huge piece of progress and it would be embraced by every single school.

The gains that would be shown in terms of information and intelligence sharing would be substantial, the increase in the multiagency bond would be obvious. The sense of security and reassurance around our schools would be palpable.

Again this is an approach that has been lost in the many numerous cuts to budgets during the austerity period – but quite frankly cutting this approach was a short term financial gain for a long term loss in terms of consequences and risks.

Recommendation 12: Budgetary grants and investments in 'designing out' teams managed through local/District level Problem Solving Groups

We have discussed the value of Problem Solving Groups and the collective results that can be achieved through well chaired and well resourced teams. We have looked at the process of designing solutions based around victimology, offender management, and adjustments made to localities where offences are committed.

County Lines and Child Exploitation is difficult in that grooming (either for sexual or criminal purposes) can happen in the virtual space – which is notoriously difficult to manage – however if tasked and equipped properly 'designing out groups' can work on identifying locations where drug exchanges are taking place, and make those locations less receptive to that form of crime by merit of quite simple steps (including CCTV, gated areas, lighting, increased visibility by cutting back certain types of trees and plants and so on).

Cyber tools – such as Qustodio – could be afforded on a subscription basis and licenses distributed to parents who need to know the whereabouts of their children, and who wish to remotely monitor social media, email, text message and telephone details.

There are technological solutions that can be introduced to local community spaces that won't (by any means) eliminate drug exchanges – but would make it significantly harder for such activity to go unobserved. Problem Solving Groups, working with Parish Councils specifically, can bring a level of local knowledge and understanding to the table that is beyond compare. The detailed understanding that they that they have – if combined with an appropriate amount of resourcing – can make a genuine difference to whether a children's play park, a local car park, or round the back of the local library is receptive and vulnerable to drop off and pick up behaviours.

Linking this type of work into law enforcement agencies could demonstrate real outcomes which would help to develop community confidence further.

Developing an innovation fund that feeds back into academic research and a learning bank held nationally on a centralised basis – such as with the College of Policing for example – and which functions to disseminate positive and creative practices nationally would help local councils and authorities in a very meaningful way in efforts to prevent crime which targets young people specifically.

444

Postscript

This has been a journey through the landscape of County Lines and Child Criminal Exploitation. In the writing of this book I have hoped to achieve several things. I never set out to document the whole problem with a comprehensive or god like omniscience – I simply do not think that is possible (and certainly not from me). This is a massive, complex and under documented subject.

What I did want to achieve was a reasonable and informed conversation with you as a reader that would help you to progress your understanding, provoke your consideration and help you to take action in the immediate sphere of your community.

I have not sought at any time to batter you with graphical horror, overwhelm you with pathos, or blackmail you emotionally. I don't think that utilising fear as a motivator is the way to move ahead on this subject. Sadly this subject is emotive and you cannot avoid that.

The truth is that a logical and ethical conversation about the realities of County Lines helps us to draw natural conclusions. It should prompt us to hold ourselves to account and to compel ourselves – as objectively as possible – to cross examination about how we arrived at this current position.

I have supplied a dozen recommendations that I think could be adopted at a variety of levels – and I accept that most of them currently sit on a wish list for local partners who would love to take a stronger material stand against this very terrible form of criminal behaviour.

You might not agree with all of the recommendations. *You might not agree with any of them*. I do hope you have read this text and that you leave agreeing that action of some meaningful value does need to be taken.

The title 'Beating County Lines and other things to do before lunch' is a tongue in cheek reference to the manner in which we are tackling this problem right now.

It is on a 'to do' list – a series of sticky notes – and one of them says "County Lines". Perhaps that sticky-note is smudged a bit, it's not as sticky as it used to be, and having found it from a couple of weeks earlier you look at it and think *"Oh shit yeah, that... what did I say I was going to do for that again?"*.

County Lines is not at the top of our agenda of daily business. We don't get out of bed in the morning, put on our clothes and say *"Today I'm going to attack County Lines"*. Few people do. It is everybody and nobody's business. Many people have a hand in it – we all share a responsibility towards it – but if I asked you who was really gripping it, focusing their determined time and effort on it – with a clear and undivided focus... nobody.

I hope that in reading the accounts that I have shared – and the content drawn specifically from disclosures made to me by children and young people, plus parents, and people who have come through County Lines (some far more damaged than others) – you will respect the disclosures I have made. I have deliberately not identified a number of people by their names – please don't try to deduce who I have been working with or referencing. This is not an exercise in *"Well I think that Gianni is actually a girl called Lindsey that I went to school with…"* I'd be upset and disappointed to think that people did that because invariably – you're likely to be wrong if you do, and you're definitely missing the point.

What I do want us to agree on is two fundamental facts (facts as I believe them to be):

Fact one is that County Lines does exist, it is a threat to all of our communities, and it is an unacceptable threat to our children and young people. It is not a threat that we can sleep on, it is not a tolerable situation, and it not something that we can write down as simply the cost of the way that we structure our society.

Fact two: We can do something about it, we can respond to it and shape our communities in a way that makes County Lines an obsolete concept, and we are under a moral and ethical duty to do exactly that. Not in the long term, not kicking the can down the street, not distracted by COVID19 or Brexit, or one-hundred-and-one things that we have to get done (some big and some small). We have to take immediate action with a portfolio of short, medium and long term measures that will force organised criminality to accept that the exploitation of children is not worthwhile, not acceptable, not effective, and is a way of conducting their affairs that belongs in the past.

We have considered this as an economic issue, as a social issue, as a criminal issue – we can attack the subject from many angles. With a matter of such prominent importance we must bring our weight to bear on the subject from every conceivable direction.

I would suggest – *and I guess that this is taking a very emotive standpoint* – that paedophiles are the most reviled of all criminals (particularly paedophile murderers). Abuse of trust and celebrity paedophiles are the absolute end of the spectrum reserved for the most vitriolic hatred of all. People responsible for Child Criminal Exploitation exist in absolutely the same sphere of harm. In many cases they open the gateway to child sexual exploitation, premature sexualised behaviours and statutory rape – while they also use their victims to carry illegal drugs, cash and weapons. They hide behind them, they use these children as insulation to protect themselves from conviction. They convince young people to never tell on or identify them – either through fear of violence and abusive reprisals, or on the falsehood of becoming some type of family or some romantic life partner.

448

We manage identified paedophiles – quite correctly – with the tightest of measures. They comply with signing on and travel permissions. They can work in only very restricted professional circumstances. They are visited and checked up on. We prevent them from having access to the internet. We map them, monitor them, and we know the cost of *not* doing so.

When we consider this – by comparison – and reflect on the way in which we deal with people responsible for County Lines, and Child Criminal Exploitation – how do we feel?

It is like a house with two doors – one door is bolted in eight different places, with deadlocks, and chains, and bars and mortis locks. That door is alarmed and monitored with every conceivable – 'money is no object' security. The back door is open though, it's a flimsy cheap door, it isn't locked, and generally we leave it slightly ajar.

There is an incompatibility between the perception of the threat posed in both circumstances. We have taught society to hate and despise one child predator, while the other child predator is broadly unknown.

What I would like to see, perhaps more than anything, is a reassessment of priority. I feel very strongly about this as an experienced professional and as a parent. There is a huge amount of investment required – but it is investment that few people would argue with – given the context and the overall availability of resources at our disposal.

Are we more at risk of a nuclear war or the victimisation and exploitation of children? Do we think that travelling from London to Manchester half an hour more quickly on a high speed train is more important than this agenda? Do we believe that the resources that we spend on global warfare and the overall budget for 'defence' cannot spare the percentile difference that it would take to making a meaningful impact (we have the second highest budget for defence in NATO at £38 billion per year by the way).

What I am going to do is include some tools and references with this book – a guide to the conversational model that I utilise with young people that I feel has helped them to open up and discuss some the issues that we have covered.

I am also going to include a useful, objective checklist that covers the signs and symptoms to spot when a child is being drawn into a criminal relationship, or might be subject to the exploitation associated with County Lines activities.

Finally, I will list the articles, documents, thesis and papers that I have referenced throughout the course of writing this particular book. I will include a reference guide to some of the best resources that I have found that are readily available on this subject.

I am grateful to everyone who has contributed to the writing of this book, and the permissions that have been granted for reproduction of pieces of research, journalism and other hard work. Nobody working within this field works alone – and this problem can only be solved through objective joined up critical thinking and action. **I encourage you to read their work first hand, buy their books, and support them as professionals in every way that you can.** *If I didn't recommend them, I wouldn't have cited them!*

Appendix A – The conversational model ('Progress and withdraw' or 'Advance and Retreat')

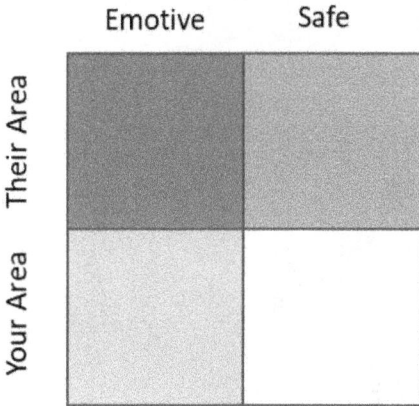

This is a basic visual guide to the engagement model that I have developed when I'm speaking to young people [above].

It serves to illustrate that conversation and dialogue, within a one to one mentoring session, is not an ad hoc process – there is a consistent method behind the approach. This is the approach that I have found to be successful where other approaches have not been.

At any given time the adult in the conversation (i.e. you or I) should know which of these 'boxes' we are functioning in. We should be able to recognise that clearly.

When you go into any engagement with a child or young person there are two halves to the engagement – your area and their area:

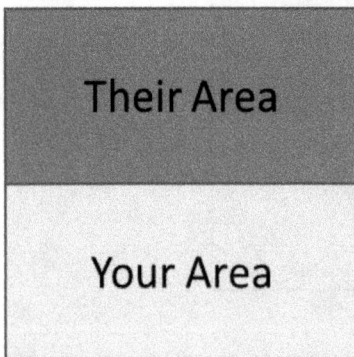

Their Area

Your Area

Your area is about the issues that you bring to the table and specifically want to talk about.

Their area is anything they *volunteer* as a subject of conversation or bring to the table without being prompted by you.

It might be that this young person has misbehaved or acted out in a specific way and you want to get in behind that and find out what that behaviour signified and what the causational factors were around that.

You might want to know if that young person genuinely understands for themselves – or if they are struggling with that level of personal awareness.

Clearly if you walk into a one-to-one mentoring session and you put that very overtly on the table you are now talking in 'your area' (you probably wouldn't – the child or young person would find that to be quite challenging unless it is done in a very adept way).

You might be confused by the whole 'their area/your area' concept because it is *about them* – that doesn't make it 'their area'. Realistically this whole session is 'about them'. So set that to one side.

If you enter into a one-to-one mentoring or talking session with a child and you invite them to tell you how their week has been, and you open it up by *getting them* to put things on the table, you are now functioning in 'their area'. You've asked them to control the session and they are clearly steering what you talk about and they have the agenda.

Visually you might think of giving them the ball. While they are holding the ball, we are in their area.

There is always a power dynamic in this relationship because they are a child, you are an adult. In a school setting they are the pupil or student, and you are a teacher or member of staff. They are always mindful of the fact that you have certain powers to direct them to go here or there, and to sanction their peers. Even without that there is a sense of you being someone who will judge them. Finally, they are in the mentoring session to improve. This isn't a mutual support group – you are the person who can help them to get stronger – and as such you have power (even if to begin with they are unconvinced about whether you can help or not).

You must do everything you can to walk a fine and appropriate line that puts that young person at ease, but keeps that boundary in place and a respectful emotional and physical distance between you.

Whether you are in your area, or their area, you are in one of two places additionally. That place is either 'emotive' – or it is 'safe':

An 'emotive area' is clearly one that is likely to trigger an emotional response – the young person my feel accused, might feel vulnerable, it might involve evocative memories or stimulus, and ultimately it could overwhelm that young person.

A 'safe area' or a 'safe zone' is a form of communication that is used to give relief to the conversation, help the young person to feel like they can have a rest, and helps you to build rapport. *You might consider this to be 'small talk'.*

Generally a safe area, within your area or side of the conversation, runs the risk of being boring and might result in the child or young person disengaging from you, checking the clock, and thinking that you are somebody that they cannot relate to.

It makes sense to choose – if you go into this area – to try to stick to content that mirrors the known interests and curiosities of the young person. This is a form of mirroring that helps to reassure them – particularly if you digress for a moment into something that *you've* had a problem with. It helps if it is something that *they've* had a problem with too.

In a safe area this will be an inconsequential issue – *"I hate it when you take a first sip of your tea and you burn your tongue – now you've got a burned tongue for the rest of the day"*. This is a fairly trivial subject matter – but don't underestimate the value. If the young person cannot find any sense of ease or safety in the conversation you won't get any value out of the other content whatsoever. **Plus you are reassuring them that you're a normal person!**

A safe area in the young person's agenda is generally characterised on a spectrum of particular interest to 'fun'. Clear example would be the young man who loves football and wants to talk about what happened on the weekend between Liverpool and Manchester United, who won the league, or who the best players in the world ever are.

If you spend the whole hour talking like this you'll come away feeling like you didn't achieve very much – but actually the bond and the rapport that exists between you (from his perspective) will be very strong. The next time that young person sees you his emotional rapport will probably be very warm and if he has problems and issues you will be one of the first people he is likely to want to speak to about it. He will begin to invest trust. You don't have to agree on everything inside that safe area – but disagreement should be light-hearted.

In children who are diagnosed on the autism spectrum the challenges of creating bonds, rapport and empathy are more challenging. I know this first-hand because my youngest son is on the ASD spectrum. What I also know is that spending time on the things that he enjoys, enjoying them with him, helps him to feel love because that is where love exists for him – it stimulates the same part of his brain.

I would dearly love to put my arms around him and share more physical affection with him – but that is an uncomfortable and threatening thing that he struggles to cope with. If we spend time doing something as simple as cooperating in a computer game environment that he loves, he will usually end up giving me a kiss and a hug – *which is a really big deal for him*.

So the section of the conversation where you are in 'their' area, and it is 'safe', you are relationship building. You might think that we should just go there and spend a lot of time there – there is a lot to be gained. You can only go there if the child or young person opens the door to you. Some are more ready to do this than others, and you can't force it. In fact, the more you bang on that door, the more inclined they will probably be to retreat away from it.

Gaining access to this area is usually a response to strong mirroring of *your* safe area. So you need to intelligently grasp the tiny opportunities to stay 'on topic' when you are in your safe zone.

	Emotive	Safe
Their Area		Favourite games console *trainers*
Your Area		*Lots of mirroring*

Examples of really easy conversations can be built around props that are placed in the meeting space deliberately, or recollections of things that everybody does. It doesn't seem to matter how random these things are because generally juvenile conversation is not as structured and as formal as adult conversation – and an abrupt change of conversation is not quite as insulting or as implicitly offensive as it is between adults.

Broadly speaking you can talk about computer games and social media because most young people have these or at least have opinions on them (safe bet). There is a greater likelihood with boys that computer gaming makes up a big part of their social time, but many, many girls enjoy gaming too.

"Are you a PS4 or an Xbox user?" is such an easy safe question with boys particularly. "What type of gaming are you into?". Even if the child or young person doesn't give you the full trust of running into their area and telling you about their gaming and online experiences – simply by saying *"I play Grand Theft Auto, FIFA and NBA 2020"* – you've got a hook to work in your own area, and stay tethered to theirs (the choices they disclose also give valuable insights into their tastes, and the levels of parental permission they are being offered).

"You're a PS4 user? Booo! I'm Xbox for life – why on earth did you go to PS4?" - *s*ome friendly and non-threatening teasing is not an inappropriate thing, it might allow a little reciprocation, which (of course) should be taken in good humour.

You use that as a foundation and start to build rapport from there. You might ask – for example – "On Xbox your headset is tethered through a headphone cable to your controller – does PS4 have Bluetooth?". This is an example of a completely safe question that is likely to get them talking, and it has the bonus of you being able to say (when they explain it) – *"Oh cheers, that sounds better actually, I always wondered about that"* and you can even move towards "What else do you like about the PS4?"

Keep in mind that I'm not being insincere, I'm sticking to a topic that I can offer something in (I genuinely do own and use an Xbox One) and I can hold up my area. There is nothing worse than coming across as being 'down with the kids', being insincere and showing yourself up as some type of imposter. A good way around this is to just say straight away – *"I don't really know a lot about that could you tell me more?"* (although clearly being well informed is probably more interesting to the young person).

Building rapport through the use of safe areas makes it increasingly possible for you to move into the emotive topics. You simply cannot go into emotive topics before that rapport and trust has been established. It is no more feasible than a perfect stranger approaching you in an abstract situation and asking you about the current state of your marriage or relationship, your sexual tastes and preferences and other intimate facts. Even if your marriage is very healthy and you and your husband or wife are super happy – the whole aspect of that intrusion is within itself just completely 'not ok'.

Within the two halves of emotive topics there is – of course – 'your area' and 'their area'.

Again the area that belongs to you is *not about you*. It is not your opportunity to speak about how unfulfilled you feel, or your existential crisis, your money worries or your relationship with your boss. The issues of an emotive nature in *'your area'* would be what you bring to the table. Perhaps you want to find out about how their relationship with their little brother is, whether everything is ok at home, or why they got into a fight with someone yesterday:

	Emotive	Safe
Their Area	"I've been smoking weed and it's getting out of control now."	
Your Area	'WHY' questions	

If you want to talk about their anger management issues – be aware that *they might not think they have an anger management issue*. The first aspect of that conversation is coming to an agreement that anger management is a relevant and important topic. You might make it less emotive by admitting that you get angry sometimes too, and in fact everyone has anger to deal with.

Their emotive areas can involve them really opening up and going into what we reference as 'free recall'. They just begin to unravel the things that have been worrying them, or recollecting adverse childhood experiences. In that situation, my advice is that you *shut the hell up* and listen.

Tools that can help in this situation are likely to depend heavily on signs of empathy – such as mirroring of body language, verbal reassurance (particularly if they get upset), and subtle methods of getting them to extend what they talk about.

A child baring their soul doesn't want to look up into the horrified expression of an adult who now seems to think they are a monster. Even if they say something shocking, it's important that our emotional volume is low and we don't react in an adverse way.

One example would be the 'repeat back' technique. This involves you literally saying what they just said, almost word for word, back to them. This helps them to know that you are paying close attention, but it generally provokes greater depth and more explanation. It sounds abstract and weird – but you can try this in any conversation.

"...and all I was doing was just sitting there, and Clare came over and said that!"

"All you were doing was just sitting there?" [tone should intimate interest and empathy]

"Yeah – minding my own business, I was reading a book about the civil war, and I was chilling"

People just respond with more detail – you have figuratively taken a step towards them, and they usually take the same figurative step towards you to reciprocate your gesture.

Being in the two 'emotive zones' is fatiguing and it can be hard work.

You get massive amounts from this – and usually when people talk about making a 'breakthrough' (for example when a young person admits that they've been taking drugs, engaged in a sexual relationship with a much older person, have been suffering some form of abuse, are being bullied or harassed) – *it is going to happen in one of these zones*.

You don't stay in one of those zones longer than the child or young person wants to, and you never try to force them into that position – which is oppressive and unacceptable.

Your responsibility as the adult in the room is to look after the welfare of the child or young person – you decide when to give them a rest and draw them back across to a safe area where they can draw breath. This is no different to a P.E. teacher getting children to run laps of the track until they collapse with burn out with exhaustion on an incredibly hot day – you let the kids take a rest in the shade, you let them sit down, you make sure everyone has a cold drink.

To use a footballing analogy – just lobbing random balls into the opposition penalty area in the hope that something ends up in the net is futile, clumsy and pointless. It demonstrates a certain desperation, it is unsettling, and even if it does open something up – I think the child or young person is only likely to be wary about ever going into a room alone with you again. The experience shouldn't feel like cross examination or being bombarded with emotive questions.

Consequently, this model is designed to give you a reference point – to know where you are operating from at any point in the conversation, and for exactly what purpose. As you get to know a child or young person better. You get to know what their tolerance and levels of comfort are.

Sequentially you are likely to begin in a soft, safe space that is yours. You can offer them the opportunity to welcome you into their safe space – *and they might* – but if they don't you have to operate with patience and empathy to eventually gain that degree of confidence and intimacy.

As you get to know a particular young person over time the weight of how much time you spend in your area versus their area might shift – *is likely to shift* – towards spending much more time in their side. The clear sign of this is that they do most of the talking. You are never going to host sessions which are 100% in their area for clear and obvious reasons and some days they feel more chatty – some days less so.

To begin with you might host lots of sessions that are heavily based in safe spaces. For some young people spending 10 or even 5% of that hour with you in an emotive zone is too much pressure and too much hard work. They get emotionally overwhelmed and cannot cope. You have to respect this. You are probably getting more out of that child than any number of other people they have in their lives. There are countless people they have refused to open up to.

You might feel that spending time in safe zones is wasted time. It really isn't. It is investment time. If you want to unknit the issues and the topics, if you want to build a genuine understanding of the child or young person and the world in which they function – you do that in the safe spaces.

This model can also contain physical activities that preoccupy you both while you chat – building Lego, drawing pictures, watching short videos. I spent an entire session with a young man who wanted to show me how he could play the drums – so we did the session in the music practice room and hardly spoke at all about emotive topics. When it got to the end of the session he implored me *"I just want to play you two more songs"*. This is a clear indication that he was gaining something important from me being there, that he wanted to impress me, and that he valued our time together.

Your challenge is to develop the skills to move gently and without announcement from one of the quadrants to another to suit what is needed in the moment. This is about what is required by the young person, interpreting their behaviour and body language, and what is in the best interests of the overall relationship that you are maintaining. That's not easy, it requires practise, and in my personal opinion it tends to be intuitive personality types who cope with this better and do it more naturally. Anyone can learn this though – and it's worth compiling notes after your session and reflecting on them and the decisions you made through that time you spent together.

Appendix B – Checklist: Signs and Symptoms

NHS England offers the following case study: 'Recognising and Acting on signs of 'County Lines' child exploitation'

It is scholarly article that tends to underline and corroborate the most serious risks around this subject by focusing on a young person 'W' who committed an act of murder shortly after being discharged from community mental health services.

I definitely recommend this as an article that should be read.

Commonly you can start to recognise symptoms of criminal exploitation in a child when you observe the following:

- Child withdraws from family and/or usual friendship group
- Arrival of new and unknown friends/friendship group
- New friends do not want to come to the house / do not like to be named or identified
- Age inappropriate relationships
- Child is secretive about possessions / whereabouts / movements and definitely mobile phone use

- Emotionally the child become disconnected and numb – but displays outbursts of anger and sometimes rage
- Adoption of a faux accent and new, foreign slang terminology
- Posture / gait change / use of gang hand signs
- Drastic change in personal appearance or image
- Erratic movements/schedule/begins to come home very late or in the early hours
- Disengagement from school, education and previously important activity
- Academic or sporting goals become unimportant very suddenly
- Emotional mood swings and behaviour changes
- Signs and symptoms of intoxication and hangover cycles
- Overt and distinctive smell of cannabis
- Adopts and new name or nick name – gets angry if you don't use it
- Unexplained injuries
- Becomes fixated about another person "He/she does this, he/she does that, he/she says this, he/she would/wouldn't…"
- Won't go to / doesn't want to be seen in specific areas of his/her home town
- Wary attitude towards unknown people
- Anti-police mentality and adversity towards authority figures

Many adolescents can display some of these symptoms without being embroiled in County Lines or Criminal Exploitation. The more indicators you observe – the greater the degree of concern I would adopt.

Considering the recommendations that all behaviours should be treated as a method of communication be mindful if the child or young person shows signs of:

- Behavioural issues at school
- Bullying, victimising or manipulating others
- Threatening behaviours / getting into fights
- Carrying weapons
- Drug misuse
- Going missing overnight
- Evidence of theft or dishonesty
- Evidence of premature sexual behaviour / 'advertising' or exhibiting themselves sexually online

If you arrive at a stage where the child or young person is offering such signs, symptoms and behaviours – verbal engagement is going to become challenging and potentially confrontational. It is not going to be a very easy situation to manage.

I recommend that – if you are a parent – you seek support from a multiagency group. You can probably gain access to such support and expertise by talking to your school (the Pastoral Lead), your G.P., by contacting the Local Safeguarding Children's Board, or Social Care. You will have enormous and understandable trepidation about doing this – but simply by taking such a step you are reassuring professionals that you are a responsible parent who is putting the needs of his/her child first.

As a professional – where you feel that there are signs of neglect or abuse surrounding any child – you should follow your organisational safeguarding procedure to raise that concern prominently and to recommend that a meeting is convened between partners to discuss the risks that you have identified.

The purpose of the meeting is to put all the pieces of the jigsaw on the table and to assemble the picture as vividly as possible so that the best decisions can be made in the interests of that child, and to safeguard any other children who are also likely to be affected.

Appendix C: Drug testing for parents

I'm not talking about drug testing Mum or Dad here!

This is a very – very brief guide for parents who are worried that their son or daughter has become involved in substance misuses. We've said before that identifying that your child is using illegal drugs is a clear indication that your child has taken steps towards the people who supply controlled drugs.

The good news is that you can find out very easily – and I'll walk you through that. There are pitfalls to avoid though, and as with most things, how you do it is just as important as the outcome of the test itself.

Covert testing is not a practical option for most parents. You're not about to steal hair from their hairbrush and send it off to a lab for root analysis (this is not an episode of 'Miami: CSI'). *So you have to be upfront about what you want to do, and why you want to do it.*

This means that you really need to have some grounds. If you have no grounds whatsoever to suspect that your son or daughter is using drugs – control your own fear because I'm 99% sure that the issue is with you and not with them.

If they are exhibiting signs and symptoms of drug misuse – which can be as obvious as coming home in a state of intoxication at an unacceptable hour with glazed eyes, reeking of cannabis – or more subtle things such as

473

rolling papers, filters, lighters suddenly appearing when you don't believe they smoke, combined with the other issues around being hung over, starting to miss school, a sudden change of friendship group and so on (see Appendix B).

If you sit down with your son or daughter and tell them that you want them to participate in a drugs test the first question you can anticipate is "Why?" with a strong likelihood of them denying that then even need to take one in the first place (particularly if they are using). They may simply say there and then that they do smoke weed (and then try to justify it). An old reliable is "I smoked it once ages ago but I didn't like it".

If you have made a decision to test your son or daughter you need to be able to furnish grounds and it's not reasonable to expect them to take the test without question. Ask yourself where your grounds appear on this sliding scale:

No grounds	Reasonable Suspicion	Balance of probabilities	Reasonable Belief	Beyond all Reasonable Doubt

As a parent it is for you to decide where your test threshold is once you have decided where your grounds sit:

No Grounds	There is nothing to suggest that your child is using any drugs.
Reasonable suspicion	You are 2/10 sure that your child is using drugs, you are uneasy about it, and something is just not right. You might only be able to attribute this to one or two things and those things are not overwhelming
Balance of probabilities	On a fifty/fifty it seems more likely that they are using that not using. You might have good grounds to understand that all their friends are now smoking weed. Do you believe that your child just stands there and watches?
Reasonable belief	This is 8/10 territory – it builds on what has come before, but maybe someone you trust a great deal got in touch and said *"I think I saw them in the park passing a roll up around and behaving strangely – I'm really sorry"*
Beyond all reasonable doubt	This is a situation like finding a bag of weed in their coat pocket, catching them smoking it red handed and so on. The question in this 10/10 situation is, why do you need to test them at all?

The only advice that I can offer here is to speak to trusted friend, try to act out of objective and rational purpose – and not out of anger. This conversation needs to remain calm and you need to reassure your child that no matter what the outcome is you still love them and you can both have a grown up conversation about it without it getting into insults or accusations.

Putting a test on the table is usually all you need to do to *pretty much know* what the outcome is going to be. How they respond to that test being in the room will tell you an awful lot. If they recoil from it in horror – refuse to engage with it offering no good reason – run from the room and slam the door, I would suggest that you've touched an emotive nerve and you can draw a certain conclusions. Think Dracula and garlic.

Explain – if you can – in the fairest way, that you do feel that you have reasonable grounds to request that they cooperate with the test, and if they don't you'll have to draw your own conclusions that they are hiding something (and that you're sorry about that). Explain that you don't want to do that.

There are two common types of test that you could use – a saliva/mouth swab test or a urine test.

Mouth swabs are best if your son or daughter comes home and you think they are stoned. Their mouth probably does contain traces of THC (which if you're testing for cannabis, that is what the test is seeking). The morning after they are likely to be hungover and very confrontational and grouchy – *I wouldn't recommend choosing that moment to ask them to take the test*. The outcome will be predictable and it won't involve them cooperating.

Mouth swabs are good for situations that are within about twenty-four to forty-eight hours after a suspected use of the drug. Teeth brushing, mouth wash, eating food, and other contaminants can mask or remove the substance you are testing for – and the longer it goes since the use, the less reliable a mouth swab test is. Mouth swabs are good because they are easy to administer and give very quick results – but if you think that your son or daughter used last weekend, and it's Thursday, I'd say that this test isn't the one for you.

Urine tests do feel more intrusive – and in law they are treated as such in police custody. While generally everyone who comes into custody for the first time will give a sample of DNA via a mouth swab based saliva sample, a sample of urine will only be requested for evidential purposes, has to be requested under the authority of a more senior officer (Police Inspector) and the detainee can refuse to cooperate with it.

A urine test is a much better indicator of the longer term history – maybe a couple of weeks in terms of certain drugs, although each drug or substance has its own half life issue and remains present in the urine for varying amounts of time. You should check the kit that you are going to use for specific guidance because that matters too (sensitivities in kits can vary).

Sticking with cannabis, and the young person you suspected was using at the weekend, I would suggest that a urine test would give you a more reliable answer. Kits generally give answers in five or ten minutes of a dip sample and most kits are pretty easy to use and interpret (although some less so, so find the kit that seems easiest for you).

Doing a drug test is a very intrusive step – no matter whether it is mouth swab or urine based. On one hand it sends a clear message about boundary setting and it can wipe away doubt and completely destroy any lies.

In one case that I witnessed the young person doubled down on the lie and said that the kit must be faulty – so she was retested again (positive) and then mum took the test herself (negative). Science removed the argument and we simply had to get to the facts that she was smoking weed regularly with friends *"...but I can't understand why it is such a bad thing"*.

The natural question is – what if they do test positive?

Well – most test kits are very affordable and test for a variety of drugs (five or six drug tests in one is not uncommon). Depending on what they test positive for you may feel like you need to respond differently.

I would advise you to be prepared for a positive outcome – after all you wouldn't be testing if you didn't think they were using (or you shouldn't be testing under those circumstances). You need to stay calm and you need to open a dialogue about what they are using, why, how, who with, how often and develop a full picture of the substance misuse issue. Try to avoid the instinct to say *"You're going to tell me everything, and you're going to tell me right now!".*

If the child or young person has developed a dependency they might not even know it yet. Even if they have a nagging feeling that they are dependent, or feel that they're not going to want to stop doing it – you really need expert help and advice. That is when I would open an honest and frank conversation with school, look to get an appointment with the GP, and/or secure a referral to CASUS in order to apply expertise to the matter in hand.

If you are inclined to punish the behaviour that you have identified – think about how that consequence serves to support the situation in a genuine way. Are you doing something merely to inconvenience and annoy or hurt them? Are you doing something to encourage reflection? Are you doing something that helps to keep them away from harm and risk? Decide whether you want to deal with this as a health issue or a misbehaviour issue. You may of course see it as both. Explaining carefully to your child that you feel let down and disappointed is one thing – but it's important that this doesn't then overshadow and obscure your ability to reassure them that you love them, and that primarily you are worried about their immediate welfare, wellbeing and health.

If you have tested a child or young person as positive for a drug you might think about doing subsequent tests over a period of time to establish if the use is continuing – but I'd recommend that you don't fall into a pattern with the tests (every Tuesday for example) because they become easier to evade or mislead.

It is not at all uncommon for a child or young person to respond with *"I knew I had to hide it because I just knew you wouldn't understand and you wouldn't be cool about it"*. It is also common to then get told *"Well Charlie smokes weed and his/her Mum knows all about it and she's really cool and fine with it – why can't you be more like her? Everyone is doing it!"*. I would be willing to wager that Charlie's mum does not know, is not super cool with it, and that in fact the number of cannabis users in your child or young person's school is certainly not 100%.

The temptation is to adopt a very 'judgemental parent' attitude about the situation – to lecture, and to get into how disappointed you are. How you thought they were better and more intelligent and more mature than that etc. This is actually also going to create boundaries because you're telling your child or young person "I don't understand you and I don't respect you". It can be particularly damaging if you point to another successful sibling and say "Why can't you be more like Andrew!". These are huge boundaries to overcome. People can end up in mediation and counselling over those two issues alone – never mind the cannabis.

Trying to encourage your child or young person into a 'grown up' discussion on an adult to adult basis is hard – but generally it is more likely that you will feel heard, they are more likely to feel respected, and generally the two of you are more likely to venture into a place where you can talk about the risks in a more constructive way. In this space *"I'm worried about you because I love you"* is more likely to feel sincere and less like emotional blackmail.

Parents who are seeking to know more about how this type of engagement works might want to read more about the subject of 'Transactional Analysis' (TA) and the work of the Canadian psychiatrist Eric Berne. His model is delivered through his best selling book 'Games People Play' which was first published in 1969 and is available from Grove Press.

Don't perform a drug test unless you've made a clear decision about what you are going to do with the outcome. Knowing that your child or young person is using drugs, and not knowing what to do about it, or doing nothing about it, undermines you completely. You paint yourself into a corner and inevitably as the situation tends to escalate you will end up in a room with a professional only for your child to turn around and accuse you:

"You've known for ages that I've been doing drugs. You even tested me for it."

Doing a drugs test does not in and of itself solve anything – it just clarifies an issue and gives you further insight. It is in effect a beginning. Before administering a test you might want to talk to your G.P. practice nurse, school pastoral leader or other professionals – and don't be afraid of being up front about your anxiety. Lots of parents feel exactly the same way.

For many young people having a parent who is testing them is a great way for them to resist peer pressure without losing face. *"I'm sorry I can't she's started making do drugs tests – can you even believe that?"*

Administering a drugs test doesn't come without a cost either (I'm not talking about the £3.99 for the kit) – it's an intrusive measure and an implicit statement that you don't trust your son or daughter. *It can undermine that bond and that rapport that you feel you have.* This being said – if you identify a legitimate issue, remove the doubt, and actually take your dialogue on drugs to a new place – it can be a cost and a risk that for many is worth taking.

Appendix D: Helpful links and resources

https://www.talktofrank.com/

This is an independent website that offers free advice and guidance about all manner of drugs and psychoactive substances. They offer free and anonymous drugs counselling without an appointment between 2pm and 6pm every day online. You can also call this service on 0300 1236600.

https://www.nspcc.org.uk/

The National Society for the Prevention Cruelty to Children is the leading child protection charity in the UK. They offer a range of resources to support parents, children and professional – including sound advice and guidance on how to spot abuse. They also have a helpline – 0808 800 5000 and trained counsellors are available to offer help, advice and support. The NSPCC also support parents who are struggling with drug and alcohol issues of their own.

https://www.childrenssociety.org.uk/what-is-county-lines

The Children's Society is another exceptional charity which promotes the health and wellbeing of children and young people. They have excellent resources explaining the threat of County Lines, what it is, who it affects, and what to do if you identify a child involved in criminal exploitation.

http://www.childline.org.uk

Any child or young person can call Childline for free on 0800 1111 (yes that's the whole number – not a typo). As well as helping young people with information about the threat of crime, Childline can help with coping mechanisms to support depression, anxiety, loneliness and feelings of isolation. Childline is very much about supporting children who have suffered early life trauma and adverse childhood experiences – they have a section for children with parents in prison, on drugs and other matters. They have a 1-2-1 secure chatroom for counselling. They have some great resources.

https://www.familylives.org.uk/

If you are a parent who is feeling overwhelmed Family Lives might be a good resource for you. They were registered as a charity in 1999, and they have a confidential helpline 0808 800 2222. They offer non-judgemental advice and guidance across a whole range of topics. Family Lives also offer advice, guidance and resources for professionals that are worth checking out.

https://www.nationalcrimeagency.gov.uk/

The National Crime Agency website is a really informative resource. This also contains links to CEOP and links that allow you to contribute information/intelligence. You can follow the Director General of the NCA on twitter – she tweets regularly - @NCA_LynneOwens – and this is definitely an account that I would recommend anyone to follow.

https://crimestoppers-uk.org/

You can call CrimeStoppers at any time on 0800 555 111 with regard to any form of criminality in any part of the United Kingdom. This is a brilliant charity and they pass information through to local police forces promptly and effectively. You don't have to give your name and you won't be traced on the basis of what you provide. For many people this is reassurance enough for them to give information that makes a critical difference to drugs enforcement in their local area.

https://www.fearless.org/en

Is a source of information for children and young people about crime and criminality. Young people can supply information with 100% confidentiality. They have a very up front but contemporary style in their presentation and they also link to other great resources (including some of the ones I have cited here). They have information on County Lines and the Criminal Exploitation of Children specifically.

https://www.mind.org.uk/

Mind are a tremendous charity that support the vital agenda of improving mental health for everyone. They have fantastic resources that reach across into the issue of drugs and psychoactive substance misuse and dependency. They have a section dedicated to children and young people which is invaluable.

http://www.marijuana-anonymous.org.uk/

Cannabis dependency is a real issue – a genuine problem – for adults and young people. MA have great resources to help you to identify whether your use of the drug has become a problem that you are struggling to get out of. They provide a pressure free environment, a non-judgemental context, and a host of information that is vital for anyone who needs to turn the corner on cannabis dependency. You can call them on 0300 124 0373.

https://www.relate.org.uk/

Relationship crisis – whether it is between parents, or parent and child directly, can be a source of emotional distress that makes it impossible for a child to seek the advice and guidance that they need. Relate are possibly the best known service for helping people to mediate their problems and sort things out.

https://www.cruse.org.uk/

In the worst case scenario you might suffer bereavement, and that can be the very worst type of emotional distress that you ever have to deal with. Unfortunately in life we will always have to deal with death and loss. Cruse are the largest and best known charity that offers support to people in all types of circumstances struggling with loss of a loved one. You can call them on 0808 808 1677.

Bibliography & References:

https://www.health.harvard.edu/diseases-and-conditions/past-trauma-may-haunt-your-future-health#:~:text=Early%20childhood%20trauma%20is%20a,stroke%2C%20cancer%2C%20and%20obesity.

County Lines': An exploratory analysis of migrating drug gang offenders in North Essex (John Hallworth, Selwyn College Cambridge, 2016);

https://www.nationalcrimeagency.gov.uk/who-we-are/publications/234-county-lines-violen-ce-exploitation-drug-supply-2017/file

https://iea.org.uk/media/uks-illicit-cannabis-market-worth-2-5bn-a-year-finds-new-report/

https://assets.publishing.service.gov.uk/government/uploads/system/uploads/attachment_data/file/448039/young-car-drivers-2013-data.pdf

https://www.nspcc.org.uk/globalassets/documents/research-reports/teenagers-at-risk-report.pdf

https://www.childrenssociety.org.uk/what-is-county-lines

https://www.gov.uk/government/news/home-secretary-announces-a-package-of-new-measures-to-tackle-county-lines

https://assets.publishing.service.gov.uk/government/uploads/system/uploads/attachment_data/file/839253/moj-county-lines-practical-guidance-frontline-practitionerspdf.pdf

https://www.theguardian.com/society/2019/jan/29/county-lines-criminal-drug-networks-rapidly-expanding-national-crime-agency

https://www.irishtimes.com/news/world/uk/how-postcode-wars-have-made-london-a-murder-capital-1.3460692

https://psycnet.apa.org/record/1943-03751-001

Niccolo Machiavelli – The Prince; Chapter 17 'Cruelty vs Mercy'

'The policing of County Lines in Affected Import Towns: Exploring Local Responses to Evolving Heroin and Crack Markets' (2019)

https://www.theguardian.com/uk-news/2019/oct/01/priti-patel-unveils-county-lines-crackdown

https://www.theguardian.com/commentisfree/2019/may/16/tories-children-poverty-britain-austerity

https://www.businessinsider.com/facebook-has-been-deliberately-designed-to-mimic-addictive-painkillers-2018-12?r=US&IR=T

https://www.bbc.co.uk/news/uk-37978582

https://www.newsweek.com/brexit-eu-immigration-ukip-poster-breaking-point-471081

https://www.pbni.org.uk/wp-content/uploads/2015/11/OrlaLynch_IPJ-13.11.17.pdf

https://www.stir.ac.uk/research/hub/publication/537905

https://www.ltai.info/about/

https://blogs.griffith.edu.au/gci-insights/2020/02/11/when-does-someone-radicalise-and-deradicalise/

https://www.pinterest.co.uk/velinow/vor-v-zakone/

National Elf Service - CBD as an Anti-Psychotic 2018

https://www.drugabuse.gov/publications/research-reports/marijuana/marijuana-addictive

www.bedrocan.com

https://www.arenapharm.com/#

Yahoo.com '25 Biggest Marijuana Companies in the World' - August 2019

https://www.latimes.com/archives/la-xpm-1996-08-08-ls-32243-story.html

https://www.nationalcrimeagency.gov.uk/who-we-are/publications/257-county-lines-drug-supply-vulnerability-and-harm-2018/file

https://journals.sagepub.com/doi/10.1177/00224278980350
03004 - Eric Baumer, Janet L. Lauritsen, Richard Rosenfeld,
Richard Wright; August 1998

Theodore Milton – Disorders of Personality (1996)

The Man Who Listened to Horses, Monty Roberts; Arrow
Books, 1997

https://www.nhs.uk/conditions/post-traumatic-stress-
disorder-
ptsd/#:~:text=PTSD%20can%20develop%20immediately%20a
fter,condition%20and%20others%20do%20not.

https://www.giftfromwithin.org/html/cptsd-understanding-
treatment.html

Nadine Burke Harris M.D. – 'The Deepest Well' - Houghton
Mifflin Harcourt, 2018

http://www.instituteofhealthequity.org/resources-
reports/social-inequalities-in-the-leading-causes-of-early-
death-a-life-course-approach/social-inequalities-in-the-
leading-causes-of-early-death-a-life-course-approach.pdf

https://www.centreformentalhealth.org.uk/sites/default/files
/2019-05/CentreforMH_EngagingWithComplexity.pdf

https://www.drugwise.org.uk/wp-
content/uploads/Highwaysandbyways.pdf

https://www.bbc.co.uk/news/uk-42403590

http://www.police-foundation.org.uk/

https://oxfordre.com/socialwork/view/10.1093/acrefore/978
0199975839.001.0001/acrefore-9780199975839-e-
1063?rskey=KYbKKK&result=13

https://www.ncbi.nlm.nih.gov/pmc/articles/PMC6025145/

https://www.independent.co.uk/news/uk/politics/priti-patel-
migrants-channel-royal-navy-record-a9659346.html

ONS Data

https://www.independent.co.uk/news/education/education-
news/school-exclusions-pupils-knife-crime-violence-pupil-
referral-units-education-barnardos-a8609046.html

https://www.bbc.co.uk/news/uk-england-london-47228698

https://publications.parliament.uk/pa/cm201719/cmselect/c
meduc/342/342.pdf

https://schoolsweek.co.uk/systematic-failure-lifts-academy-
trusts-deficit-to-2-4m/

https://www.theguardian.com/politics/2009/jul/13/boris-
johnson-second-salary-chickenfeed

https://www.nytimes.com/2019/02/24/world/europe/britain
-austerity-may-budget.html

https://www.edp24.co.uk/news/health/east-of-england-
ambulance-service-staff-deaths-whistleblower-warning-1-
6392546

https://www.unison.org.uk/content/uploads/2017/03/CC-SocialWorkWatch_report_web.pdf

https://www.theguardian.com/global-development/2020/jan/27/its-incredible-what-they-see-housing-associations-take-on-county-lines

https://www.telegraph.co.uk/news/uknews/1574927/Tories-attack-something-for-nothing-culture.html

https://www.channel4.com/news/factcheck/factcheck-cameron-caught-out-on-frontline-police-cuts

https://en.wikipedia.org/wiki/Peelian_principles

Independent article August 2018

https://www.college.police.uk/What-we-do/Standards/Guidelines/Neighbourhood-Policing/Pages/definition-of-neighbourhood-policing.aspx

https://www.legislation.gov.uk/ukpga/2003/44/schedule/15

https://www.ft.com/content/1f1c5c48-33d8-11ea-9703-eea0cae3f0de

https://www.justiceinspectorates.gov.uk/hmiprobation/wp-content/uploads/sites/5/2020/01/NPS-central-functions-inspection-report-1.pdf

https://assets.publishing.service.gov.uk/government/uploads/system/uploads/attachment_data/file/871302/Action_Plan_PDF.pdf

https://www.bbc.co.uk/news/uk-48288433

https://www.theguardian.com/business/2020/may/04/the-inside-story-of-the-uks-nhs-coronavirus-ventilator-challenge

https://www.ft.com/content/4bf155c8-fc8e-338b-9f7c-e41b7f5e3ba4

https://www.theguardian.com/society/2020/mar/01/dwp-criticised-for-incredible-secrecy-over-deaths-of-benefit-claimants

https://www.theguardian.com/commentisfree/2020/feb/04/errol-graham-welfare-uk-benefit-cuts-disability-deaths

https://www.theguardian.com/commentisfree/2020/jan/30/death-errol-graham-dwp-benefits-ill-disabled
https://www.instituteforgovernment.org.uk/explainers/departmental-budgets

https://www.youtube.com/watch?v=3yEi72XfNbA

https://yjlc.uk/wp-content/uploads/2018/02/Modern-Slavery-Guide-2018.pdf

https://anyoneschild.org/get-the-facts/

https://www.independent.co.uk/news/people/derren-brown-explains-how-to-reduce-a-mugger-to-tears-using-nothing-but-words-9859017.html

https://www.independent.co.uk/voices/uk-drugs-addiction-marijuana-crime-government-nhs-a8529731.html

https://ocs.ca/collections/balanced?product=4571297777484&sort_by=products_custom_pricing_desc

https://iea.org.uk/media/uks-illicit-cannabis-market-worth-2-5bn-a-year-finds-new-report/

https://www.independent.co.uk/news/uk/politics/trident-replacement-cost-nuclear-submarines-205-billion-independent-trident-commission-cnd-caroline-a7025956.html

SUBVERSIVE MEDIA

PUBLICATIONS

Publisher's Cataloguing-in-Publication data:
Priestley, Philip
Beating County Lines (and other things to do before lunch) / Phil Priestley

ISBN: 978-1-8382131-2-1

1. Main category of the book - No-fiction
2. Other category - Child Protection
3. Sociology
4. Self-help

FIRST EDITION

www.ingramcontent.com/pod-product-compliance
Lightning Source LLC
Chambersburg PA
CBHW070857030426
42336CB00014BA/2242